Praise for *First into Nagasaki*

"An invaluable historical resource for those seeking the truth . . . Weller, impersonating a colonel, sneaked into Nagasaki and brazenly demanded the help of Japanese military authorities. . . . Weller interviewed eyewitnesses, survivors, doctors, and imprisoned Allied POWs and wrote a brilliant series of reports. . . . These exceptionally important eyewitness accounts, collected and organized by a tireless war reporter dedicated to making the horrible truth known to the American public . . . vividly relate the everyday inhumanity of the Pacific war. Despite the sanitizing impulses of U.S. military censors, George Weller's words continue to speak eloquently about the horrors of war across a gap of sixty years."
—*Boston Globe*

"A powerful set of historical documents . . . [Anthony Weller's] intelligent concluding essay provides the framework for his father's raw copy."
—*Wall Street Journal*

"One of the great foreign correspondents of the twentieth century. Gutsy and enterprising . . . Weller wrote with a literary flair."
—*Chicago Sun-Times*

"Unearthed at last after six decades, George Weller's daring reportage from the ruins of Nagasaki has made an unforgettable and momentous book. From the remains of a scorched, fractured city to the unfathomable tragedy of Allied POWs in Japanese custody, he channeled his five senses straight to the page, giving eloquent testimony to the martyrs, American and Japanese alike, who were trapped in the Pacific war's bloody fun house."
—James D. Hornfischer, author of *Ship of Ghosts* and *The Last Stand of the Tin Can Sailors*

"Gripping . . . harrowing."
—*International Herald Tribune*

BY GEORGE WELLER

NOVELS

Not to Eat, Not for Love
Clutch and Differential
The Crack in the Column

HISTORY

Singapore Is Silent
Bases Overseas
First into Nagasaki

TRANSLATION

(as Michael Wharf)
Fontamara, by Ignazio Silone

BY ANTHONY WELLER

NOVELS

The Garden of the Peacocks
The Polish Lover
The Siege of Salt Cove

TRAVEL

Days and Nights on the Grand Trunk Road:
Calcutta to Khyber

FIRST INTO NAGASAKI

The Censored Eyewitness Dispatches
on Post-Atomic Japan
and Its Prisoners of War

GEORGE WELLER (1907–2002)

Edited and with an Essay by Anthony Weller
Foreword by Walter Cronkite

THREE RIVERS PRESS
NEW YORK

Library of Congress Cataloging-in-Publication Data

Weller, George, 1907–2002
First into Nagasaki : the censored eyewitness dispatches on post-atomic
Japan and its prisoners of war / George Weller.
1. Nagasaki-shi (Japan)—History—Bombardment, 1945.
2. Prisoners of war—United States.   3. Prisoners of war—Japan.   I. Title.
        D767.25.N3W45   2006
    940.54'252244—dc22   2006011345

ISBN 978-0-307-34202-7

Printed in the United States of America

Design by Lauren Dong

10 9 8 7 6 5 4 3 2 1

First Paperback Edition

Contents

Foreword

This is an important book—important and gripping. For the first time in print we can read the details of the nuclear bombardment of Nagasaki, Japan, as it was written by the first American reporter on the terrible scene.

George Weller's dispatches from Nagasaki, just four weeks after the bombing, were censored and destroyed by General MacArthur. Weller salvaged his carbon copy but, in his subsequent travels to many corners of our troubled globe, the copy disappeared. His son, an honored writer in his own right, has only recently uncovered it and this book is the result.

George Weller was not only one of our best war correspondents but he had that quality that imbued his copy with lasting importance. He wrote in the present tense but always with the recognition that he was writing the history of his time. Many major honors, including the Pulitzer Prize, attested to this quality.

Although not in Weller's original report, this book by his son underlines the important historical note regarding General Mac-Arthur's total censorship of all dispatches from Nagasaki. We can only speculate as to his motive in imposing this total blackout to keep the United States and the rest of the world ignorant of the horrors of nuclear war. With those bombings, first of Hiroshima and then, in short order, Nagasaki, the Japanese sued for peace and the war was over. Why then such rigid, total censorship? Was it perhaps simply MacArthur's swollen ego that led him to believe that the Pacific war was his alone to win? Or perhaps was it more complicated? Was there a hope in MacArthur's headquarters and perhaps in Harry Truman's White House that our victory (and, certainly, the American lives that had been saved) would overshadow and justify beyond condemnation the mass destruction and casualties we had caused?

This total blackout, of course, depended on keeping reporters and photographers from the scene. George Weller was both reporter and photographer, and his daring and secret entry into Nagasaki just four weeks after the atomic attack threatened to destroy that hope. He wrote and photographed the still-smoldering and dying city and its dead and dying population. His reports, so long delayed but now salvaged by his son, at last have saved our history from the military censorship that would have preferred to have time to sanitize the ghastly details with a concocted, fictional version of the mass destruction and killing that man's (read that "America's") newest weapon had bestowed on civilization.

Or possibly was it one of those vastly unreasonable hopes held in the American high commands that by imposing silence in the press they might protect longer the secrecy of our atomic arsenal?

Also delayed by MacArthur's censorship were Weller's dispatches from his visits to American prison camps within a forty-mile radius of Nagasaki. There he uncovered the Japanese military's savage treatment of their American prisoners. Among those stories is that of a Japanese prison ship that once packed into the freighter's hold 1,600 American prisoners. When the hold was finally opened 1,300 of the prisoners were dead—only 300 had survived.

There is so much in this volume that we never knew or have long forgotten. It comes at a time when our nation is again at war and our citizenry can only guess as to how thick are the blindfolds of censorship that distort the truth of our military engagements and our international commitments.

This volume of the last generation's history is an important reminder, a warning to inspire civilian vigilance. Yes, indeed, this is an important book.

—Walter Cronkite

It is through knowing the truth that the people discover their hidden will.

—George Weller
Singapore Is Silent (1943)

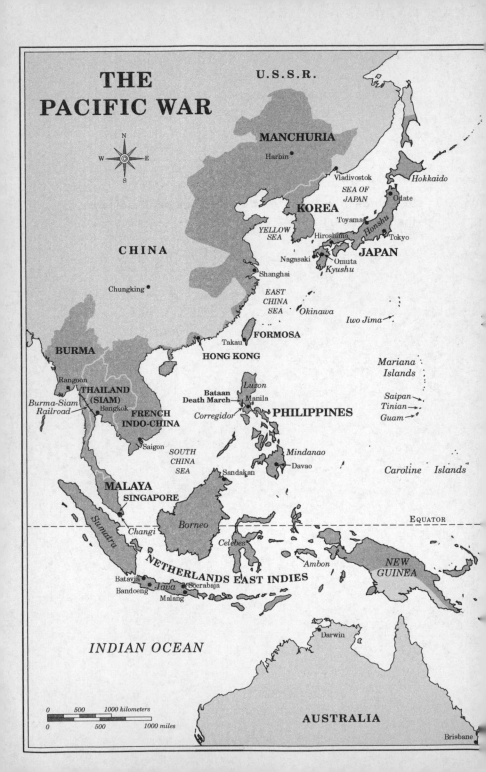

THE PACIFIC WAR

U.S.S.R.

MANCHURIA

Harbin

Vladivostok

Hokkaido

SEA OF JAPAN

Odate

KOREA

Toyama

Honshu

YELLOW SEA

Hiroshima

Tokyo

CHINA

Nagasaki

JAPAN

Omuta

Kyushu

Shanghai

Chungking

EAST CHINA SEA

Okinawa

Iwo Jima

FORMOSA

Takau

Mariana Islands

HONG KONG

Luzon

BURMA

Rangoon

THAILAND (SIAM)

Burma-Siam Railroad

Bangkok

Bataan
Death March

Manila

Saipan
Tinian
Guam

FRENCH INDO-CHINA

Corregidor

PHILIPPINES

Saigon

SOUTH CHINA SEA

Mindanao

Davao

Caroline Islands

Sandakan

MALAYA

SINGAPORE

Changi

Borneo

Celebes

EQUATOR

Sumatra

Ambon

NEW GUINEA

Batavia

Java

Soerabaja

Bandoeng

Malang

NETHERLANDS EAST INDIES

INDIAN OCEAN

Darwin

0   500   1000 kilometers

0   500   1000 miles

AUSTRALIA

Brisbane

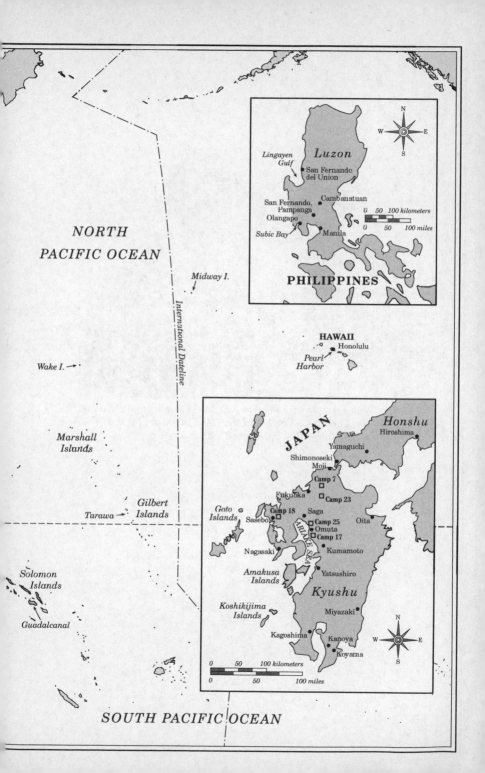

NORTH
PACIFIC OCEAN

International Dateline

Midway I.

Wake I. →

Marshall
Islands

Gilbert
Islands

Tarawa →

Solomon
Islands

Guadalcanal

SOUTH PACIFIC OCEAN

Lingayen Gulf

Luzon

San Fernando
del Union

Cambanatuan

San Fernando,
Pampanga

Olangapo

Subic Bay

Manila

N
W   E
S

0   50   100 kilometers
0   50   100 miles

PHILIPPINES

HAWAII

Honolulu

Pearl Harbor

JAPAN

Honshu

Hiroshima

Yamaguchi

Shimonoseki
Moji

Fukuoka

Camp 7

Camp 23

Goto
Islands

Camp 18

Sasebo

Saga

Camp 25
Omuta
Camp 17

ARIAKE SEA

Oita

Nagasaki

Kumamoto

Amakusa
Islands

Yatsushiro

Kyushu

Koshikijima
Islands

Miyazaki

Kagoshima

Kanoya

Koyama

N
W   E
S

0   50   100 kilometers
0   50   100 miles

George Weller (*right*) with John S. Knight (journalist and owner of the *Chicago Daily News*) on board the U.S.S. *Missouri* for the treaty signing, Tokyo Bay, September 2, 1945.

Introduction

On December 7, 1941, a Sunday morning, Japanese dive bombers launched a surprise attack on the U.S. base in Hawaii at Pearl Harbor, destroying much of America's fleet in the Pacific. Within a week the United States was at war with the Axis powers: Japan, Germany, and Italy.

Within six months the Japanese controlled Malaya, Singapore, the Philippines, Formosa, the Netherlands East Indies, Indo-China, Burma, Korea, Thailand, and strategic Pacific islands like Guam and Wake. They also controlled large parts of China.

In the prior world war, the majority of the losses had been combatants—meaning civilians turned soldier. World War II made mass civilian deaths central to the equation of modern war, to force an enemy to capitulate. When it was over, civilian deaths (55 million) were more than double those of combatants (22 million).

Beginning near the end of 1944, the United States waged a punishing air assault against Japan. Its industrial areas were all heavily populated cities that were largely made of wood, ideal for incendiary bombs. For example, in a three-hour air raid on Tokyo in March 1945, sixteen square miles of the city were destroyed, a million people made homeless, a hundred thousand torched to death—and nearly a fifth of the city's industrial capacity obliterated. This was known as area bombing, and years of Japanese atrocities against civilians and soldiers all over the Pacific and across Asia were thought ample justification. Since Japan knew only the concept of "total war," now it was receiving the same in return.

Throughout the war the atomic bomb was being developed with great determination and speed under President Franklin Roosevelt, who died in office in April 1945. He was succeeded by his vice president, Harry Truman.

Following Hitler's suicide, in May 1945 Germany—what was left of Nazi Germany—signed an armistice with the Allies, ending World War II in Europe. Japan was now choosing to go it alone against the United States, Britain, Australia, and the Netherlands.

In late July the Allies issued the Potsdam Declaration, asking Japan for unconditional surrender. Japan, still in the political grip of its military, refused.

At this time there were around thirty-five thousand Allied prisoners of war being held in Japanese camps, under extremely harsh conditions.

On August 6, 1945—a Monday morning—after nearly four years of war with the Japanese, the United States dropped an atomic bomb code-named "Little Boy," with a warhead of uranium 235, over the city of Hiroshima, on the island of Honshu. It killed about one hundred thousand people, mostly civilians, either that day or during the next few weeks.

On August 8 the Soviet Union declared war on Japan and launched an enormous, successful blitzkrieg against the 2 million Japanese soldiers occupying Manchuria.

A few hours later, on the morning of August 9, the United States exploded a second atomic bomb—this one code-named "Fat Man," armed with a warhead of plutonium 239—over Nagasaki, a port city devoted to military industry on the island of Kyushu. It killed about forty thousand people that morning and throughout the coming month.

On August 14, after lengthy discussion with his cabinet, the Japanese emperor Hirohito agreed to surrender. The terms resembled those proposed several weeks earlier, except that it was understood the emperor would remain in power.

In Tokyo Bay on September 2, on the U.S. battleship *Missouri,* in front of hundreds of reporters arrived from around the world, the Japanese foreign minister signed a treaty of surrender with General Douglas MacArthur, now commander of all Allied forces in the Pacific.

My father, George Weller (1907–2002), one of the most experienced American World War II correspondents, was among those present. The war was over; the last chapter of his war was about to begin.

—ANTHONY WELLER

I

First into Nagasaki

(1966)

W henever I see the word "Nagasaki," a vision arises of the city when I entered it on September 6, 1945, as the first free westerner to do so after the end of the war. No other correspondent had yet evaded the authorities to reach either Hiroshima or Nagasaki. The effects of the atomic bombs were unknown except for the massive fact that they had terminated the war with two blows in three days. The world wanted to know what the bombs' work looked like from below.*

I had just escaped the surveillance of General MacArthur's censors, his public relations officers and his military police. MacArthur had placed all southern Japan off limits to the press. Slipping into forbidden Nagasaki, I felt like another Perry, entering a land where my presence itself was forbidden, a land that now had two Mikados, both omnipotent.

When I walked out of Nagasaki's roofless railroad station, I saw a city frizzled like a baked apple, crusted black at the open core where the searing sun born at Alamogordo had split open the blue sky of midday. I saw the long, crumpled skeleton of the Mitsubishi electrical motor and ship fitting plant, a framework blasted clean of its flesh by the lazy-falling missile floating under a parachute.

What irony, I thought, in a war of competing velocities, that this slowest-borne of all weapons, falling at a speed little greater than my own descent when I took training as a paratrooper, should in the end out-destroy all the fleetest of the winged killers. The bomb of Nagasaki reversed the rule of war, getting there last and slowest but with the most, a terminal blow riding under a silk handkerchief.

---

* See closing essay, pp. 252–269 and p. 277. Weller wrote the present piece for a 1967 anthology of reporters' memoirs.

Even now I see the scorched hills ringing the bottleneck of the port. Along the blistered boulevards the shadows of fallen telegraph poles were branded upright on buildings, the signature of the ray stamped in huge ideograms. I can never forget the hospitals where I heard from X-ray specialists the devouring effects of the ray on the human bloodstream and viscera, analyzed as impassively by the little men in white coats as if it had happened to someone else, not themselves. In the battered corridors of these hospitals, already eroded by man's normal suffering, there was no sorrowful horde. The wards were filled. There was no private place left to die. Consequently the dying were sitting up crosslegged against the walls, holding sad little court with their families, answering their tender questions with the mild, consenting indifference of those whose future is cancelled.

I felt pity, but no remorse. The Japanese military had cured me of that. After years of unchallenged domination, they were bending a little under the first after-wind of the bombs, a national mistrust, almost contempt, for having led Japan into war. A few sought escape in hara-kiri. The majority blamed the enemy for using weapons that were "unfair."

Had Japan got these weapons first, would they have been unfair, I asked? Was Pearl Harbor an act of Japanese chivalry? The crafty eyes under the peaked brown caps turned unblinking and blank.

In the harbor, I remember, there still burned the last altar kindled by the fireball. A small freighter, crisped like dry bacon down to the waterline, still smoked, glowed and puffed. She was a floating lamp, untended, with all her mooring ropes burned outward till the ends fell in the water. But her hot pink hawsers still held. Bobbing there among the debris-littered dark waters, she spread a light that flickered in eerie unison with the candles and kerosene lamps and little flashlights ashore.

I felt I had a right to be in Nagasaki, closed or not. Four weeks after the two bombs, with no riots or resistance in Japan, it seemed reasonable that MacArthur should lift his snuffer from the two cities. There was a sort of reason for delay, but it had nothing to do with the public's right to know. As something to fall back upon in the event of the failure of the bombs, MacArthur's planners had arranged that the Japanese archipelago was to be invaded in one-two time, first the northern islands and the Tokyo-Yokohama area, and then the south, with the two atomic cities. Japan's surrender made little difference. An incredible six weeks was announced as the interval before the southern islands were to be occupied. MacArthur had fought a slow, cautious, methodical war, taking no chances with his postwar target, the presidency. His peacemaking was its twin, with censorship prolonged after victory long after the slightest pretext for it existed.

After submitting to the censors of the MacArthur command ever since I had escaped from Java in March, 1942, I felt I could not take much more. I remembered how his censors, perhaps eager not to offend or alarm the White House, killed a dispatch I wrote criticizing Roosevelt's defeat by Stalin at Yalta. With security no longer in question, I was not going to be stifled again. But I was not unaware that in planning to slip into an atomic city first, I was also risking repudiation by the conformists in my own profession. Four years earlier they had ceased bucking the communiqué-fed hamburger grinder, and they disliked—while perhaps secretly admiring—anybody who kept on trying to report the war, to make the public think as well as feel.

My plan of extrusion formed itself a few hours after we all sat on the gun turrets of the *Missouri*, watching Japan surrender to MacArthur and Nimitz. This measured rite over—almost wrecked by a Russian photographer in Lenin cap who was chased around like Harpo Marx—the correspondents were summoned ashore to a press conference. The war was ended, as we had reported, but the censorship was not. There was no chance, therefore, to ask from Tokyo why the Kurile Islands, regular patrol grounds of the U.S. Pacific Fleet, were to be handed to Russia. What the command wanted covered was the prison camps of northern Japan. The dam was to be opened to one last orgy of home town stories, more mindless and more alike than the slow molasses drippings of four years of sloppy, apolitical, dear-mom war. Everything had been arranged: destroyers and planes were to take the correspondents north. North, north, north, away from where the war had been decided a month before.

Once, in midwar, I had been able to escape the darkrooms of the four main theaters of war by going home and running off a book called *Bases Overseas*, claiming for the United States a worldwide network of small strong points where her men had died and her treasure been expended. I did not feel that the right way to end this war was to be herded north, away from Hiroshima and Nagasaki, to chew more fodder about what-beasts-the-Japs-are and Jimmy-looks-skinnier-today. Only a few days before, but after the Mikado's surrender, a *Saturday Evening Post* writer who wore colonel's leaves refused to pass my story about the 503rd Paratroops on Corregidor, my old outfit, that revealed there were still Japanese bodies unburied in the tunnels. "That's contrary to the Geneva Convention, and might make the Japs cancel their surrender," he said. . . . The American psychological grasp of the Japanese was shallow.

I listened as the chief conducting officer, rod in hand, pointed out on a map the prison camps where the newsmen were to be allowed to land and play savior. "Southern Japan remains closed. However, there is a little place down here"—he pointed to the southern end of Kyushu—"where their navy had a kamikaze base. Anybody interested in the divine wind?"

"Geisha schools next door?" asked a jaded voice.

"Nuh-uh. And the pilots are all in the stockade, I'm afraid." Ah, no interviews, then. Enemy personnel, minimize glorification of.

"What happened to their planes?" asked a hopeful photographer.

"Not much left after the flyboys worked 'em over. But we do have the strip working again. That's a story in itself." Nobody seemed to agree. For *Stripes,* perhaps. **SUICIDE STRIP OPERATIVE— ENGINEERS IN OVERNIGHT MIRACLE.** Full of bewildering unit numbers, and ten terse words from the colonel.

No hand was raised for the kamikaze junkpile. Everybody signed for a prison camp, or nothing, and walked out. At the door I turned back to have another look at the map. The kamikaze hole was named Kanoya. While the officer was sorting out his camps and correspondents, I cased Kanoya. A railroad came down to it. Kyushu, in fact, was covered with little railroads. But were any operating?

Hiroshima and Nagasaki were a long way north, and it was partly mountain country, where bridges had been knocked out.

And then I felt rising in me, like a warm geyser, a jet of confidence. It is like the moment when a poem unties your mind.

"I might kill a couple of days with that Kanoya thing," I said. "Who's conducting?" He told me the name of a captain, new to me, not one of MacArthur's little foxes I had been dodging since Buna and Moresby.

"Okay, I'll take a chance."

"Sign here."

The conducting officer, when I met him later, turned out to be a young, friendly captain who had earned a late overseas assignment by impeccable performance somewhere back home. He had already dutifully pulled together everything about Kanoya that could be wrung out of intelligence. Next morning,* as we got aboard the plane, I asked him: "What made the general take Kanoya and leave out all the rest of southern Japan?"

He knew, because he had asked. "He had to give back to Eisenhower and Marshall all the C-54s he borrowed to bring our headquarters in from Manila. So we're down mostly to C-47s. They need fuel between Atsugi and Okinawa."

I wanted to get some idea how hard this eager officer was going to press me to produce. "No pain for you, I hope, if I don't find a story in traffic safety," I said.

"It's a gamble," he said cheerfully. "No pain, no strain."

Neither of us mentioned the conspicuous nearness, in flying distance, of Hiroshima and Nagasaki. There had been just enough atomic ferment at the press conference to warn the command that the reporters could not much longer stall off the editors at home. The look-Mom, I'm-free stories couldn't last forever.

As we buzzed south at a safe five thousand feet, keeping offshore as if Japan would strike again, I asked myself how I could shake off this earnest, able officer without souring the end of his war, late and

* Two mornings later, in fact. (Sept. 4)

little as it was. What gave me trouble was that I liked him. He really wanted to help me, not throttle me.

When we landed at Kanoya the strip was stiff with Japanese soldiers, drawn up in honorific array. Perhaps they were expecting MacArthur himself. They were ready, if need be, to surrender their ancestral swords. What they got, instead, was a natty, cheerful captain leading a rumpled laundry bag of a correspondent. It was obviously a letdown.

Politely we inspected the smashed hangars, the bomb racks, the dormitories where the pilots slept for the last time before taking off for Iwo and Okinawa. We got almost too much attention. It bonded us together, preventing me from looking around to find a way to escape. . . . Had I had enough of Kanoya? my guide wanted to know. "Because I've made arrangements for us to fly back tomorrow." This was alarming. Unable to think of a reason to stay longer, I began to fear that the trip was all a sterile gamble.

Working around the edge of the base that afternoon, I found that the least conspicuous way to get to the mainland was to hire a motorboat. It was only a few hundred yards. I managed to dig up a railroad schedule. All I could read was the numbers. Kanoya was stiff with ambitious Nisei who could have read it at a glance. But I feared that these loyal patriots would turn me in for an extra stripe.

The help I needed appeared suddenly in a tall thirty-year-old sergeant in Army Airways Communications intelligence named Gilbert Harrison, later the organizer of the American Veterans' Committee, and later still the editor of *The New Republic*. By his easy irony and barbed distaste for military authority, I guessed he might be the outrigger I needed. After some wary soundings to make sure he would not turn me in, I spilled my plan to him. "Can I come?" he said instantly. . . . We arranged for me to get away by motorboat under cover of night and pointed for a rendezvous over on the mainland.

I shook off my captain early, tapped away at my typewriter until he went to bed in a nearby room, and then went to bed myself, fully dressed. In case he ran a bed check, I left my shoes outside the door. Not long before dawn, I slipped past his door, out under the stars. I felt faint pangs. What punishment might MacArthur's dutiful colonels wreak on a trustful, gentlemanly, dewy-fresh captain who was given only one, repeat one, correspondent to watch and lost him? To avoid generating alarm and despondency, I put aside my guilt as I stepped into the boat to cross the stream.

When I landed on the opposite shore, the village lights were just winking out. Nobody was awake but a few fishermen, coiling their nets on the beach after the night's catch. I don't remember Harrison being with me, and I think he spent the night in camp, to avoid causing any alarm. As I remember we formed up at the railroad station in Koyama, the end of the line. The gentle captain seems to have assumed that I went out for an early morning walk and got lost, delayed or shacked up.

Harrison protected his disappearance by sending a dutiful service story about Kanoya's redemption to his commanding officer in Manila. Actually the sergeant was in better legal shape than I was. He had orders allowing him five days to reach Tokyo, means unstated. The orders didn't say that he couldn't visit southern Japan any more than a powder room says "Ladies, No Men." So he chose to imagine that his superiors didn't care how he went. Nothing happened to him, indeed, until ten days later when his colonel found him in the officers' mess in Tokyo and asked: "Are you enjoying yourself here, sergeant?"

The first train north did not leave until four in the afternoon. We kept worrying that the Americans on Kanoya might be willing to smudge their image as liberators by asking the Japanese police to pick us up. These police were ubiquitous, the only government Japan had. By train time I felt confident enough to order the soldiers around the station to carry our bags.

For the conquerors to choose to travel in third class, which was crowded as a cage of monkeys, seemed puzzling to the soldiers, passengers and train crew. But we had no Japanese money and it seemed to me that there, where a fuss would cause maximum trouble, we had the best chance of brazening our way through. We also were protected, by this eccentric self-abasement, from the prying questions of passengers of rank who might have the brains and mischief to turn us in.

Harrison had brought a box of rations, including plenty of coffee, a means of barter better than gold. Spectacled students kept pegging us with questions. Where were we going? I refused to say. I wanted to leave a cooling trail. Fumbling for direction, we changed four times. At one junction, all lanterns, rumors and whispers, we found that we had to make the decision: Hiroshima or Nagasaki. The nearer to Hiroshima was the nearer to Tokyo. I was afraid that there we might run into some party of bombing assessors. Nagasaki, being remoter from MacArthur, seemed safer.

Already I had a formula that held off the most officious questioners. I looked them in the eye and said very softly, "Please consider your position." When they did, they blanched and departed.

We were aristocrats in a series of slow rattlers whose locomotives and coal cars were draped with clinging deadheads, mostly homebound soldiers. Each time we changed trains, at Shibushi, Yatsushiro and Tosu, the good-humored trainmen saw that we were protected by soldiers with fixed bayonets. The trains were filthy and we were hoarse with soot, our arms weary from opening and shutting windows at tunnels. The trainmen filled our canteens with clean water and showed us the *benjo,* or latrine. At Shibushi we met our first escaped prisoner, a private from Utah. He was not eager to accompany us to a bombed city, feeling that we were inviting a necktie party.

We decorously refused to take any gifts, but we traded intensively, giving hard candy for rice and coffee for small sweet cakes, meanwhile plying our customers for information about where we were. A few hours after daylight we reached Yamaguchi. Here, after eighteen hours of travel, we picked up the train for Nagasaki. We also took in tow three Dutch prisoners captured in Java—as I almost had been, too—four years before. A week earlier, two weeks after Japan surrendered, on August 28 their camp of six hundred starving men had been "bombed" by B-29s with food and pamphlets warning them not to eat too much. MacArthur's cautious pace in liberating Kyushu excited their derision more than their anger. They were simply ignoring orders to stay in the camps, and wanted to see Nagasaki.

We needed numbers. I accepted them. The trainmen moved us to a baggage car, roomy and airy. As we click-clicked along, it occurred to me that the authorities of Nagasaki might be more difficult than train crews. Here we were, an atomic mission, highly classified, but also oddly bereft of orders. Nor did we have sidearms. We were headed by an untidy reporter and a gangling sergeant, with three alien privates whose rice-gray faces and merriment revealed their ex-prisoner status. I saw that the first Japanese official who guessed our real identity would get the police to put us in custody "for your own protection," exactly as MacArthur was doing with my colleagues, and telephone to Tokyo for the MPs to come and pick us up. Lacking even a revolver, we could not defend our mission with force. There was only one protection we could assume: rank.

Rank! In war it will get you everything but mail.

I therefore awarded all members of my command spot promotions, starting naturally with myself. I became Colonel Weller. In hardly an hour, between Yamaguchi and Nagasaki, Harrison rose from sergeant to major. He could not have done better in Cuba. The three Dutch privates became lieutenants in an inter-Allied working party so dense with secrecy that they communicated with me part of the time in German, the enemy language. We removed all our tabs that were detachable, dipped handkerchiefs in canteens and washed away the soot. We even cleaned our nails.

I felt small guilt at this lightning round of promotions. In the U.S. Army correspondents carried only the assimilated rank of lieutenant, a painful disparity with Italy's fascist forces, where they were splendid colonels with orderlies. Still, I could hardly expect MacArthur and his colonels to promote me. After all, I had refused to promote them.

I took off my brass shoulder tabs, lettered "War Correspondent," and put them in my back pocket, ready for use if Colonel Weller were compelled, by some emergency appearing out of the fog of war, to turn his force around and lead it back into humbler status. The needles kept pricking me in the behind during the following week in Nagasaki. They hurt especially whenever a Japanese called me "Colonel." I felt like one of those Caesars in triumph, who had an elderly slave standing behind him in his chariot, murmuring, "Remember thou art only a man."

On September 6, exactly four weeks almost to the hour since the bomb dropped on Nagasaki, our little train of toy cars flustered its way into the remains of the station. For the last ten miles the buildings were in ruins on both sides of the track, and I assumed the whole city was flat. I was wrong. The blast had traveled out along the railroad gulch, instead of being deflected upward as it was by the hills in the city's heart.

My heart sang with an immense, selfish sense of possession. What happened from now on did not matter much. Even whether it was written did not matter much. I was here. Nagasaki was waiting to be recorded, and I was here to do it.

There were no taxis, no rickshaws, no wagons. Defeat had leveled the Nagasakians into a city of walkers, except for the lucky officials, who had bicycles. By firm language with the police sentries and introductions from the trainmen, we managed to intercept a truck. I asked to be taken to the military commander. The volunteer pointed up to a hill flecked with villas: "The general lives up there." "Get him down here. I must talk to him," I said. The police were impressed. It seemed good riddance to take us up to him. I showed annoyance, but consented.

As we climbed the graceful curves into the little-damaged suburb of the executive class, Nagasaki came alive. The long inlet of the main harbor looked eerily deserted, with the floating lamp of a single freighter smoking off the blistered, sagging piers and twisted derricks. We could see the main Mitsubishi plant, a long fallen zeppelin of naked, twisted steel, bent like a child's structural toy crushed by a passing foot. Its form was still almost intact, though it was almost directly under the bomb. The sturdiness of the ceilings had taken the blast and blocked the ray. The workers were more fortunate than their families in the one-story bungalows around the plant. They did most of the dying.

When we arrived at the arch-roofed villa of the major-general, I left my staff outside and marched up the broad front stairs. Leading me was the general's aide, a sharp lieutenant around twenty-five with an eye full of cool appraisal. He guided me into the general's office. He was a square-built, impassive man in his forties, guardedly cordial, warily courteous. I explained my mission: to obtain the facts about Nagasaki. I did not say for whom.

The lieutenant translated, and appended a suggestion of his own. The general nodded. "General say he like to see your orders," said the lieutenant.

I did not look at the general, but I spitted the lieutenant with a glance. "If the general doubts our authority," I said icily, "I suggest that he telephone directly to General MacArthur for confirmation." The general, who understood more English than he let on, glanced at the lieutenant, inviting comment. The lieutenant scrutinized me a shade more respectfully. "But in making such a call," I said, "the general should *consider his position.*" Now I looked at the general. There was a nervous pause. The general said something low and rapid.

"General says you are very welcome in Nagasaki, Colonel. He will give orders to show you everything." I nodded casually, as if no other result was ever thought of.

"You have only three cars left, I understand," I said directly to the general, to let him know I realized he had notions of English.

"General says that is true," said the lieutenant at my shoulder.

"Then my party will take only two of them, the two Fords," I said. "I realize that the general must have one car for himself. He has the very important task of keeping discipline and order, and preventing looting." This remark seemed to reach the general. He nodded with vigor. "And I shall require two Kempeitai [military police] every evening to take my daily reports to Tokyo."

"This is a difficulty," said the lieutenant. "Many of our men have gone—have been released. Why two? One is enough."

"One is not enough," I said. "One Kempeitai must be awake while the other sleeps. My reports go straight through Tokyo to Washington."

A consultation. "General says it is difficult, but you will have two Kempeitai."

"Good. Now would the general give us the two cars and send us to our quarters?"

The general sent us down to a hotel. This was our baptism in the new Japan, where the army was spurned. The manager simply refused to book us. He did not like the vagueness about who was going to pay, and who we were. The lieutenant, abashed, called the general. Colonel Weller and his staff were transferred to a villa of their own where we bathed and lived on lobster, rice and sweet little slices of canned tangerine.

Before this muddle about quarters cooled him, the lieutenant took me out on the terrace of the general's villa. We stood at the top of the long, temple-like flight of steps, overlooking the prostrate, battered city from which rose only the tinkle of bicycle bells. The arrogance habitual to the military caste, sitting uneasily on him as an educated civilian, was now plated with a new veneer, freshly applied, of compassion for the bomb's victims. He was not cringing. The Japanese had studied Americans for enough years to know that Oriental cringing was not the way to subdue them. You had to play at being American. He was aiming at that underlying strain of compassion that makes the American review all his acts of force, even against assassins.

He pointed at the sky at a point not much higher than we stood. "One enemy plane fly right over city," he said. "We sound no alarm. Think maybe he is lost. Another plane off there. Seem like he watch first plane. But maybe he lost, too. No formation."

Did the people take shelter? "No. Only some prisoners lie down in slit trenches. No alarm, so good people keep working." Did they know about the Hiroshima strike three days before? "We know. General and I know. Police know. But few people know."

This was a lie, I learned later. At first the Nagasaki newspapers were ordered to censor out Hiroshima, but this was pointless. The trains were still running—nothing can stop the Japanese railroad system, which has a life of its own—and too many people were moving around. Hiroshima was terribly and mysteriously stricken, that much was known. But it did not seem worse than the great fire raids on Tokyo.

Nagasaki, people felt, would be spared. Why? Because in the face of all logic, it had been spared so far. It was a complex of industrial plants. It was a feeder port for the campaign in Southeast Asia. It was the nearest major Japanese city to the American bombing bases. And yet it had been left almost intact. Streams of B-29s flowed north and south around it, but this prime target remained mysteriously untouched. Perhaps, people guessed, it might be because it had a large Roman Catholic population. But Rome's railroad yards had been bombed, with Catholic bombardiers at the pips. More likely, they thought, it was being saved as the logical port for a coming invasion, a Cherbourg. They did not know MacArthur had decided to hit the north first, then work down. That decision put Nagasaki on the bombing list.

"Police ring our telephone," said the lieutenant. "They say me: 'Tell general enemy plane drop parachutists. Please to watch the falling.' I see big parachute, with man hanging underneath, not moving legs, falling like dead. He seem about eight hundred meters tall. Plane flying away fast, not watching. Very strange, to drop spy over city in daylight. Not fool anybody. Police say, 'You watch, tell us where parachutist fall.' I find binoculars quick and watch. Lucky, because binoculars save me from blindness for my life." He gulped.

He closed his eyes, then went on. Suddenly he was talking like a civilian. "Big light. Too much. I drop glasses. Fall down. Blind. Fall right there." He pointed, "General in back. He all right, I think. When get up, still cannot see. Parachute should still be falling. But gone. Man gone, too. Police phone not working anymore. I go tell general. He say it is big bomb, like Hiroshima. We come back on terrace. My eyes better. We can see damage to buildings, bodies in streets. Ships sinking, sailors swimming. Mitsubishi plant, roof gone. General say, very bad."

Did a wave of fire sweep the city?

"No wave. Only little fires. No big ones. Just a few little ones where workers live next to plant. There, see?" He pointed to the still, lifeless acres of charred beams and blackened walls, a hopeless tangle of burned-out debris.

The vision of the outside world of the bomb as whipping the city with a single, all-killing sheet of flame was wrong. Even the awful heat of the bomb, being only instantaneous, did no more harm than an opened furnace door to anyone who had any solid protection: a roof, a wall, a door. Yet most of the dead had been incinerated right there in the ruins. If not the bomb, what killed them?

He explained. The bomb fell almost at the noontime break in the factory, when wives were preparing rice over charcoal fires in kitchens and tiny gardens. The flame burst on high. The ray swept their roofs. Neither did much harm in themselves. But the blast pressed the roofs down, broke the timbers, sent the ceilings crashing onto the open hearths, scattering red-hot embers amid bodies and firewood.

People not wounded tried to fight the first small fires. But the water lines were broken. Firemen got as far as the edge of the district, then were stopped. They could not get inside, either with hoses or shoulder-pack chemicals. Walls had fallen across streets. Alleys were flaming tunnels. The wounded nearest the edges were dragged or crawled out. Inexorably the smoke spirals turned to flames. The flames spread. In half an hour it was out of control, a broad, orange-red, crackling pyre. By then the last cries had long ceased, as suffocation mercifully preceded incineration.

Now came the lieutenant's epilogue. "What do you think, Colonel," he said, "of the culture of a people who could drop such a terrible weapon on the people of Japan?"

I wanted to cut this experiment off early. I waited a moment. Then, as gravely as I could, I said, "To give you an honest reply, I would have to ask my own people. And of course I would have to begin with those who were walking to church on Sunday on Red Hill in Hawaii when your planes struck them."

We got along much better after that.

NAGASAKI was never, strictly speaking, "destroyed." Nagasaki had about 300,000 people, about the size of Worcester, Peoria or Tacoma. About 20,000 died right away, the majority by concussion from falling buildings or by burning in ruins, not by concussion of air or direct singeing. I was told 35,000 had been hurt, mostly by burns. Harrison's figures were 25,000 and 40,000. About 18,000 homes, mostly two-room bungalows, were destroyed, for perhaps $20 million worth of total replacement.

Soon after the Soviets consolidated their booty in the Kuriles and the Rosenberg spy case developed, the atomic bomb became a "horror weapon." The ideology of the Japanese army became that of the Communist International. Since then, Nagasaki's casualties have been rising in multiples of five and ten thousand. At the most recent ban-the-bomb meetings the dead tripled to 65,000.

Before the bombs fell, Nagasaki was getting ready to lose the war but win the psychological recovery. American prisoners working in the Mitsubishi plant were naturally told that if defeated, the entire nation would commit hara-kiri. But the executives of the plant had taught their foremen some highly unsuicidal terms, such as, "How are you today?" and "We workers want to save our plant." They had also shown disbelief in Nagasaki's immunity by moving their most expensive machinery to a hole in a hill two miles away.

I found these instructors, many of whom had brutal records in prison camps, now fawningly eager to serve the new colonel in town. They mistook me for their bridge into the MacArthur command. The general himself saddled me with the most repulsive of these double-tracked vehicles, an unctuous character who, Harrison discovered, had been one of the roughest straw bosses over the Allied prisoners. These swarming aspirant-interpreters did not, like those in Germany and Italy, try to prove that they had been oppressed democrats all the war. They imitated the army's pitch: that the United States had won unfairly and owed Japan generous help to come back. Their hands were out to collect the first slice for themselves.

When we entered the ruins, I had my first showdown with my interpreter. The ruins were "poisoned" and "dangerous," he said. Luckily, in the hospitals I had asked the X-ray specialists. "We don't think so, not if you wear thick-soled shoes like yours," they said. When I led the way in, he tried to take my camera. "Photos are forbidden," he said. "Not to me," I said.

I got rid of the interpreters in the hospitals because their officious manner got between me and the doctors—earnest, dedicated scientists, with nothing to sell. As fast as the pathetic patients squatting in the corridors died, the interns took them into the back rooms and dissected them for the doctors. Already they knew precisely what the effect of the ray was.

A doctor who had survived Hiroshima explained to me: "The main effect seems to be on the bloodstream. People say that the red and white corpuscles are killed. But we do not find it so. What are killed are the platelets. Do you know what they are?" I didn't. "They are the third important element of the blood, which gives it the capacity to coagulate. See that man?" He pointed to a thin figure with a paper-white face propped against a wall, surrounded by kneeling, intense relatives. "He was already a tuberculosis case, with minor hemorrhages. He was exposed about a quarter mile from the explosion. He was knocked down, but not apparently hurt. Then, after a few days, his coughing began to increase. He began raising more and more blood. We looked at it, and found the platelets were all dead." "Is there nothing you can do?" His eyes fell, as if in apology for his inadequacy. "Nothing," he said.

The most valuable thing I got in Nagasaki was a careful analysis of the effects of the ray on each organ: heart, lungs, kidney, liver, stomach. In all cases there was some deterioration. But often they were almost intact, and the patient died of some insignificant scratch whose bleeding could not be stemmed.

When darkness fell I spent three hours each night tapping out my stories by lamplight. Then, about a half hour before the train left on its twenty-four-hour journey—at least—to Tokyo, two Kempeitai arrived at my door. I addressed the stories to "Chief Censor, American Headquarters, Tokyo."

I considered trying to smuggle my stories out of Japan, but rejected it. I had made the point I wanted by getting into Nagasaki and proving it could be done safely. Now I wanted to give the MacArthur command the least possible excuse to hold up my research. I eschewed all horror angles. I intended within five days to be in Tokyo myself. I wanted to be prepared to defend every line. If the stories were blocked as reprisal against me, I intended to take the case to MacArthur himself. Only if he blocked them would I consider smuggling them out myself.

One thing that made me feel extra secure in my laboratory, able to work methodically and broadly, was that Nagasaki's airfield was supposed to be damaged beyond repair. And then, on the fourth day, when I had pumped off about ten thousand words to Tokyo— research, interviews, damage reports—my laboratory was burgled, my monopoly ended. The lieutenant phoned me the awful news. "Many American reporters have landed," he said. "They have two planes." I hurried downtown with my staff. Indeed there they were, about two dozen old friends from all the war theaters of the world, wandering up and down the pitted boulevards in their go-to-hell Air Force caps, talking Pentagonese. They looked like yacht passengers who have stopped to buy basketry on an island. I had an impulse to hide, but they already knew about Colonel Weller. "You dirty dog, how did you get here?"

I told them. "Well, you better not go back to Tokyo. They're sore as hell at you. Get aboard with us. We've got two Forts—yes, two, one to ride, one to transmit our stories. We take off and sling them straight into Washington. The straight stuff, no censorship."

How could I close up my atomic laboratory, with the work only half finished? Where were they going? "Right down the line, Hong Kong, Hanoi, Saigon, Singapore, Indonesia, maybe even Bali."

Up sauntered the small slim commander and deviser of the expedition, Tex McCrary, former New York editorial writer turned colonel, a friendly, dynamic wheeler-dealer who married Jinx Falkenberg and later made himself into a breakfast-hour TV star. "Did MacArthur clear you for Nagasaki?" I asked hopefully. There might be a loophole there for me. He shook his head. "Never asked him. Didn't have to. We're flying right out of Washington, under worldwide orders from Joint Chiefs. We can go anywhere, write anything. We have our own censors, and we transmit while airborne. No local clearances."

"We just throw it over their heads into Washington," growled a voice. "In three hours from now, all our Nagasaki stuff will be on the desk."

"Stuff"! I felt like a Robinson Crusoe, reluctant to be rescued, but half-sensing, from these new-dateline-every-day boys, that my obsession with history was getting out of hand. My Dutch forces had

quit Nagasaki and gone back to their camp, where movie projectors and films were now being dropped in. Harrison had run out of time and was leaving. One of my cars had disappeared, and the night before the lieutenant had sent only one Kempeitai, not two. Was it time to cut my losses and go?

But the deep fullness of the Nagasaki story was still emerging. I was beginning to look ahead to something free, big and formal. I considered deferring fighting the censorship in Tokyo, and going north to Hiroshima. My mind was fumbling for something ample, leisurely and magnificent, such as John Hersey was to do several months later for *The New Yorker*.

McCrary, kindness itself, offered to take carbons of my stories and file them when airborne. In my stubbornness I refused. First, my work wasn't over. Second, I had spent four years bucking the MacArthur blackout (minus intervals in European and African fronts). This was my fight and I was going back to see it through. The circus shook their heads as if I were mad, and they were right.

When I looked up, alone again in Nagasaki, and saw the two B-17s swing over the city, and imagined the typewriters talking as they swept southward, I had that bite of shame that comes when you have missed your communications. A few hours later, on the old radio in the villa, the playback of the "the first correspondents in Nagasaki" began to come through.

What remained fascinating for me was the constant revision of my own ideas of total-devastation and no-escape-from-the-bomb. The sharpest correction came from 120 prisoners I interviewed on an island in the harbor, and another camp of workers—Americans, British, Dutch, Australians and Javanese—next to the Mitsubishi plant. Of these several hundred men, only eight had been killed by the bomb. Why so few, when so near the supposedly all-pervasive doom? "Those eight wouldn't have got it, either," explained an American dentist, "but they poked their heads out of the slit trench to watch the parachute falling. Just too curious."

They showed me the slit trench, hardly two hundred yards from where the bomb went off high above their heads, and barely four feet deep. "Whenever there was an air raid warning, we would bugger off and hunker down in the slit trenches till the all-clear sounded, or the foremen drove us back. That's what saved us. For the last weeks there were so many planes passing north and south around Nagasaki that the warnings and all-clears got all mixed up. The workers stayed at their machines, but we claimed our rights. And they needed our skilled work so much they didn't force us."

Blast and ray flew harmlessly over their heads. They had lain prostrate almost directly under it, and only forty claimed to be wounded, few severely.

A few, who had happened to be looking that way, saw the mushroom cloud climb over Hiroshima. But they had then been in the mad camp at Omuta, where an insane Japanese captain with a mania for baseball kept the diarrhea patients running bases in a lavatory league of his own. It was a week after Nagasaki's bomb, when the prison authorities began burning the medical records, that they knew the war was over.

Not a word came back from Tokyo about my dispatches. The Kempeitai returned to Nagasaki, but they had no message for me. A feeling of hopelessness about my stories began to drag me down. Perhaps they were already locked in some censor's safe. If so, what sense was there in leaving southern Japan for Tokyo, to start this tedious battle? Why not, instead, mine what there was around me? The camps of southern Japan, six weeks after the Mikado's surrender, were still not opened.

So, about four days* after McCrary's flying circus departed, Colonel Weller packed his bag and started up country, sans staff. Two American officers who had wandered into Nagasaki furnished me with a list of unopened camps, each with its weird story. For a week I roamed from camp to camp. Then the grapevine of errant prisoners brought me another blow. The Marines had landed in Nagasaki. I raced back south. What a change!

In three days Nagasaki had undergone the full transformation from crushed worm to brave yellow butterfly. A ruin was changing into a hostess city. Destroyers, transports, LSTs crowded the harbor.

---

* One or two days, in fact.

My floating lantern was gone. Salvage operations had begun. Jeeps and trucks hustled through the stream of bicycles. Marines leaned on the sagging sills of the harbor buildings, lovingly cleaning their carbines.

But still there were no correspondents. The Navy had landed, but even they were under MacArthur. And still, going on seven weeks after the bombs, the world was waiting. What was the reason? To keep the victory of two nuclear weapons from eclipsing a general? To prevent its being said that the Pacific war was finally won in the Manhattan Project, not in Manila? I could imagine the two hundred correspondents, still bottled up in Tokyo, being told that there were "no facilities" for them in Nagasaki, and that the ruins might be infected. Meantime I was leading Navy doctors and nurses through the now cleared, sorted, arranged embers.

By this time it was not really necessary to become a casualty of Nagasaki myself, but I managed to do so. On a hospital ship's deck I caught a medicine ball thrown by a burly Navy doctor, and felt something crack. In an hour Dr. Malcolm Stevens, the former Yale coach, had me mummified in a plaster cast from neck to hips. The ship carried me off to Guam.

But I still had my smudged carbons. A month later I started trying to get them through the Navy censorship. "We can't clear this stuff, but we'll be glad to send it to Tokyo for you. I'm sure they'll release it there." "Thanks, but never mind."

As soon as I was able to walk, I received orders to go back to China. I was somewhere in Manchuria, I believe, when I received news that parties of correspondents were now being taken to Hiroshima, and yes, Nagasaki, too.

They won. At least I was not busted by my organization for bucking the system, like dour, funny Ed Kennedy, who was too early for Eisenhower with the signing of the armistice. Ed, who had covered the fall of Greece with me, had set up communications that were too good. I threw away my one good chance to communicate, trying for a fuller, more perfect story.

O, Nagasaki! What a way to lose a war!

II

Early Dispatches

(September 6-9, 1945)

From September 6 until September 10 Weller stayed in Nagasaki, exploring the blasted city each day, writing his dispatches far into each night, then sending them off to MacArthur's military censors in Tokyo, hopeful that they were being cabled onward to his editors at the *Chicago Daily News* and thence to a vast American readership via syndication. These dispatches have remained unpublished for sixty years; it appears that the U.S. government destroyed the originals. Weller's own carbon copies were found in 2003.

nagasaki 62300 herewith follows first known eyewitness
account results atomic bomb dropped nagasaki by
american ground observer chicagonewses george weller
who reached crippled city three days after first american
troops landed southern kyushu

Nagasaki, Japan—Thursday, September 6, 1945
2300 hours

Walk in Nagasaki's streets and you walk in ruins.

It is thirty-three days* since two American planes appeared in a clear midday sky and let fall the blow which clinched Japan's defeat and decided her surrender. The mystery of the atomic bomb is still sealed. But the ruins are here in testimony that not only Nagasaki but the world was shaken.

The last two or three of what were scores of fires are burning amid Nagasaki's ruins tonight. They are burning the last human bodies on improvised ghats of rubbish. Flames flicker across flattened blocks from which planks, lathes and timbers have been removed as a fire menace, and only shapeless piles of plaster remain.

Yet the atmosphere is not precisely dolorous. Nagasaki cannot be described as a city of the dead. The unquenchable Japanese will to live has asserted itself. Though the smashed streets are as barren of production or commerce as Pompeii's, yet a living stream of humanity pours along them, looking with alert, shoe-button eyes for today's main chance.

After a 24-hour trip on what seemed like dozens of trains, the writer arrived here this afternoon as the first visitor from the outside Allied world. Trains coming from both Honshu and southern Kyushu were so jammed with returning human beings that the writer was able only to fight his way into the baggage cars. Some

---

* Twenty-eight days, in fact; Weller miscounted.

refugees rode the locomotives' cowcatchers. Nagasaki has only about one hundred fifty of its normal three hundred thousand inhabitants, but they are coming back. By the hundreds they streamed along the concrete platforms which alone remain of Nagasaki's station, their belongings tied in big silk scarves or shoulder rucksacks. Painstakingly these Nagasakians ignored the soot-stained American trudging beside them. Fear or merely resignation may have accounted for their indifference. What looked like disinterest amid Nagasaki's peace-imploring debris was the suppression of personal feeling in obedience to the emperor's order.

The first thing you learn as you walk amid the flattened houses, and the cordwood that was once walls piled with Japanese neatness, is that the atomic bomb never really "hit" Japan. If the Japanese are right, the bomb exploded over Japanese soil. They can only tell what they saw and try to guess much of what really happened.

At about 11:30 o'clock on the morning of August 9th, a lieutenant who is aide to Major General Tanikoetjie, commanding the district, was walking through the headquarters on the hill above Nagasaki's long waterfront. The lieutenant heard a high faint moan of aircraft motors, found his fieldglasses, went to a porch and trained them to the sky. What he saw was two B-29s at about 22,000 feet, flying in echelon. No anti-aircraft fire was around them; they were too high for Nagasaki's batteries.

Suddenly there broke from the forward plane three parachutes. Their canopies unfolded and what they bore earthward seemed to be three oblong boxes. The boxes looked about thirty inches long by eight inches wide. Demurely as *The Mikado*'s three little maids from school, the canopies sailed downward. The lieutenant took them for some new form of pamphlet propaganda.

The three parachutes had reached the point where the lieutenant could begin sending auto crews to confiscate their freight when something violent happened. With the parachutes at perhaps a five thousand feet level there suddenly occurred below them, at about fifteen hundred feet, a burst of flame. Almost instantly the flame, yellow as gaslight, fell in a widening cone to earth, at the same time spreading wider in hoopskirt fashion.

This skirt of flame fell across the bottleneck creek which is a dead end for Nagasaki's tremendous shipping industry. Nothing human or animal that was above ground there at that moment survived.

As the fiery skirts swept the ground there suddenly burst upward a cumulus cloud of black dust. This cloud climbed high into the sky, visited by a terrible atomic heat erecting a pillar of warning over death's city. The lieutenant saw this as it began but immediately fell flat on his face, letting the concussion pass over him. When he rose up the parachutes were gone, and Nagasaki was afire.

The lieutenant never saw the atomic bomb or any other in the air, perhaps because its bulk is reportedly small. His theory is that the parachutes were not carrying bombs, but were carrying machinery for controlling the altitude at which a free-dropped bomb would be exploded by its companions.

Dropping the atomic bomb on Nagasaki, after Hiroshima's bomb, was like hitting Pittsburgh after Detroit. The puff of death quickly scurried up the valleys of hilly Nagasaki. Whereas Hiroshima was a plain, these small hills tossed the blast from crest to crest like a basketball. Winds of terrible force churned about in the valleys, stripped the roofs in many homes and brought the greatest number of dead in houses where they had been sheltered two and three miles from the explosion, in a fashion resembling a hurricane. Roofs fell on weak foundations, burying those beneath.

Nagasaki had had its first air warning only on July 5th and only one earlier serious raid. The so-called "long" or constant warning had been in effect since 7 o'clock but most people had ignored it.

At constabulary headquarters tonight, little Lieutenant Colonel Tokunagawa told the writer that as catalogued up to September 1st, 19,741 deaths had been positively and officially counted, plus 1,927 missing. Wounded requiring treatment number 40,093.

[ends weller]

please acknowledge receipt this story by radio to weller and whoever's else in tokyo, mcgaffin or thorp.

george weller

Nagasaki, Japan—Friday, September 7, 1945
2400 hours

Two Allied prison camps in Nagasaki harbor number nearly 1,000 men, who have just one question they want answered.

It is: "How does the atomic bomb work?"

They have seen what it does. The Japanese placed one camp amidst the giant Mitsubishi war plants and the other at the entrance to Nagasaki, where it would be impossible for it not to be shelled by any attacking task force.

Seven Dutchmen—including camp leader Lieutenant Kick Aalders of Bandoeng, Java—and one Britisher died from the atomic bomb attack. The writer visited their camp this afternoon as the first outsider in years.

American, British, Dutch and Australians each had their national preoccupations of which I was able to settle the American and British, but failed completely at the Dutch and Australian. Their questions were as follows:

The Aussies, "Who won the Melbourne Cup?" (with Aussies it is always *who* for horses.)

The British, "Is Winnie still in, or did Britain go labor?"

The Dutch, "Is Juliana's third child a boy heir to the throne, or another girl?"

The Americans, "B-29s dropping us food keep enclosing Saipan newspapers with stuff about some guy named Sinatra. Who is he and what's his racket?"

Nagasaki, Japan—Saturday, September 8, 1945
0100 hours

The atomic bomb may be classified as a weapon capable of being used indiscriminately, but its use in Nagasaki was selective and proper and as merciful as such a gigantic force could be expected to be.

Such is the conclusion which the writer, as the first visitor from the outside world to inspect the ruins firsthand, has drawn after an exhaustive though still incomplete study of this wasteland of war.

Nagasaki is an island roughly resembling Manhattan in size and shape, running in a north-south direction with ocean inlets on three sides. What would be the New Jersey and Manhattan sides of the Hudson River are lined with huge war plants owned by the Mitsubishi and Kawanami families. The Kawanami shipbuilding plants, employing about 20,000 workmen, lie on both sides of the harbor mouth on what corresponds to Battery Park and Ellis Island. That is about five nautical miles from the scene of the explosion's main blow. B-29 raids before the atomic bomb failed to damage them and they are still hardly scarred.

Proceeding up the Nagasaki harbor, which is lined with docks on both sides like the Hudson, one perceives the shores narrowing toward a bottleneck. The beautiful green hills are nearer at hand, standing beyond the long rows of industrial plants, which are all Mitsubishi on both sides of the river. On the left or Jersey side, two miles beyond the Kawanami yards, are Mitsubishi's shipbuilding and electrical engine plants, employing 20,000 and 8,000 respectively. The shipbuilding plant was damaged by a raid before the atomic bomb, but not badly. The electrical plant is undamaged. It is three miles from the epicenter of the atomic bomb and repairable.

It is about two miles from the scene of the bomb's 1,500 foot high explosion, where the harbor has narrowed to the 250 foot wide Urakame River, that the atomic bomb's force begins to be discernible. This area is north of downtown Nagasaki, whose buildings suffered some freakish destruction but are generally still sound.

The railroad station—destroyed except for the platforms, yet already operating normally—is a sort of gate to the destroyed part of the Urakame valley. Here in parallel north-south lines run the Urakame River with Mitsubishi plants on both sides, the railroad line, and the main road from town. For two miles stretches this line of congested steel and some concrete factories with the residential district "across the tracks." The atomic bomb landed between and totally destroyed both, along with perhaps half the living persons in them. The known dead number 20,000, and Japanese police tell me they estimate about 4,000 remain to be found.

The reason the deaths were so high—the wounded being about twice as many, according to Japanese official figures—was twofold: that Mitsubishi air raid shelters were totally inadequate and the civilian shelters remote and limited, and that the Japanese air warning system was a total failure.

Today I inspected half a dozen crude short tunnels in the rock wall valley, which the Mitsubishi Company considered shelters. I also picked my way through the tangled iron girders and curling roofs of the main factories to see concrete shelters four inches thick but totally inadequate in number. Only a grey concrete building topped by a siren, where clerical staff worked, had passable cellar shelters, but nothing resembling provision had been made.

A general alert had been sounded at seven in the morning, four hours before the two B-29s appeared, but it was ignored by the workmen and most of the population. The police insist that the air raid warning was sounded two minutes before the bomb fell, but most people say they heard none.

As one whittles away at embroidery and checks the stories, the impression grows that the atomic bomb is a tremendous but not a peculiar weapon. The Japanese have heard the legend from American radio that the ground preserves deadly irradiation. But hours of walking amid ruins where the odor of decaying flesh is still strong produces in this writer nausea, but no sign of burns or debilitation. Nobody here in Nagasaki has yet been able to show that the bomb is different than any other, except in the broader extent of its flash and a more powerful knockout.

All around the Mitsubishi plant are ruins which one would gladly have spared. Today the writer spent nearly an hour in fifteen deserted buildings of the Nagasaki Medical Institute hospital which sit on a hill on the eastern side of the valley. Nothing but rats live in the debris-choked halls. On the opposite side of the valley and the Urakame River is a three-story concrete American mission college called Chin Jei, nearly totally destroyed. Japanese authorities point out that the home area flattened by the American bomb was traditionally the place of Catholic and Christian Japanese.

But sparing these and sparing the Allied prison camp, which the Japanese placed next to an armor plate factory, would have meant sparing Mitsubishi's ship parts plant, with 1,016 employees who were mostly Allied. It would have spared an ammunition factory connecting, with 1,740 employees. It would have spared three steel foundries on both sides of the Urakame, using ordinarily 3,400 but that day 2,500. And besides sparing many sub-contracting plants, now flattened, it would have meant leaving untouched Mitsubishi's torpedo and ammunition plant employing 7,500, and which was nearest to where the bomb blew up. All these latter plants today are hammered flat. But no saboteur creeping among the war plants of death could have placed the atomic bomb by hand more scrupulously, given Japan's inertia about common defense.

More pieces to the broken mosaic of history are supplied by prisoners in the liberated but still unrelieved camps on Kyushu, Japan's southernmost island. While waiting for General Walter Krueger's army to arrive, the inmates are receiving humble bows and salutes from the Japanese officers who formerly ruled them with a rod of iron. By exchanging visits with prisoners from other parts of Kyushu, they are able to find out what happened in the blacked-out periods of the past.

Camp #14, which was inside the Mitsubishi war factory area until the atomic bomb fell upon it, is now moved inside the eastern mouth of the Nagasaki harbor. Here you can meet Fireman Edward Matthews of Seattle and Everett, Washington, and of the American destroyer *Pope,* who bummed his way here on the Japanese railroad from Camp #3 near Moji in northern Kyushu. He fills in the unknown story of how the *Pope* fought, trying to take her cruiser *Houston* through the Sunda Straits in the face of a Japanese task force of "eight cruisers and endless destroyers. We contacted the Japs at seven in the morning. They opened fire at 8:30 a.m. We held out until 2 p.m., when a Jap spotter plane dropped a bomb near our stern and watched us go down. The Japs saw us sink. It was a perfectly clear day. They let us stay in the water—154 men with one 24-man whaleboat and one life raft—for three days. We were about crazy when they picked us up and took us to Macassar."

From Camp #3 at Tabata near Moji in northern Kyushu come three ex-prisoners who have found the lure of the open roads irresistible after three years' confinement and have come to Nagasaki in order to view the results of the atomic bomb.

Charles Collings of Northeast, Maryland, says, "The *Houston* was caught on the eastern, or Java side, of the Sunda Straits near Bantam Bay. Three hundred and forty-eight were saved, but they are all scattered."

Chicago-born Miles Mahnke, of Plano, Illinois, who looks all right, though his original 215 pounds dropped to 160, says, "I was in the death march at Bataan. Guess you know what that was."

Here is Albert Rupp of Philadelphia, from the submarine *Grenadier.* "We were chasing two Nip cargo boats four hundred fifty miles off Penang. A spotter plane dropped a bomb on us, hitting the maneuvering room. We lay on the bottom, but the next time we came up we were bombed again. We finally had to scuttle the sub. Thirty-nine men of forty-two were saved." Another from the submarine is William Cunningham, of Bronx, New York, who started with Rupp on his tour of southern Japan.

Another party of four vagabond prisoners from camps whose Japanese commanders and guards have simply disappeared are Albert Johnson of Geneva, Ohio, Hershel Langston of Van Buren, Kansas, and Morris Kellogg of Mule Shoe, Texas—all crew members of the oil tanker *Connecticut.* Now touring Japan with a carefree Marine from the North China Guard at Peking, Walter Allan of Waxahachie, Texas, these three would like a word with the captain of the German raider who took them prisoner. The captain told them, "In the last war you Americans confined Germans in Japan; this war we Germans are going to take you Americans to Japan and see how you like a taste of the same medicine."

Kyushu has about 10,000 prisoners, or about one-third of the total in all Japan, mixed in the completely disordered fashion the Japanese used and without any records.

At Camp #2, by the entrance to Nagasaki Bay, are living in comfortable air-fed circumstances 68 survivors of the British cruiser *Exeter* which sank in the Battle of the Java Sea while trying to escape the Japanese task force. Eight-inch shells penetrated her waterline. Five of the supposed total of nine survivors from the British destroyer *Stronghold,* sunk near the Sunda Straits at the same time, are also here. There are also 14 Britons of an approximate 100 from the destroyer *Encounter* lost at the same time, besides 62 R.A.F. mostly from Java and Singapore.

Among the 324 Dutch here from the Battle of the Java Sea are 230 Navy men. They include one officer and eight men from Admiral

Doorman's flagship cruiser *De Ruyter.* This officer told the writer that two Dutch cruisers, the *Java* and *De Ruyter,* were sunk at 2330 and 2345 hours on the night of Feb. 27, 1942, by torpedo attacks which the Japs boasted were staged not by destroyers or submarines, but by cruisers. There is also a Dutch officer from the destroyer *Koortenaer,* torpedoed by night in the Battle of the Java Sea.

Husky Corporal Raymond Wuest of Fredericksburg, Texas, told how 105 members of the 131st Field Artillery poured 75-caliber shells into the Japs for six hours outside Soerabaya [Surabaya] before Java fell, killing an estimated 700. To this correspondent's eager questions about this outfit which he had seen go into action in Java, Wuest said that 450 members fought in western Java and were now scattered throughout the Far East. Eighty-five reached Nagasaki, whereof most were moved to Camp #9 near Moji.

Nagasaki, Japan—Saturday, September 8, 1945
0300 hours

A Dutch doctor and an American dentist are commandants of two Allied prison camps at the mouth of the harbor of Nagasaki, the seaport of the southern island of Kyushu partly crippled by the atomic bomb. The Dutch doctor is thin, energetic Army Lieutenant Jakob Vink, who is assisted by a Dutch flying ensign and Singapore Brewster flying expert, Paul Jolly. Vink is expert at curing wounds from the atomic bomb.

The American dentist, Captain John Farley of Raton, New Mexico, was one of five American prisoners here who saw the atomic bomb and observed it more fully than any of the others.

Controlled and quiet in his account, Farley said, "I was looking up the harbor toward the Mitsubishi plants five miles from here when I saw a terrific flash. It was white and glaring, very like a photographer's flare. The center was hung about 1,500 feet from the ground. Light was projected upward as well as downward, something like the aurora borealis. The light quivered and was prolonged for about thirty seconds. I instantly caught the idea that it was something peculiar and hit the ground. The building began to shake and quiver. Glass shattered around me; about one-third of the windows in the camp broke. After the blast passed, I saw a tall white cumulus cloud, something like a pillar, about four or five thousand feet high. Inside, it was brown and churning around."

The week before the bomb fell, as a consequence of B-29 raids late in July, Dr. Vink went to the Japanese with Dutch Lieutenant Kick Aalders and protested against the prisoners being obliged to live in a camp next door to the Mitsubishi shipfitting plant where they worked. This camp, #14, numbered about 200, three-quarters being Dutch. The Japanese said that the Allied prisoners must be ready to take the same risks as the Japanese.

Later the Dutchman renewed his plea and asked for the right to build an underground shelter because the plant's were so few and inadequate. The plea was denied, but later granted. The prisoners had only had time to start their hole when the atomic bomb fell. Forty-eight were wounded, four instantly killed, and four, including Aalders, died.

Visiting the camp's old site with the Japanese police, the writer found it flattened. Vink and Jolly were both in the blast. Jolly said, "Some say three, but I saw four parachutes falling. While I watched, I heard a separate hissing sound of the bomb."

Harold Bridgman, a civilian workman from Witten, South Dakota, who has been imprisoned ever since Wake Island fell on December 23, 1941, saw the atomic bomb hanging in Nagasaki's sky and told the writer, "To me the light looked sort of bluish, like a photographer's light bulb. It was so powerful that the blast behind it seemed to suck your breath right away."

Another Wake Island civilian, Fred King of Legrand, Oregon, who is troubled with prison abscess, said, "I was in bed. The light seemed to me like a gun flash. It tore plaster down and broke the fixtures—that was from five miles away."

Corporal Raymond Wuest of Fredericksburg, Texas, captured in Java with the Texas 131st Field Artillery, said, "We thought the Nagasaki power plant must be blowing up. It was a huge electric flash which sent us all to the floor. Then came the concussion. But we never understood until the food bombers also dropped us an explanation."

Vink is one of eleven Dutch medical officers who have survived of the thirty-eight captured in Indonesia. He was aboard a prison ship torpedoed on June 24, 1944, sixty miles off Nagasaki. From 770 prisoners, 212 survived including 10 Americans. Two drowned in Nagasaki harbor when, despite their pleas of an inability to swim, the crew of a Jap destroyer kicked them overboard with seven swimmers, ordering them to make their own way to another boat.

According to Vink, Camp #14 has had 512 prisoners, of whom 112 died in Nagasaki, mostly from pneumonia induced partly by malnutrition. Vink pointed out that the Japanese incidence of pneumonia is also high.

Nagasaki, Japan—Saturday, September 8, 1945
2300 hours

In swaybacked or flattened skeletons of the Mitsubishi arms plants is revealed what the atom can do to steel and stone, but what the riven atom can do against human flesh and bone lies hidden in two hospitals of downtown Nagasaki. Look at the pushed-in facade of the American consulate, three miles from the blast's center, or the face of the Catholic cathedral, one mile in the other direction, torn down like gingerbread, and you realize the liberated atom spares nothing in its way. Those human beings whom it has happened to spare sit on mats or tiny family board-platforms in Nagasaki's two largest undestroyed hospitals. Their shoulders, arms and faces are wrapped in bandages. Showing them to you, as the first American outsider to reach Nagasaki since the surrender, your propaganda-conscious official guide looks meaningfully in your face and wants to know: "What do you think?"

What this question means is: Do you intend writing that America did something inhuman in loosing this weapon against Japan? That is what we want you to write.

Several children, some burned and others unburned but with patches of hair falling out, are sitting with their mothers. Yesterday Japanese photographers took many pictures of them. About one in five is heavily bandaged, but none are showing signs of pain.

Some adults are in pain as they lie on mats. They moan softly. One woman caring for her husband shows eyes dim with tears. It is a piteous scene and your official guide studies your face covertly to see if you are moved.

Visiting many litters, talking lengthily with two general physicians and one X-ray specialist, gains you a large amount of information and opinion on the victims' symptoms. Statistics are variable and few records are kept. But it is ascertained that this chief municipal hospital had about 750 atomic patients until this week and lost by death approximately 360.

About 70 percent of the deaths have been from plain burns. The Japanese say that anyone caught outdoors in a mile and a half by one mile area was burned to death. But this is known to be untrue because most of the Allied prisoners trapped in the plant escaped and only about one-fourth were burned. Yet it is undoubtedly true that many at 11:02 on the morning of August 9th were caught in debris by blazes which kindled and caught fire during the next half hour.

But most of the patients who were gravely burned have now passed away and those on hand are rapidly curing. Those not curing are people whose unhappy lot provides an aura of mystery around the atomic bomb's effects. They are victims of what Lieutenant Jakob Vink, Dutch medical officer and now Allied commandant of Prison Camp #14 at the mouth of the Nagasaki harbor, calls "Disease X." Vink himself was in the Allied prison kitchen abutting the Mitsubishi armor-plate department when the ceiling fell in. But he escaped this mysterious "Disease X" which some Allied prisoners and many Japanese civilians got.

Vink points out a woman on a yellow mat in the hospital who, according to hospital doctors Hikodero Koga and Uraji Hayashida, has just been brought in. She fled the atomic area but returned to live. She was well for three weeks except for a small burn on her heel. Now she lies moaning, with a blackish mouth stiff as though with lockjaw, and unable to utter clear words. Her exposed legs and arms are speckled with tiny red spots in patches.

Near her lies a fifteen-year-old fattish girl who has the same blotchy red pinpoints and a nose clotted with blood. A little farther on is a widow lying down with four children, from age one to about eight, around her. The two smallest children have lost some hair. Though none of these people has either a burn or a broken limb, they are presumed victims of the atomic bomb.

Dr. Uraji Hayashida shakes his head somberly and says that he believes there must be something to the American radio report about the ground around the Mitsubishi plant being poisoned. But his next statement knocks out the props from under this theory because it develops that the widow's family has been absent from the wrecked area ever since the blast, yet shows symptoms common with those who returned.

According to Japanese doctors, patients with these late-developing symptoms are dying now—a month after the bomb's fall—at the rate of about ten daily. The three doctors calmly stated that Disease X has them nonplussed and that they are giving no treatment whatever but rest. Radio rumors from America receive the same consideration with the symptoms under their noses. They are licked for a cure and do not seem very worried about it.

Nagasaki, Japan—Sunday, September 9, 1945
0020 hours

Watching Americans die from a lack of medicine—while Japanese bayonets denied them the use of a warehouse full of needed supplies a hundred and fifty yards away—was only one experience of two doctors, veterans of the Bataan death march, who reached Nagasaki today.

No pity for the Japanese digging themselves out from the ruins of the atomic bomb was expressed by dentist Lieutenant William Blucher of Albuquerque or Lieutenant Vetalis Anderson of Denver. The two physicians with the 200th Coast Artillery were cheerful, though worn by their more than three years of bitter captivity at infamous Camp O'Donnell and Cabanatuan in the Philippines and more recently at Camp #3 near Moji in northern Kyushu.

How helpless they were to aid 8,000 Americans and 30,000 Filipinos dying respectively at a rate of twenty-five and three hundred daily was retold by the two young doctors. As Lieutenant Blucher recounted, "On the death march we saw men drink from cesspools with dead bodies in them. Any men who dropped out were shot or bayoneted. At O'Donnell we had hundreds of cases of malaria. From a warehouse jammed with Red Cross supplies, the Nips issued us enough quinine for only twenty men. We became the arbiters of life and death. We simply had to decide who would be kept alive and who would be allowed to die. We used rags for dressings."

According to Lieutenant Anderson, "The Japanese always enjoyed keeping us without water, and forcing us to sit in the sun in order to get thirsty and dizzy quicker. I saw with my own eyes a Filipino bayoneted for trying to offer us water. When the Filipinos saw they'd be killed for this, they set five-gallon tins of water along our marching route. The Jap commander sent ahead a special detail of men to knock the tins over. I saw a Jap kick in the stomach a pregnant Filipino woman who tried to give us riceballs. She fell, and I went past with her lying there. The Filipinos were magnificent all the way through. At O'Donnell they sent us three trucks full of food and medicine. The Japs turned them back at the camp gate, though men were dying so fast we could not bury them. Later, when the Japs allowed us to go into the jungle to gather guava leaves for tea, the Filipinos used to find our parties and sneak them little packets of medicine."

Without any medicine or instruments, both doctors tried to treat the fractured skulls of men beaten by the swords of Japanese officers standing in trucks during the death march. "It was hard to march and keep ducking these blows when you wanted to fall down anyway," they said.

Lacking any sick bay, Anderson and Captain Louis Snyder of Portland, Oregon, began to outfit an abandoned Japanese latrine. The result was that Camp Cabanatuan's Marine commandant, Lieutenant Colonel Manuel Freeman of Maryland, was confined for allowing the unauthorized use of Japanese property. At one time Anderson and Snyder unaided were treating twenty-five hundred men.

Anderson told how after reaching Moji he tried to persuade the Japanese to part with some hoarded diozane for those dying Americans with pneumonia. Only when two died and a third was beyond help did the Japanese commander give his consent. Oxygen was denied to another ailing man and Anderson heard the Japanese commandant say that the man was "no damned good if he needed oxygen." He was refused digitalis for an elderly Indian with this remark by a Japanese doctor: "He cannot work; let him die."

Both Americans agreed that some Japanese doctors were humane but said that American doctors had to submit to the lowest Japanese corpsman. Japanese peasant soldiers would go along through sick bay, ordering men to their feet to work.

Japanese officers always took a Red Cross package each and forced the prisoners to feed Japanese soldiers from theirs. During last winter's early bitter cold, the commandant at the Moji camp had seven Red Cross blankets and all his soldiers three to four, while the American prisoners had less than enough to go round.

They told how Major John Bennett of Luresa, Texas—after being slapped repeatedly by a Japanese sergeant—attempted to see the

Japanese commandant and was beaten until lacerated by the same sergeant.

Both doctors were under orders to salute all Japanese except for the capless, when they were obliged to bow deeply in Nipponese fashion. They told how new Japanese soldiers distributed Red Cross sweaters among themselves and let the Americans shiver last winter. Men with a cold or influenza were not allowed to lie down in the sick bay but forced to stand up. If otherwise unoccupied, their job was to catch bedbugs. "The goal was fifty daily, and if we caught less we were sent to the fields."

At Moji's camp the Japanese forced pharmacist's mate Stanley Shipp of Hay Springs, Nebraska, to falsify the records in order to prove that there had been proper medical treatment. Nevertheless, on August 15th the Japanese removed and burned the camp records.

Nagasaki, Japan—Sunday, September 9, 1945
0100 hours

The atomic bomb's peculiar "disease," uncured because it is untreated and untreated because it is undiagnosed, is still snatching
away lives here. Men, women and children with no outward marks
of injury are dying daily in hospitals, some after having walked
around for three or four weeks thinking they have escaped. The doctors here have every modern medicament, but candidly confessed in
talking to the writer—the first Allied observer to reach Nagasaki
since the surrender—that the answer to the malady is beyond them.
Their patients, though their skins are whole, are simply passing
away under their eyes.

Kyushu's leading X-ray specialist, elderly Dr. Yosisada Nakashima,
who arrived today from the island's chief city of Fukuoka, told the
writer that he is convinced these people are simply suffering from
the bomb's beta, gamma, or neutron rays taking a delayed effect.
"All their symptoms are similar," said the Japanese doctor. "You
have a reduction in the white corpuscles, constriction in the throat,
vomiting, diarrhea and small hemorrhages just below the skin. All
these things happen when an overdose of roentgen rays is given.
Bombed children's hair falls out, and some adults'. That is natural,
because these rays are used often to make hair fall artificially and it
sometimes takes several days before the hair becomes loose."

Nakashima differed with general physicians who have asked the
Japanese government to close off the bombed area, claiming that returned refugees have been infected from the ground by lethal rays.
"I believe that any after-effect out there is negligible, though I mean
to make tests soon with an electrometer," said the X-ray specialist.
The suggestion by Dutch doctor Lieutenant Jakob Vink (taken prisoner in Java and now commander of the Allied prison camp here)
that the drug pentnucleosan—which increases white corpuscles—
be tried brought the rejoinder from Nakashima that it would be
"useless, because the grave X-ray burns are incurable."

43

At Emergency Hospital #2 the commanding officer, young Lieutenant Colonel Yoshitaka Sasaki, with three rows of campaign rib-
bons on his breast, stated that 200 patients had died of 343
admitted, and that he expects about 50 more deaths. Most severe ordinary burns resulted in the patients' deaths within a week after the
bomb fell. But this hospital began taking patients only from one to
two weeks afterward. It is therefore almost exclusively "Disease X"
cases and the deaths are mostly from this.

Nakashima divides the deaths outside simple burns and frac-
tures into two classes on the basis of symptoms observed in nine
post-mortem autopsies. The first class accounts for roughly 60 percent of the deaths, the second for 40 percent.

Among exterior symptoms in the first class are: falling hair from
the head, armpits and pubic zones; spotty local skin hemorrhages,
looking like measles all over the body; lip sores; diarrhea but without blood discharge; swelling in the throat areas of the epiglottis and
retropharynx; and a descent in the number of both white and red
corpuscles. Red corpuscles fall from a normal five million to half or
one-third, while the whites almost disappear, dropping from seven
or eight thousand to three to five hundred. Fever rises to 104 and
stays there without fluctuating.

Interior symptoms of the first class revealed in the post-mortems
seem to show the intestines choked with blood, which Nakashima
thinks occurs a few hours before death. The stomach is also choked
with blood, and also mesenterium. Blood spots appear in the bone
marrow, and subarachnoid oval blood patches appear on the brain
which, however, is not affected. Upgoing parts of the intestines have
little blood, but the congestion is mainly in downgoing passages. The
duodenum is drained of blood, but the liver, kidney and pancreas remain the same. The spleen is hard but normal, though the urine
shows increased blood. There is little blood in the colon but much in
the jejunum or upper intestine.

Nakashima considers it possible that the atomic bomb's rare rays
may cause deaths in the first class, as with delayed X-ray burns. But
the second class has him totally baffled. These patients begin with
slight burns which make normal progress for two weeks. They differ

from simple burns, however, in that the patient has a high fever. Un-fevered patients with as much as one-third of their skin area burned have been known to recover. But where fever is present after two weeks, the healing of burns suddenly halts and they get worse. The burns come to resemble septic ulcers. Yet patients are not in great pain, which distinguishes them from any X-ray burn victims. Four to five days from this turn to the worse, they die. Their bloodstream has not thinned as in the first class, and their organs after death are found in a normal condition of health. But they are dead—dead of the atomic bomb—and nobody knows why.

Twenty-five Americans are due to arrive on September 11th to study the Nagasaki bombsite. The Japanese hope that they will bring a solution for Disease X.

III

Among the POWs

(September 10-20, 1945)

On September 10, the day after the U.S. military press junket came and went in mere hours, Weller left Nagasaki to explore the POW camps about forty miles north. He probably got there using a car and driver commandeered from the general.

None of Kyushu's Allied camps, whose prisoners worked as slaves, had yet been "opened"; few camps were aware the war was over, although many Japanese guards and officers had fled. Some camps had received food drops from B-29s. The prisoners—mainly American, British, Australian, Dutch— were diseased, weakened, yet reluctant to risk leaving, fearful for their lives after years of indiscriminate torture and deliberate starvation.

The Japanese POW camps are one of the great omissions in World War II memory. Despite the large numbers involved— 140,000 Allied prisoners through the war—they have not been portrayed in films, chronicled by historians, or officially documented as the Nazi camps have been, though they were seven times deadlier for a POW. The Pacific war was as much a tribal struggle of race, with all its mutual incomprehensions, as a struggle of nations.

Weller's dispatches are full of prisoners talking who often had realized only that very day that they were suddenly free men, now telling how it felt to be at the receiving end of that struggle. These men were the lucky ones, the survivors. All were brought to the camps from overseas: captured on Java or

Singapore, put to work in Burma or Thailand, imprisoned as one of MacArthur's abandoned eighty thousand from Bataan and Corregidor who endured the death march to O'Donnell and Cabanatuan and somehow survived. A third of the prisoners in any camp died.

Many of Weller's POW dispatches concern Omuta #17, the largest camp of all. Weller arrived there unescorted and went directly into the commander's office; shortly afterward an assembly was called, with American POWs on one side and rifleless guards on the other. Speaking from a platform, the Japanese commander said, "Japan has laid down its arms in favor of a great nation."

Then Weller spoke, and told of the two atomic bombs, the recent surrender, and how U.S. troops for the occupation of Kyushu were arriving down in Kanoya daily, airlifted from Okinawa. "I have no authority to tell you what to do," he said, "but why should those planes go back empty?" That day, men began to leave.

Omuta, Japan—Tuesday, September 11, 1945
1800 hours

Allied Prison Camp #17, Omuta, Kyushu

Midwesterners now impatiently awaiting their return home saw a pillar of cloud following the atomic bomb form across Nagasaki Bay. Today they told their impressions to a *Chicago Daily News* correspondent. They are members of the 1,700-strong Allied camp which is probably the largest in Japan. Many have been working eight to ten hours daily in a low-ceilinged coal mine owned by Baron Mitsui, who is still residing unrestricted and roaming at large here.

Albert Dubois (Webster, Wisconsin): "Smoke from that atomic bomb made Nagasaki look like a mass of blackness for six hours afterward."

Lester Tennenberg (Chicago, Illinois): "We saw the cloud rising up from the ground over Nagasaki and admired it, but only learned after the surrender that it was an atomic bomb."

Sergeant Wallace Timmons (Chicago, Illinois): "I think the Japs were seriously frightened by the incendiary bombing before the atomic bombs."

Stanley Lukas of Chicago, a civilian employed by U.S. Army Ordnance in Corregidor, said, "I only heard about the atomic bomb, because the Japanese had me underground in the coal mine."

Sergeant Harold Fowler of Peoria and *Sergeant David Garrett of Carbondale,* both mechanics with the 17th Pursuit Squadron, said, "At evening roll call after coming out from the mine, we saw a strange haze over Nagasaki. That was all we saw of the atomic bomb."

Sergeant James Bashleben (Park Ridge, Illinois): "About seventy-five percent of Maywood Company were living after Bataan, but I lost track of things after the long death march to Camp O'Donnell."

Robert Johns (Pekin, Illinois): "On Bataan, with the 200th Coast Artillery, I weighed 170. The Japs had me working in 'meso nooky.'

That's the water-covered portion of the mine floor. My weight went down to 115, but I've added some since our planes began dropping us rations."

Stanley Kyler (Dekalb, Illinois): "I've been working twenty-two months for Baron Mitsui. Four months was driving hard rock, and eighteen months was shovelling coal, twelve to fourteen hours a day. The Japanese often made us extractors work two hours extra."

Sergeant Warren Lackie (Aitkin, Minnesota), said: "When the Japanese brought me from Bilibid Prison in the Philippines, we were bombed off Olangapo and I got crushed in a falling hatch cover. I thought I was done for when I was carried ashore at Moji, in Japan. I've thrown away the crutches now and manage well on canes. I've gone from 82 to 135 pounds."

Annapolis graduate *Lieutenant Edward Little (Decatur, Illinois),* captured on Corregidor: "I saw the atomic bomb over Nagasaki, when from a red ball suspended in the air it began to mushroom upward like an ice cream cone. The core stayed red for about twenty minutes. I got the impression that a fire was burning in the cloud. The Japs were very concerned, they kept pointing their swords toward Nagasaki and jabbering. They knew about the first one at Hiroshima and were as worried as we were ignorant."

Omuta, Japan—Tuesday, September 11, 1945
2200 hours

Allied Prison Camp #17, Omuta, Kyushu

Within view of the cloud rising up from the atomic bomb over Nagasaki, prisoners from the New Mexican 200th Coast Artillery at this, the largest Allied camp in southern Japan, are waiting eagerly for orders sending them homeward. They have worked twelve-hour days for many months in Baron Mitsui's coal mine on their hard road from Bataan, but liberty is now at hand.

Benny Daugherty (Alamogordo): "When I saw the atomic bomb's smoke over Nagasaki it was one hour after it had been dropped at eleven o'clock. We were marching to work in the Mitsui coal mine and I saw the smoke turning from grey toward black. Our eyes rose up because fires were catching in the town."

Robert Dunlap (Carlsbad): "We discussed the smoke rising over Nagasaki and wondered whether it was bombing or a cloud, and could not make up our minds."

Corporal Agapito Silva (Gallup): "I missed the bomb by being in the mine. Our work was so long, so dangerous and so rough that it caused some men to deliberately get their arms broken in order to escape from being underground."

First Sergeant Manuel Armijo (Santa Fe): "To us, Japanese treatment meant frequent beatings and being ill-clothed and ill-fed, which caused some stealing due to hunger. We passed a very hard winter."

Valentine Dallago (Gallup): "I've seen at least a score of men whipped underground by Japanese overseers with a length of dynamite fuse, or struck by a shovel."

Thomas Barka (Gila): "Our main troubles were a water freshet in the mine, stooping for the low roofs, being obliged to carry heavy timbers and being continually beaten by the Japanese bosses."

Corporal Ben Montoya (Taos): "Cave-ins came about once a week. Seven months ago a cave-in broke my right leg, and I'll be glad to get some American treatment."

Corporal Jesus Silva (Santa Fe): "It was so bad underground that your friend would ask you to go off into a dark lateral passage with him, hand you a crowbar and reach out his foot or arm, and whisper, 'Will you, please?' You knew that meant for you break it, which would mean thirty or forty days' rest for him. For asking the Japanese foremen to remove the timbers preventing my crew from building a wall face, I was severely beaten by three overseers who took turns smashing their fists into my face. They wanted me to go to my knees and ask for mercy but I refused. Finally one took a club and knocked me out."

Evangelisto Garcia (Hot Springs): "My biggest thrill was June 18th and July 27th by night, when B-29s burned practically all this mining town. I only regretted that they failed to put the mine out of order, because it was hell. I lost track of the times I was beaten up for simply not understanding the Japanese language. They took full advantage of our being prisoners, unable to strike back."

Sergeant Thomas Nunn of Albuquerque was preparing a lateral passage in the Mitsui mine when he went to fill his flask at a place where water dripped from the coal ceiling. When he returned the overseer was angry, with Corporal George Craig standing helplessly by. He dragged Nunn to the superintendent's office. The superintendent and overseer gave him a preliminary beating with fists and a small stick, then handed him over to soldiers on the surface. "The soldiers beat me with the handle of a spade, about fifty cutting blows on the buttocks, which left them bleeding. I missed my shift that night. The mine boss complained. Soldiers came and dragged me to jail. They practiced a bamboo torture, forcing me to kneel on a piece of bamboo placed on the floor. I had to keep my toes stretched out behind me, resting all my weight on my knees. I stayed that way, kneeling, for two days and two nights without rest. To weaken me they balanced a pail full of water on my bent thighs in order to increase the weight on my knees. I had to hold the pail with my hands and not let it fall off my thighs. Finally, to increase the pressure even more, they put my head through a short ladder with the long sections resting on my shoulders. They'd take turns pulling down on the ends of this ladder. Then they removed the water bucket and the ladder. The *gunze*—that's sergeant—took a mallet like a croquet mallet and hammered me all over my head and face till one eye was completely closed and the other only barely open. Then they forced me go back to work in the mine. I worked for one day. Finally, on July 4th they let me return to my bunk."

Fred Starnes (Silver City): "I'd been sick and so I was not strong. That increased my beatings. If there was a big nugget and they ordered you to pick it up and you couldn't, they'd beat you."

Faustino Olguin of Albuquerque bears a scar on his scalp from a sabre blow by the camp commandant, who still rides about Omuta undetained and unrebuked. Olguin needed a pencil to make out a receipt for the light worn on his mining cap, and borrowed one from the mess sergeant. Possession of pencils or paper was forbidden by the Japanese. The Japanese commandant saw him and began beating him with a sheathed sword. He was then thrown into jail by soldiers who held him foodless for two days. "They kept me kneeling on bamboo at attention all day. Because it was in March, and cold, the Japs also took me out in the wind and poured buckets of water over me, which gave them a great laugh."

Joe Medina (Taos): "I'm a blaster or explosive man. I've seen plenty of Japs killed in the mine with a cave-in. But I've been fortunate; they never laid hands on me."

Omuta, Japan—Tuesday, September 11, 1945
2300 hours

To: Commanding officer, Recovered Personnel section,
    Yokohama
From: George Weller, Chicago Daily News correspondent,
Prisoner of War Camp 17, Omuta, Kyushu

september eleven twentythree hours message begins
todays drops gratefully received stop unfortunately
personnel were injured and installations damaged
including two kits on dispensary stop therefore aiming
point for camp seventeen containing seventeen hundred
persons been moved halfmile southward stop drop
ground for camp twentyfive containing four hundred
prisoners remains same

paragraph chinese camp containing roughly two thousand
received seven drops today which was their first help
since surrender stop chinese especially need general
issue medicine

paragraph chinese buildings were hitherto unmarked due
failure japanese inform chinese of manila agreements
conditions regarding marking prisoner war buildings for
air drops

paragraph as of september twelfth northward facing roof
markings of all three prisoner war camps near omuta will
bear under prisoner war inscriptions their respective
designations seventeen twentyfive and quote china
unquote message ends

Allied Prison Camp #17, Omuta, Kyushu

American and Chinese prisoner coal miners emerging from under-ground darkness in central Kyushu are discovering for the first time that their prison camps are adjacent.

For nearly one month since the surrender the Chinese have been going foodless because their Japanese guards have departed from the camp. Their serious medical condition was discovered today by two parties headed by American doctor Captain Thomas Hewlett, of New Albany, Indiana, and Crystal River, Florida, who was captured on Corregidor, and Australian Captain Ian Duncan, of Sydney, captured in Singapore.

B-29s today dropped the Chinese their first food supplies since the surrender.

Hewlett reported that the nearest Chinese camp commander is a remnant of a party under American-trained Airman Lieutenant Colonel Chiu, which left North China two years ago, then numbering 1,236. Three hundred men died on reaching Japan. The Japanese never provided a camp physician and the Chinese have none. Thus in the Chinese camp every man regardless of condition has been considered by the Japanese fit for underground work. Fifty are seriously ill, about half of these with deficiency disease.

This Chinese camp counted 70 men killed by Japanese guards in two years, plus 120 dead of disease, with 546 still living.

The other coal miners' camp of Chinese consists of what remains of 1,365 who left China eighteen months ago; 54 have been executed or otherwise beaten to death by the Japanese, and 60 died of mining injuries.

Many of the surviving Chinese are "as thin as skeletons," with bandages made of rags or newspapers. The camp has one Chinese doctor who possesses neither a scalpel, forceps, thermometer nor stethoscope.

Both those Mitsui mines worked by Americans and those worked by Chinese are defective, "stripped" mines, dangerous to operate because their tunnels' underpinnings have been removed to obtain the last vestiges of coal.

Another Chinese camp is known to exist somewhere in Kyushu and is being sought by a party headed by Medical Warrant Officer Houston Sanders, of Hartwell, Georgia.

Omuta, Japan—Wednesday, September 12, 1945
0230 hours

Allied Prison Camp #17, Omuta, Kyushu

For hundreds of Americans held in Kyushu prison camps, the atomic bomb bursting over Nagasaki in full view was a signal of their liberation from serfdom in Baron Mitsui's cruel and dangerous coal mine. Some Bataan and Corregidor prisoners were worked to death here. Captain Robert W. Schott, an energetic dentist from What Cheer, Iowa, has succeeded the Japanese commander. Here are G.I.s' comments on their coal mine slavery, and on the bomb ending it.

James Small (Gate City, Virginia): "The mine was hard not because of the work, but because the Japanese insisted on our carrying impossible burdens. Many times we took beatings just in order to have two men carry one roof support."

Sergeant James Bennett (Monongahela, Pennsylvania): "I lost my thumb trying to protect my detail from being beaten up by a Japanese soldier. Rushing things to make the Jap cease his beating, I fell forward and a mine car rolling forward caught my hand."

Corporal Junious Carroll (Thornton, Washington), who had his hearing impaired by an explosion on Corregidor, has lost his left leg at the shin: "A Japanese overman borrowed my cap lantern, leaving me to go through the tunnel to get another. Seeing no light where I was, the mine train ran over me."

Joseph Valencourt (Lawrence, Massachusetts): "After the atomic bomb I saw a cloud lit up like a sunset over Nagasaki. But not understanding, I paid no attention."

Corporal Gerald Wilson (Clovis, New Mexico): "The atomic bomb cloud looked like a giant thunderhead. It kept boiling, getting larger."

Corporal Richard Burke (Chicago): "The atomic bomb cloud seemed to me like the dying embers of a sunset, but all in one spot."

Elmer Swabe (San Francisco), captured on Wake Island: "I've been in Japan for three years and had just one letter—from my wife."

Sergeant Gail Herring (Los Angeles): "Most of my outfit, the 60th Coast Artillery, have had at least one letter since being captured on Corregidor. But I've had none."

Robert Fortune (San Francisco), captured on Wake: "I worked for twenty-six months in a steel mill at Yahata near the camp at Moji and got pneumonia and beriberi. But since coming here in January I've gained some weight."

Larry Sandoval (Albuquerque), his right leg missing two inches from the knee, is one among the American prisoners who paid for the Japanese insistence that this old and dangerous mine be exploited. "I was building a supporting wall opposite the coal face when the ceiling came down."

Robert Case (West Terre Haute, Indiana) is another victim of Baron Mitsui's enterprise, with his left leg gone between knee and ankle. "I got caught in a coal-carrying transmission chain, and was carried into the motor."

Edgar van Imwagen (Palmyra, Ohio), with his left leg amputated two inches above the knee: "The Japs always shoved us in against the coal face without testing whether it would hold, because they wanted to not lose any time. Last December 12th, when I weighed 100 pounds after forty-five days in the mine, the overseer shoved us into an untried coal face. The roof's pressure, being unbraced, blew the wall in on us. I was bending over, shoveling, and got buried completely. A half hour later the Japanese doctor took off my leg, which healed in sixteen days. A whole bunch of Koreans were buried alive the year before in the same place, and are still there. When Japs came to my bed at Christmas and offered me a gift of two cigarettes, I just lay there and laughed."

Sergeant Calvin Elton (Dividend, Utah): "I live in a mining town and I knew for all my two years around the Mitsui mine that the Japanese were just using Americans to remove the pillars from an old mine, leaving tunnels unsupported. Accidents were the natural result of such dangerous work."

James Voelcker (Wetmore, Texas): "In February I got so weak with diarrhea I couldn't work, and mine overseers handed me over to the military who threw me into the *aeso*—that's Japanese for guardhouse. It was cold and the Japanese made me carry water for them. My feet were always wet and finally froze. Gangrene set in and an Australian doctor had to amputate all my toes and both feet."

Kenneth Vick (Oklahoma City): "I've been able to run the camp toolroom, working above ground, because I got hit by three machine gun bullets on Bataan."

Air Corps Sergeant Ben Lowe (Knoxville, Tennessee), captured on Bataan, who lost his right leg halfway between the hip and the knee: "Our Buntai Joe—that means overseer—refused to go in under this bad coal face, but sent my crew in to dig. When the coal fell the first nuggets knocked me down, then the whole face buried me. Three weeks later Captain Hewlett amputated my leg."

Alfred Schnitzer (Portsmouth, Virginia), captured at Corregidor: "I've always tried to give the Japanese my best, and when the military put me in the guardhouse, the sentries refused to punish me."

Sergeant James Justice (Gaffney, South Carolina), taken on Bataan: "I was lifting a heavy coal trough when the foreman began yelling at me. I made some remark in English. He hit me with a piece of coal. I knocked out two teeth on him. He reported me to the military, who slapped me and beat me with a board. Captain Hewlett got me declared unfit for underground work. Two months ago the camp commander beat my head with a two-by-four for not replacing a door after a typhoon blew it in." Justice is wearing a bandage on his head, where Captain Hewlett took out four stitches.

Earl Bryant (Anaheim, California): "I saw what might have been the first atomic bomb, in the direction of Hiroshima. It was a white cloud, big at the top and narrow at the bottom, on what seemed a bed of black smoke."

Corporal Dale Frantz (Canton, Ohio): "I missed Nagasaki's bombing, but I saw the cloud in the opposite direction, toward Hiroshima, on the first bombing. The cloud started small but built up high and fast. It was pure white, with a pinkish tinge. I could see airplanes circling between me and the cloud and suppose now that they were photographic planes. At the time we were puzzled by the whiteness of the smoke and supposed that it must be from a chemical plant."

Charles Butler (Smithdale, Mississippi): "It was a clear day, with other clouds all high strata. We could see this unnatural thunderhead with straight sides instead of being pyramidal-shaped, and airplanes seemed be circling around watching it."

George O'Brien (Wascott, Wisconsin): "I saw a reddish glow in the sky over Nagasaki and at first I thought it was a fire after the bombing. But it lasted too long for just Japanese shacks, and I was puzzled."

Joseph Collins (San Antonio), captured on Corregidor: "The next morning after the noonday bombing of Nagasaki, I climbed on a waterboiler platform with Stanley Peterson of Los Angeles, and we could see flames over in Nagasaki, leaping up and dying and rising again like an oil fire, but with a peculiar absence of black smoke."

Corporal Lee Dale (Walnut Creek, California), who visited the Nagasaki atomic bombsite: "Those flattened buildings made you want to cry, not on account of the lives lost, but because of the destruction involved."

"The Japanese Little Theater Gives a Red Cross Benefit"

Allied Prison Camp #17, Omuta, Kyushu

A cold brook runs through the tunnel of the Mitsui coal mine at Omuta, on Kyushu, but the air 1,440 feet underground is thick and hot. Your feet are ankle-deep in the rushing, icy water; at the same time your head swims with fatigue, and the sweat-towel around your brow is soaked with perspiration. "For almost two years we worked here twelve hours a day," the G.I.s tell you. "We got a little less than a cent a day. Pretty good for the Mitsuis. Till we came along, they never thought the mine could be made to pay again. Our officers only knew about the mine what we told them. The Japanese never let them go down."

But how about the neutral inspector from the International Red Cross?

"They never let him go underground, either."

Whenever a new shipment of American prisoners was seen shambling down the tunnel to work, backs bent under the low ceiling and cap-lamps bright, the weary old shift would break away from the "long wall"—the most advanced face of coal—and ask those arriving, "What's new topside?"

The incoming shift, skinny-legged and pale as the old on the same three half-bowlfuls of rice a day, would say, "Nothing, same as usual. Except the Japs strafed the new Red Cross packages today."

"What'd they get?"

"They took all the meat and fruit cans, and the condensed milk and most of the chocolate."

"What'd they leave?"

"Same as usual: the raisins and the prunes."

"Whatsa matter with those raisins and prunes? Why do they always leave them?"

"Search me." A minute of wordless thought on both sides; being

a prisoner is submission, but sometimes you have to remind yourself. "Any ceilings fall today on anybody?"

"Not yet, but look out for that mushy one over there. She shifted
twice this afternoon. Our *shotai Joe* made us work under the
cracked beam, but she's just about ready to let go and come down."

Stripping the abandoned mine of the Mitsui barons, removing its
last supporting coal pillars, was work for men who had already written off most of their future. But that did not mean that they had surrendered the present. Nothing that Captain Fukuhara, the camp
commandant, could do was able to silence the horselaugh that rip-
pled through the tunnels every six months or so, on the day after the
visit of the International Red Cross inspector.

Underground in the mine you could always tell when the B-29s
were making a visit overhead. The main power plant on the surface
closed down, the weaker auxiliary pumps went into action, and the
air grew gluey and hard to breathe. In a slightly different way you
could tell, while underground, when the Red Cross man was making
a visit. From every section gang the strongest American was told off
and ordered to take the mine train to the surface. He had ceased
being a miner; he was now an actor. He had a role in a play that the
mine authorities were going to put on for the benefit of the audience
of one: the Red Cross inspector.

Two or three days before the Red Cross man—usually a Swiss
or Swede—actually arrived, secret rehearsals had already been
begun by what might be called the leads: the Japanese authorities
of the camp. But for the real fibre of the performance the Japanese
counted on their unrehearsed extras, the Americans.

Show day comes. A one-shot performance can be as good as its
scenery, rarely any better. What is this extraordinary change that
has overtaken the filthy little clinic, where operations without anesthesia have often taken place? It is transformed. Not only ether
and morphine, but other medicines have appeared, the very medicines that were unobtainable 24 hours ago. . . . And look at the
notice board! What are those neatly typewritten sheets fluttering
from its black surface, now suddenly innocent of punishment records? It is the *Daily News Bulletin,* no less. ("We do what we can,

Mr. Inspector, to satisfy the extraordinary American curiosity about current events.")

And here comes the Red Cross visitor, walking like a prisoner himself in a phalanx of potbellied Japanese colonels and majors. Has he been underground? He has not. Will he get a view of the barracks? Well, a quick one, maybe. But first he is shown documents for three hours, till his eyes ache. Then the place for him to go is to the hospital. After all, a hospital is the great index of humanity. If the hospital in a prison camp is all right, everything else must be all right, too.

And everything in the little hospital *is* right, as superlatively right as the last canto of Scrooge's Christmas. Just the entrance alone is beautiful. On each side of the door, Red Cross boxes are piled tastefully in twin pyramids—medicines, food, a cornucopia of abundance. The military interpreter opens the door and the inspector enters. Order and cleanliness, a lovely sight. The faces of the men on their cots are turned toward him. Sick? If these men are the sick, confined to the hospital under medical treatment, then it is hardly necessary to see the healthy, now working down in the mine. For these men, as prison standards go, are not badly off at all. Their faces—though wearing a peculiar quizzical, stolid expression—are round and full. Their eyes are clear. A Japanese doctor would call them robust.

The visitor, stroking his moustache, turns to the Japanese nurse, one of several chubby little starched creatures who have been placed at even intervals the length of the ward, like markings on a clinical thermometer. "How are the prisoners doing?" he inquires through the interpreter. "Oh, very well, very very well," she says, with a shining nursely smile.

The inspector observes there are white sheets on the mattresses. Really not bad, altogether. Each man has a can of salmon or of pears at the same geometrical point near his bed. Not quite within reach, perhaps, but nearby.

Gently Captain Fukuhara suggests that perhaps the official party had better not delay too long in the hospital. Luncheon is already waiting. Would the inspector like to see what the prisoners are eating? The party passes rapidly through the kitchen to the mess hall, where the prisoners are lined up, waiting to be seen. Their faces still bear looks of unmistakable pleasure and anticipation, in which a sharp eye might detect strong traces of astonishment. There is no doubt that this is a happy camp. Look at the faces of the prisoners as they scan the miracle that lies waiting for them in their wooden mess gear: three camp rolls with a dab of margarine, bean soup with a bit of pork, a spoonful of Japanese red caviar, and a baked apple.

(It is the baked apple, though the visitor does not know this, which has really bewitched them. This baked apple is more than remarkable; it is historical. It is the only baked apple ever seen at Camp #17 in two years.)

The inspector has now seen the camp. But he must not go away without talking to one or two individual prisoners. So he is led to the Japanese headquarters, he is settled in the comfortable chair of the commandant, and several handpicked Americans are brought to him. The room is full of Japanese military and police; the only non-Japanese are the prisoner and the Red Cross man.

"We were selected for health, first," Sergeant Joe Lawson of Klamath Falls explains it. "Then, when they knew the inspector was at the railroad station, they double-timed us to a bath, clean clothes and a shave. We went in that room and only needed to look around at the familiar faces to know what we were up against. We'd had plenty of stickwork done on us already. We knew that to get plenty more, all we needed to do was open our mouths."

Now the last monosyllabic prisoner has walked out. The inspector rises. It is all over. Everybody is smiling. Nobody has said or heard anything disagreeable or discordant. Even the prisoners back in their quarters are happy in a way, for their fears that the visitor would ask penetrating questions and make it impossible for them to conceal the truth have been dispelled. The lie is still intact. How cheerful everyone is! Captain Fukuhara—on whose hands is the blood of five Americans beaten and starved to death in the *aeso,* the guardhouse—is geniality itself. He suggests a photograph to perpetuate the occasion. His lieutenants take up the proposal with an acclaim like bacchantes. A picture, a photograph of everybody! We must have it!

A table is decorated with cigarettes, cookies and fruit from the mess of the *kempeitai,* the military police. A Japanese Cecil Beaton runs around, all dithery excitement until he finds what he wants to put on the table with the edibles: a trumpet, a harmonica and a guitar. A suggestion is made that some of the irreproachable prisoners might be summoned back to get in the picture, but the picture is too crowded already, and the suggestion falls flat. . . . "All smile, prease!" (It is a little joke, for the fussy photographer to use the language of the prisoners, and all smile at it.) "Sank you! All finish!"

The military motorcar is waiting for the Red Cross man. Perhaps, in this last moment of shaking hands, he may be troubled by some inner doubts. But there is no time to sift them. He must hurry off, for he is to catch the train for Moji, connecting with the express for Tokyo. See you next year!

If he had seen the prisoners the next day, instead, the inspector would have learned more. If his officer escort would allow him to get off at the first station, turn around and go back to the camp, the inspector might see how the pageant of his welcome, as insubstantial as Prospero's, faded into nothingness as soon as he left.

What has happened in the camp? The pyramids of Red Cross packages are demolished. The boxes are in Captain Fukuhara's closet, and the key is in his pocket. The cans of fish and pears have disappeared. Gone, too, are the white sheets from the hospital beds; where, nobody knows. The little nurses are climbing into their truck to be taken back to the local hospital in Omuta, swans never seen before in camp, unlikely to be seen again. The *Daily News Bulletin* is gone without a trace from the notice board, and a *kempeitai* is frowningly nailing back the punishment schedule. In the kitchen the Navy cook, Woodie Whitworth of Bourne, Texas, is preparing supper. The menu is the same as usual: one-half bowlful of plain rice, laced with millet to make it cheaper.

A column of prisoners dressed for work, with cap-lamps and

sweat rags, is marching past the god of the mine.* As their guards command them, they all bow to his exalted, unsmiling image. These miners are the extras of the benefit performance, who were patients in the hospital until a few minutes ago.

Having arrived at the entrance shaft they adjust their lamps for the last time, hug their mess-gear full of cold rice, climb into the roller coaster–like iron train and hold on. The cable starts moving. The train slides down the slanting chute into the sooty, echoing tunnel. For a while its roar is loud, but soon it dies away. After five minutes or so a bell rings. The cable slows, tightens, and finally stops. The patients from the hospital have reached their normal level of operation, 1,440 feet below ground. The sideshow is over. The Mitsui show is on once more.

---

* A giant, greenish-black statue of an idealized Mitsui miner, towering in the prison yard above the buildings.

Omuta, Japan—Wednesday, September 12, 1945

Allied Prison Camp #25, Omuta, Kyushu

The atomic bomb, seen bursting over Nagasaki by British prisoners from Camp #25 in central Kyushu, astonished and mystified them.

Captain Douglas Wilkie (Fairlight, England) said that it "seemed like a huge, ever-swelling mushroom-shaped whiteish cloud, with a glowing center and stem reaching to the earth. I was queerly uneasy and very puzzled, and thought it was perhaps a new type of incendiary bomb."

Lieutenant William Miller (Glasgow, Scotland): "The bomb appeared like a growing ball of white smoke, with a red ball inside, giving me an impression of vague terror as an unaccountable phenomenon."

Warrant Officer James MacIntosh (Invercargill, New Zealand): "It started as a white puff of smoke, swelling and growing to a mushroom shape, and suddenly lit up inside. It was terrifying, as if clouds had caught fire."

Staff Sergeant George Duke (Lahore, India): "After a flash, white smoke expanded to the shape of an enormous parachute with an orange glow in the center. It remained suspended for half an hour and I thought it was possibly a prematurely detonated landmine. It gave me an empty feeling in the pit of my stomach."

Company Quartermaster Sergeant Norman Jones (Hartlepool, England) remembered "a huge white cloud, intermingled with orange flame spurting in all directions. I felt completely dumbfounded."

Sergeant Albert Young (London, England): "I saw a flash—as if a mirror had shone into one's eyes—followed by a white puff in the sky spreading to a huge ball of cloudy fire. I felt uneasy and frightened at something unknown."

Corporal Hubert Fyfe (Edinburgh, Scotland) described it as "the top half of a colossal hourglass, with red flame inside instead of sand, rapidly increasing in size. I thought a chemical works had been bombed."

Corporal William Lunan (Glasgow, Scotland): "I saw what looked like an enormous white wheel in the sky, with a glowing hub and axle pointing towards the ground. I felt unhappy about it, not knowing what to think."

Private Ernest Newsome (Barnsley, England) recalled "a huge ball of fire suspended in the air, growing larger and larger. It was still there after half an hour. I thought it was perhaps a new kind of gas. And I was upset."

Lance Corporal William Angus (Nuntley, Scotland): "A flash in the sky was followed two minutes later by a white puff growing to a mushroom shape, with a bright red glow inside. I thought it might be a new secret weapon, and was very bewildered."

Gunner Denis Maguire (Merthyr Tydfil, Wales): "It looked like a revolving ball of cloud in the sky, with a red glowing center, becoming momentarily larger. I had never before seen its like, and was thunderstruck."

Private Thomas Jones (Nieuport, Wales): "Following the explosion I saw a beautiful pure white cloud, which changed to red inside and commenced expanding. I thought it was a bomb raining red hot stuff down like a volcano."

Sergeant Johnny Sherwood (Reading, England) saw what seemed "an enormous white parachute poised in the sky. But I did not think any further of it and went on with my work."

Warrant Officer Richard Ranger (Auckland, New Zealand) said that the explosion "started as a small cloud, burning red in the center but fading to the edges. It gradually grew larger, with sheet lightning in the middle."

Gunner Leslie Hughes (London, England) compared it to "a huge, whiteish parachute burning inside, like a Crystal Palace firework display."

Warrant Officer Eddie Kuhn (Wellington, New Zealand) recalled: "I saw a ball of fire with a billowing white cloud at the edges. After a few minutes it became completely red-tinged, as if reflecting some huge city fire on the ground below. I was bewildered at this new horror."

Gunner Ian Wiley (Pudsey, England): "I saw a white cloud

suspended in the air, with tracers coming from it. My impression was that it must be a new type of anti-aircraft defense."

Gunner Fred Dillon (London, England): "It seemed like a ball of fire giving off white smoke in the sky, and suddenly bursting out in all directions. I thought it was a new type of bomb."

Gunner Leslie Huson (London, England): "I saw a parachute-shaped cloud with a red flame in the center, spreading sideways. It remained in the sky for about thirty minutes."

And *Corporal Stan Thompson (London, England)* remembers that "it appeared as a glowing turbulent cloud, expanding at the edges. I considered that it might be a new bomb. But I felt it best not to express my opinion, for fear of alarming the others."

Nagasaki, Japan—Wednesday, September 12, 1945
0130 hours

Allied Prison Camp #25, Omuta, Kyushu

This camp has received a note dropped with food from a relief-carrying B-29 by Lieutenant Joseph Rose, bombardier of the nine-man crew.

The note reads, "Hello Fellows, I happen to be co-pilot, but I am trying to express the thoughts and feelings of the whole crew—many of them could probably do the job more eloquently.

"We sincerely hope you won't need these supplies, but if the same conditions prevail in your camp as have been reported about others, you are sorely in need of them. Already some P.W. camps have been liberated and I want to assure you that every effort is being put toward getting you back home to rest camps and hospitals. Some crew members of our own bomb group have already been liberated and we are hoping more of them.

"Since they have sacrificed so much, it is with humility that I offer a short history of our crew. We arrived in the Marianas in March, 1945 and since that time have flown 33 combat missions. With this 37th mission, we have had our share of rough ones but by the grace of God our crew remains intact with no purple hearts to our credit.

"Again we wish you all the best luck in everything you undertake and if any of you live near any of our crew, or ever come close to where we live we want you to drop in and we will treat you as royally as possible."

The co-signers were the pilot, Captain John Mapes; navigator, Lieutenant Joseph Andrews; radioman, Sergeant O. C. Cushing; Engineer Sergeant Ardia Vorley; Flight Officer Harry Gordon; Sergeant James Aretakis; and two gunners, Sergeants H. A. Hecleworth and Samuel Thrower.

Today Camp #25's all-American medical staff, Captain William

Brenner of Selmo, California, and Gilbert Cotner, of Riverside, California, are replying by courier from this radioless camp:

"Received your air drop and needless to say everything was appreciated. Only a prisoner knows what it means to sit down to eat an American meal after rice and soup for the last three years.

"Our camp consists of 396 men: 3 New Zealanders, 1 South African, 2 Americans and the remainder are from the British Isles. The men have been fortunate in working in a factory instead of a mine and the general health, while only fair, is now rapidly improving.

"After our short period of active service on Bataan, we felt that we had done very little when we consider what occurred during our term as prisoners.

"I wish to express thanks to British prisoners both for supplies and the risks and dangers incurred in their delivery. When we reach civilization a feast will be in order and not a Japanese feast!"

Omuta, Japan—Wednesday, September 12, 1945
1800 hours

Allied Prison Camp #17, Omuta, Kyushu

The following is an exclusive-name story of British prisoners, witnesses of the atomic bomb, for *The Daily Telegraph* and possible Canadian newspapers.

The atomic bomb falling on Nagasaki and Hiroshima released from servitude 250 Britons working in the Mitsui zinc factory and a few in the Mitsui coal mine along with some 700 Americans. Beatings were frequent and the death toll high. The Britons had been mostly captured in Singapore and the Philippines.

Here are characteristic statements from those who saw the atomic bomb explode thirty miles away in Nagasaki, not realizing at the time that it meant their freedom.

Driver H. Dinn (Wolverhampton): "Thanks to this new bomb, the war is ended."

Warrant Officer T. C. Simons, Indian Army: "An astounding flash and smoke, and a fitting climax to Singapore, Thailand, and my experiences in the zinc works."

Corporal D. E. Poynton (Newport): "When I saw the billowing smoke and flames over Nagasaki, I thought it was just another raid."

Driver L. Stokes (East Acton, London): "It was a pleasure to see and hear those bombs dropping."

Driver T. W. Ewins (Worcester): "I am overjoyed at this sudden end to the war due to the new atomizer bomb."

Driver George Fuller (Dundee, Scotland): "Bless the atom bomb. Plum duff soon."

Driver S. Harrison (Radcliffe, Lancashire): "It is amazing what fire and atom bombs can do."

Britons who spent the atomic bomb raid in the shelter underneath the zinc factory commented as follows over the release from their bondage:

D. H. Batton (Blackburn): "Living conditions were appalling. Our food was poor and Japanese treatment very bad."

Sergeant at Arms J. Jardine (Cavan, Eire): "The Japanese are a sadistic race. Their brutality and torture is beyond all comprehension."

Corporal W. Campbell (Inverness): "I experienced and witnessed inhuman treatment, and feel lucky in my misfortunes."

Sergeant Major J. W. Heathcote (Wealdstone): "Living one year as a prisoner of war in Japan was much harder than two in Thailand."

Sergeant W. Cartwright (Coventry): "Over three years of mental and physical torture, disease, starvation and death."

Corporal G. Murdock (Dundee, Scotland): "Good luck to the atom bomb. A mighty package with amazing results."

Private McEvoy (Waterford): "The sooner I leave this god-forsaken country, the better."

Driver Bain Norwich: "The parents of all the Japanese I have met could never have been married."

Lance Corporal Blair (Aberdeen): "Bombs or no bombs, I am coming home for Christmas."

Driver Spiller (Leicester): "Life as a prisoner was hell on earth."

Sergeant Alfred Hammond: "Starvation, humiliation and brutality was the treatment given to all."

Sergeant Scott E. Fakenham (Norfolk): "We were slaves for over three years, with little food or medical supplies."

Gunner G. V. Newton (Blackpool): "Blood, sweat and toil; reward—starvation."

Driver Jim Gordon (Buckie, Scotland): "Soon debts to the Japanese will be squared."

Driver Cameron (Glasgow): "The Japanese are a disgrace to humanity."

Driver Ralph J. Burnley: "I can still hardly believe we are free from these hateful people."

Private Pattison (Coventry): "Being animals themselves, they tried to bring us to their level."

Private Albert Monks: "An orange peel was a luxury."

Private Herbert Guppy (New Washington): "Men murdered and tortured; living skeletons."

Private Robert Booker (Wotvester Park): "These nasty yellow people have no saving grace."

Driver Thomas Wood (Salford): "Work, disease and starvation. Death was a liberation. There was never a sign of civilization."

Driver Lawrence (Luton): "Home for Christmas, thanks to the bomb."

Lance Corporal Starkey (Sapcote): "I would sooner die than do it again."

Lance Corporal McLean (Glasgow): "We have been degraded, tortured, starved, insulted and treated like rats."

Private James Bradley (Leeds): "They enjoy seeing men suffer. The best is a barbarian."

Private Fred Roberts (Bolton): "A nation of hateful people."

Private A. K. Glover (Crewe): "Years of hell, like a Karloff horror film."

Driver A. J. Gay (Taunton): "Their treatment was inhuman, devoid of all pity. We were overworked and on insufficient rest."

Sergeant N. Gallager (Birr, Ireland): "Years of torture, indescribable to a civilized world."

Driver Newton (Lancaster): "Freedom is a dream come true."

Private R. W. Tinkler (Grantham): "We Britons were slaves, but only for three years."

Private George Allen (Derby): "A nightmare at the hands of these merciless, uncivilized barbarians."

Corporal J. Symon (Great Yarmouth): "Being a prisoner under the Japanese is an experience I would not wish on my worst enemy."

Driver Clarke T. Rochdale (Lancashire): "Lucky to be alive. Bad treatment by Japs. Shelled and bombed by our own forces."

Driver Wilkinson Harleston (Norfolk): "We were worked to the breaking point even when sick."

Corporal H. Jones (Chesterfield, Derbyshire): "The atomizer bomb blasts us back to civilization. Three and a half years of hell are over at last."

Corporal N. F. Haigh (Darwen, Lancashire): "Little soup and rice, many fleas and lice, home . . . what price?"

Driver T. R. Bevan (Bridgend, Glamorgan): "The atomizer bomb gives us freedom from suffering at last."

Driver G. Cross (Chester): "Only two raids destroyed the whole town of Omuta by fire."

Driver W. R. Howden (Sheffield): "The Japanese are unfit to rule over animals, least of all men."

Driver R. Woods (Manchester): "I am lucky to be alive after such bad treatment and the new bomb."

Private W. Coman (Coltishall, Norfolk): "Three and a half years of hell in the hands of sadists."

Private T. Eldridge (Welling, Kent): "Thanks to the atomizer bomb, rice and soup is off the menu."

Private J. H. Griffiths (Twickenham): "The Japanese take great delight in torture of all types."

Private T. Jackson (Torquay): "I did not realize people could be treated so badly. The Japanese are not human."

Private W. Carlton (New Ross, Ireland): "The most wicked people on earth."

Private W. Walpole (Manchester): "I cannot express on paper the mental and physical torture I have experienced."

Sergeant W. A. Underwood (Peterbourough): "*You* beat the Japanese. *We* beat malaria, plague, dysentery, cholera and beriberi."

Sergeant T. Archie (London): "Over three years ago I ceased to be a human being."

Sergeant D. M. Boorer (Surrey): "Three years of hell. Now for England and heaven."

Private A. J. Peppall (London): "After years of misery, we are coming home for Christmas."

The following is an exclusive-name story for the *Australian Mirror* syndicate.

The atomic bomb falling on Nagasaki and Hiroshima released from servitude 420 Australians laboring in the Mitsui coal mine and zinc factory, having been captured in Singapore, Java and Timor. 300 worked in the coal mine beside 700 Americans, with the death toll high from disease, injuries and undernourishment.

A few saw the Hiroshima bomb cloud bellying high into the sky, but more saw the Nagasaki bomb. None guessed its meaning.

Here are characteristic statements as these Aussies await the coming American transport planes which will take them to liberty. Some have already taken "French leave" via the airbase at Kanoya, in southern Kyushu, and are now in Okinawa or Manila.

The Aussie camp commandant, Lieutenant Reginald Howel (Wolseley): "I believe I saw both Hiroshima, a hundred thirty miles away, and Nagasaki, about forty. Hiroshima was a white cloud formation rising endlessly in billows flecked with orange fire throughout the cloud. To me, the Nagasaki bomb, though nearer, made a less impressive pillar, although it was the same white formation, colored crimson."

Captain Ian Duncan, camp physician (Killara): "Even after our experiences in Thailand building the railroad, I was still able to feel awe at the atomic bomb's pillar of fire and smoke."

Sergeant Robert Dodsworth (Tranmere): "There was a flash, and a fiery white cloud billowed into the air. As it rose it rolled in ever-increasing circles, assuming at its peak gigantic dimensions that were sustained for several hours."

Vernon Benjamin (Natteyullock): "Glowing clouds of smoke billowing up like a huge volcanic eruption."

Driver C. Pickstone (Brisbane): "The atomic bomb did not kill half enough. Air supplies have been our life saver."

Driver Jack Farrell (Melbourne): "The atomic bomb was a godsend, but it did not destroy enough."

Sergeant Noel Robins (Centennial Park): "A huge multicolored cloud rose upwards, giving the impression of an extraordinary bombing. I cannot visualize a punishment harsh enough for the vultures of the east."

Sergeant Arthur Cyrne (Brisbane): "My view of billowing fire and smoke from the atomic bomb brought me full satisfaction, owing to our brutal treatment by the Japanese."

Private R. N. Lamb (Caulfield): "After three and half years in the dark, we live in the sun again."

Signalman Dan N. Laurie (Castlemaine): "From a land of filth and hardship, back to paradise again."

Private Frederick A. Forcina (Melbourne): "At last a release from the bonds of slavery, building railroads on rats and rice, digging coal on dogs and frogs. Our present airborne food is a godsend."

Driver Reginald Nagor (Kalgoorlie): "The bomb saved many lives."

Signalman Dave Rodda (Melbourne): "A month of freedom and good food has made new men of us."

Navy Signalman Foze (Victoria Park): "Our positions are now reversed—the Japs do all the work."

Loading Aircraftsman Power (Maylands): "With the temperature below zero, they still gave us no boots to wear."

Warrant Officer Wyllie (Sydney): " 'Once I built a railroad . . .' "

Able Seaman Strange (Sydney): "Waiting for the Yanks and tanks."

Driver Ted Knight (Perth): "Once again under Aussies' banner, doing well on Uncle's manna."

Loading Aircraftsman Dean: "I'm a vegetarian no longer!"

Warrant Officer Percy Mann (Brighton): "Our lads can take hell when it comes to treatment. The little yellow men are now getting theirs."

Driver Herb Harrison (Melbourne): "They are the most inhuman race you can imagine."

Private Bill Eames (Crows Nest): "Hell is but heaven to any prisoner of war."

Signalman Mayberry (Ormond): "Coal mining under the yellow dogs was no cop. They starve, work, and murder you, then pray for you. But the rising sun has set."

Staff Sergeant Laurie Jonas (Melbourne): "Survival as a prisoner was more hazardous than dodging bombs, shells, etcetera. Atrocity stories by the hundreds can be told by all."

Corporal Gowers (Sydney): "The B-29s certainly made a bonfire of this joint. Now it looks like a rubbish dump."

George Scott (Manly): "One of my friends lost his legs as a result of Japanese torture."

Gunner Viv O'Sullivan (Bundaberg): "Men stripped of all their clothing in the depth of winter were stood to attention for days, with cold water thrown over them periodically."

Gunner Francis Scriven (Brisbane): "With a man's hands tied, cigarettes were placed in each nostril and mouth and allowed to burn down until they burned the prisoner."

Corporal Robson (Sydney): "Many men are returning legless and armless because of the Japanese ill treatment."

Sapper Dave Young (Sydney): "Just a story of torture, starvation, and more torture."

Corporal Herd (Sydney): "A race of barbarians."

Sapper Nicholson (Sydney): "The new bomb must be a whizzer."

Emmett McGee (Wollongong): "I witnessed the savage treatment of Dutch women whilst in Java. I saw them beaten into unconsciousness with rifle butts."

Private Bob Wright (Marryatville): "Hundreds died of starvation while food rotted in store houses. They were bombastic while 'might was right,' but now they are most humble. May they rot on their own dunghill."

John Miller: "Men suffering from cholera were buried before they were dead."

Sidney Ionn (Kogarah): "No punishment is too severe for the Japanese."

Bombardier Tommy Uren (Wollongong): "Three metres a day on the hammer and tap under a blazing tropical sun, with a pick handle to caress your head in over-amorous affection at any cessation of labour."

Private Norman Sunderland (Armidale): "We have been bombed by Allied planes because of the Japanese violations of the Geneva Conventions."

Gunner Falk Arncliffe: "Withholding permission to go to the air raid shelter, during air raids at the zinc works, resulted in several casualties."

Sergeant Douglas Faherty (Sydney): "Captain Lumpkin, a young married officer of the U.S. medical department, gave his life while rendering medical service to the sick in Burma. For endless days and nights he treated thousands of men, tirelessly and courageously, for the many pestilences and diseases rife in that country. Handicapped by a lack of medical supplies he fought fearlessly on. Weakened by sickness and overwork, he finally succumbed. This man—this great American—really deserves recognition for his marvelous work."

Private Jay Mears (Preston): "We saw Chinese women in Singapore outraged before the eyes of helpless prisoners by Nipponese soldiers."

Private Gill Gore (Parkside): "For having my hands in my pockets while walking back from work, I was beaten unconscious by naked bayonets, then kicked back to consciousness."

Private Norman Ablett (Fremantle): "We prisoners were beaten to insanity."

Private Donal McClelland (Saint James): "Prisoners were forced to kneel on stones with bamboos behind their knees for long periods."

Private Harry Lucas (Bridgetown): "At one camp I was in we originally had 3,000 men. 1,000 died, and 200 had their legs or arms amputated."

Driver Garnet Dixon (Phillip Island): "It's great to be free from these heathens, but we have much to avenge."

Driver Robert Dayble (Melbourne): "Like starting life all over again."

Private Walter Bush (Dubbo): "The Japanese can dinn it out, but they can't take it."

Private Charles Burell (Brisbane): "The Japanese nation plays God, makes the blind see and the limbless walk. Their method? Punishment. The result? A failure of the miracle."

Private Neal Smith (Ellorne): "Officers and doctors were thrashed for trying to prevent the sick and dying from working."

Private John Holman (Sydney): "Sick men were left to die on the road during our march up through Thailand."

Corporal Stone (Devonport): "Men were beaten to death with pick handles."

Private Charles Veness (Queenstown): "Hara-kiri should be encouraged in this country."

Private Alf Adames (Ma Wollumbi): "The large numbers of prisoner deaths often necessitated the use of communal graves."

Private N. Moylan (Kyogle): "We were forced to work even with bodily temperatures of one hundred and three to one hundred and five degrees."

Private Don Tweedie (Willoughby): "I am deaf from vitamin deficiency, and often have been beaten because of it."

Private Tom Kershaw: "Electrical torture was an amusing game for the Jap guards."

Private Viv Doland (Derwent Park): "Live wires were tied around the stomachs of prisoners for punishments."

Sergeant Wilkinson (Wollstonecroft): "A Jap officer walked into a hospital ward and said, 'Hurry up and die, I need your clothes and boots for the other men to work in.' "

Private Lyle McCarthy (Sydney): "Bootless prisoners were thrashed for not moving quickly over sharp stones."

Private Ronald Marshall (Inverell): "I witnessed a friend beaten unconscious because he was too sick to hold a jackhammer."

Corporal Taylor (Mossvale): "No spark of humanity burns in these people."

Officers' Steward Donald McLean (Sydney): "East is east and west is west and never the twain should meet."

Sergeant Robert Thomson (Hackney): "I'm now an unemployed coal miner!"

Sergeant Edward Head (Adelaide): "Japanese civilians must be happier now that the army yoke has been lifted from their shoulders."

Sapper Arthur Moore (Newtown): "Our release is a godsend, thanks to the atomic bomb."

Driver Pat Lynch (Warracknabeal): "Not enough Japanese were killed."

Sergeant Louis Trouchet (Perth): "Drop more atomic bombs after the evacuation of all prisoners of war."

Able Seaman Percy Bullivant (Sydney): "Three and half years in Burma, Thailand and Japan—now headed for heaven."

Private Thomas Campbell (Melbourne): "The death roll of prisoners is a monument to the treatment we received."

Able Seaman Alec Murphy: "Uncle Sam's air supplies are a godsend."

Private Joseph Lonsdale (East Perth): "Let us not forget those lads down under the earth. The Japanese have a big debt."

Private Roy Hamilton (Epping): "We who are left are very fortunate, but let me also remember the boys the Japanese have murdered."

Gunner Robert Carroll (Leeton): "No punishment could be too severe for the Japanese camp commanders and guards."

Gunner Anatole Voevodin (Brisbane): "Three and half years of torture and starvation, yet they still could not break our spirit."

Gunner Neville Daniels (Lidcombe): "Civilized people cannot imagine the treatment received by prisoners of war."

Driver Fred Ward (Norseman): "There were numerous acts of cruelty. Prisoners bashed into unconsciousness, electric shocks passed through the body."

Private Alan Beattie (Perth): "The Japanese made prisoners drink water in large quantities, and then jumped on their stomachs."

Gunner Tasman Knight (Hobart): "War maims, slays, and cripples men. But not to the extent of Japanese treatment."

Sergeant John Brosnan (Sydney): "Dutch women were flogged with rifles for trying to get food to their husbands."

Private Starcevich (Grasspatch): "When the temperature was below zero, prisoners were stripped and stood to attention for hours."

Private W. Haynes (East Coburg): "Since the surrender we have found our Red Cross medical supplies hidden in the coal mine."

Private Alan Nicholls (Tintaldra): "The lack of medical supplies killed many of my mates."

Private Pat Oregan (Wagga Wagga): "Exterminate them, and please the prisoners of war."

Corporal Robson (Sydney): "Save the atomic bomb for the Japanese."

Private Norm Gough (Loederville): "Everyone is asking, will all this be forgotten?"

Omuta, Japan—Thursday, September 13, 1945
0100 hours

Allied Prison Camp #17, Omuta, Kyushu

Freedom is at hand for 700 Americans and 1,000 other Allies at this large prison camp dominated by Baron Mitsui's dangerous and worn-out coal mine. Men are still dying here from the effects of Japanese neglect—three since the surrender—but parachutes floating food and clothing down from the sky have improved life for the men, mostly veterans of Bataan and Corregidor.

Regarding an Australian and an American who died today, *Lieutenant Theodore Bronk of Irwin, Pennsylvania,* a graduate of the University of Pittsburgh and the George Washington School of Medicine, said, "Our malnutrition and dysentery deaths could have been prevented if the Japanese merely gave us the medicine belonging to us which they had kept under lock and key. Our men have often died puffed up with edema or suffering from a vitamin or protein deficiency. Our death toll of 125 would have been halved if the Japanese had given us what was needed."

Ship's Cook Robert Bickley of Fort Worth served on *Fisheries II,* one of the Navy's three wooden ships which fought until the end at Corregidor, the others being the yacht *Mary Ann* and the customs boat *Prairie.* "Our job was to act as advance lookout for raids by Bulkeley's PT boats behind Japanese lines. We went ahead, and served as the radio contact with Corregidor for radioless PT boats. Our skipper was Ensign Petritz, a 220-lb. football player from Marquette who ended his voyage in December 1944 aboard the *Oryoku Maru.** Through three years of imprisonment, including two years cooking for Baron Mitsui's coal mine, of the American prisoners I've

---

* Ensign George K. Petritz actually survived the sinking of the *Oryoku Maru.* All the men aboard assumed that he had drowned, but he managed to swim to shore and escape. See "The Death Cruise: Seven Weeks in Hell," later in this volume.

always remembered [Lt. John D.] Bulkeley as the bravest, most efficient officer I've ever known."

Joseph Niespodziani (Bridgeport, Connecticut): "I spent thirteen
months wandering in Luzon after Bataan fell, before the Japanese,
along with pro-Japanese Filipino soldiers, caught me when I was
down with my second day of malaria."

Tall *Corporal John Bruer of Eau Claire, Wisconsin,* who fought
at Bataan and Corregidor: "Because I'm six feet three, the Japs put
me and other big men in the lowest-ceilinged tunnels, right down to
three feet. Last August a piece of Mitsui's defective equipment broke
loose, pinning me against the wall. The injury to my back was very
painful, making me unable to stoop. Though American doctors pronounced me unfit, the Japs had a rule that no accident without
bloodshed could allow your release from the mine. I was forced to
continue working underground until April, when they allowed me to
change to gardening."

Corporal Oliver Ard (Pensacola): "The miners got a breakfast of
rice and soup and a small box of rice to keep them going during the
twelve hours underground. Some were so hungry they ate both rations before going down, either because they knew that the hot gases
down there would sour their food, or because they just could not
control their hunger. Those guys always got a beating, because the
overseers feared they could not keep digging all day."

George King (St. Louis): "We had an overman, during one of my
two years underground, who specialized in extra beatings which
took place when the gang withdrew into side tunnels waiting for dynamite to go off. This overman named Yumamitsan would say in
Japanese, 'You want a present?' then let you have it. I saw him order
Corporal Jesus Silva of Santa Fe to kneel down because he was not
working fast enough building a rock wall. Silva is tall, and being
small, Yumamitsan smashed him in the face with a wooden pillar
wedge until his face was covered with welts."

Corporal Ray Brookshire of St. Louis, a redhaired, baldish veteran of the Bataan death march: "In eighteen months underground here, I was beaten about six times—once by an overman
named Denki until the pick handle broke. I'd started eating my

rice before he told me, because I saw other men eating. The longer he beat me, the madder he got. I went down three times and finally the left side of my head was covered with blood and I couldn't rise again. I was working as a gardener when the atomic bombs went off over both Hiroshima and Nagasaki. Hiroshima we saw from the beginning, when it was a flash, then opening like a white chute upward. Nagasaki we noticed only when the cloud was fully developed and airplanes were flying overhead. We overheard Japanese civilians looking toward Nagasaki say, 'They're giving us a present.' "

Corporal Isadore Sabbota (Detroit): "Our worst overseer was one we called Flangeface. He would sleep for an hour while we worked, then get up, look at the trough where were shoveling, slug us with anything handy, then go back to sleep."

Corporal Robert Bailey (Italy, Texas): "I got along fairly well with most of the overmen, but Flangeface always beat me whenever he could. Another who we called Sugarlips often beat me with a stiff wire or a *noko,* which means saw."

Corporal James Brock (Taft, Texas): "I was most often overworked by a boss we called Shitbird, usually with a hammer handle or a *mairugi*—that's a small timber. He hit everybody who passed him, whether you belonged to his shift or not. I'm sorry he's disappeared since the camp was liberated."

James Ball (Rochester): "Due to my feet swelling with beriberi and my bad eyes, the Japs allowed me to change from the mine to gardening. I saw the big white cloud rising after the bomb, but I never guessed what it was."

Corpsman Dean Pronovost of Missoula, Montana, a Flathead Indian: "I saw the atomic bomb cloud over Nagasaki, white and funnel-shaped, coming down to a point with odd, faint overlaying colors—rose, yellow, and purple—which we thought must be gas from bombed chemical works."

Boatswain Clarence Taylor of Cloverdale, Virginia, and Long Beach, California: "At first it was a wool-packed white cloud, then it turned blue inside in five minutes, then after five minutes more turned red."

Sergeant Joe True of Cheyenne and a New York lawyer, *Bertram Friedman of Mount Vernon,* were the most capable saboteurs. The Japanese posted a red-lettered sign in the cap-lamp room warning that both men were dangerous. According to True, "We were beaten with hammers, saws, and wrenches. Friedman's left hand was broken. I once was able to ruin an expensive 350-foot conveyor belt by allowing rocks to fall in the machine. The Japs finally gave up trying to catch us or beat us into submission and just removed us from the mine. Once Friedman and I did the bamboo-kneeling punishment for destroying property." Both had been on MacArthur's clerical staff, and were taken on Bataan and Corregidor.

Sergeant Hughy Cox (Alocomb, Alabama): "Overmen seldom hit you with their hand; it was always with a club, because they could reach you better and it made them bigger. The worst was Haikara, whom we called the Fox because he was a good coal miner himself, quick in movements, with a sharp eye for faulty ceilings. When ceilings fell on our men, the nimble Fox always got out from under. He beat me with a wrench and an iron drill, and for fun he would throw coal dust in my face."

Sergeant Jack Wheeler of San Francisco—a onetime insurance underwriter, and on Bataan and Corregidor a sergeant major—has borne probably more administrative responsibility than any American prisoner in Japan. He was sergeant major at two Philippine horror camps, O'Donnell and Cabanatuan, and a hero of Camp #17 at the Mitsui coal mine center here at Omuta. "Our worst period was at first, because as horrible as this mine camp has been, the Philippines were tragic. I'm glad that the atomic bomb spared us prisoners all that an invasion would have meant: further starvation and probably more exposure to battle conditions. When we get home we will have a new appreciation for what America means."

Sergeant Russell Sayan (Hermosa Beach, California): "We were underfed in the Mitsui mine and overworked, being gone always from eleven to thirteen hours. I was beaten once by a guard we called Brown Bomber for taking a bath in a fishpond when the water system stopped after an air raid. Brown Bomber hit me fifteen times with a stick six feet long and three inches square. He made me stand straight up, hands extended, in order to prevent my reaching back and blocking blows."

Oscar Otero of Los Lunas, a husky New Mexican captured on Bataan, learned Japanese by being chauffeur to a colonel. By refusing to allow him to talk any Filipino, the Japanese furnished the coal mine prisoners with their ablest unofficial interpreter.

Chief Machinist Walter Smith of San Diego and Mount Pleasant, South Carolina: "Like most Navy men here, I never received a letter from home."

Pharmacist Jeremiah Crows of Cleveland and San Diego: "My greatest thrill was August 7th, when I saw eighteen B-29s unload bombs on the zinc factory nearby. But just when we were all feeling happiest, the last plane was hit by an anti-aircraft shell. It turned on its wing and slid downward, falling in pieces. Only one chute came out."

Chief Machinist's Mate Louis Vacchiano (South Langhorne, Pennsylvania): "From weighing 280 I sank to 130 by the first day of peace, thanks to the Japanese comfort system. I never thought reduction was possible, but three bowls of rice daily did it."

Chief Boatswain's Mate Charlie Hammon of Oakland and Signal Mountain, Tennessee: "I escaped the coal mine by breaking my leg in two places in a cave-in. The Japs might have sent me back down, but my muscles became paralyzed due to beriberi, and I was able to hold out until the surrender."

Henry Sublett of Cisco, Texas, a Marine captured on Corregidor: "I was down with pneumonia and worked in the mine both after and before. Our first Buntai Joe, or overseer, used to be drunk all the time and beat me every day for my first three months. He always used to start the day off with a few *savas*—meaning 'gifts'—of blows."

Chief Commissary Steward Leonard Weidel of San Diego, age 43: "In nine months' work in the mine, my weight—which before the war was 208—fell to 109. I was so weak I couldn't stand, so the Japs put me to work making straw shoes."

Curtis Polk of Biloxi, Mississippi, and Bogalusa, Louisiana: "The coal mine here is tough, but at Nichols Field I've seen men drop rocks on their feet or drive picks through them in order to escape the Japs. I saw a Jap boss at Nichols, whom we called the Wolf, beat to death a New Mexican named Coco. Coco came to Nichols with the same rice-bloated 300 prisoners from Cabanatuan as myself. He was too weak to push heavy dump-cars at Nichols so the Wolf first beat him with a stick, and then at roll call with a blackjack. A former Japanese naval officer we called Cherry Blossom finished Coco off the next day when he found him recovering consciousness. Cherry Blossom kicked him around the room until Coco fell and died. The Japs also killed a man named Quattroni, who had cerebral malaria, by putting him in mud and force-feeding him water, then jumping on his body."

Chief Petty Officer Harvey Massingill of Oakland, taken on Corregidor: "I don't weigh much anymore, but I've done better with mail than most Navy men."

Chief Yeoman Theodore Brownell of Fort Smith, Arkansas, and San Francisco: "The best words I've heard in Japanese were two officials on a telephone, saying, 'B-29s and many, many dead.' "

Seaman Daniel Rafalovich of San Pedro, a signalman from the U.S.S. *Houston* who was one of four Americans transferred to Admiral Doorman's flagship *De Ruyter* for the Battle of the Java Sea: "I was picked up by a Nipponese gunboat after sixteen hours in the water with three Dutchmen. A British Navy signalman also in the water with us disappeared just as the gunboat reached us. The Japs placed us aboard the cruiser, then used us for labor in unloading near Rembang for five weeks. I saw some Texas 131st Artillerymen in the so-called 'Bicycle Camp' outside Batavia, and also in Singapore at Changi Prison."

Marine Harold Peterson (Pasadena): "I've worked in the Mitsui coal mine only a little, being sick from the beginning with beriberi and dysentery. Luckily I got thrown down by a cave-in the day before Christmas and got a useless hand, removing me from the mine. My life was saved by a pal, Floyd Singer of Anaheim, California, captured on Bataan. He was digging me out before the whole coal face toppled."

Corporal Leon Cleboski of Houston and *Alexander Katchuck of Brooklyn,* both Marines from Corregidor, told how one overseer, the

Fox, used to beat up Cleboski. According to Katchuk, "The Japs used to push around Cleboski because he was moving slow and thinking slow as a result of undernourishment, having lost thirty-five pounds. The Japs liked to throw rocks at him, kick him, and hit him with a ceiling wedge." Cleboski showed this writer patches gone from his scalp where the Fox had hit him with a pick while remarking, "Six-foot box for you."

Chief Yeoman Winfred Mitchum (Houston): "While working in the coal mine I took two tomatoes from the galley and they were found under my pillow. In the *aeso* [guardhouse] the Japanese gave me the electrical treatment, consisting of fixing a wire in an electric light socket and forcing me to hold on to the other end, then switching the current on and off. The mine guards did this for five nights, taking turns and laughing. I was in the guardhouse with absolutely nothing to eat at the special order of camp commandant Fukuhara, who—though I confessed that the tomatoes were from the galley—insisted they came from his private garden. The guards made the electrical shocks sharper by pouring water on me in order to increase the conductivity all over my body."

Yeoman Daniel Ebbert of Wheeling, West Virginia, showed the writer tropical ulcers on his legs and said, "One overseer we called the Airedale used to enjoy kicking these sores. The night that peace came I weighed 120 against my normal 170, and I was too weak to pick up a jackhammer from the tunnel floor."

Seaman Raymond McDonough of Columbus, Ohio, captured at Fort Hughes after being on the U.S.S. *Mindanao,* flagship of the Souchina patrol: "The Japanese seemed to ignore the fact I was deaf, and beat me repeatedly across the face and head for not understanding their orders. I could not even hear what they said."

Seaman John Yoder (Des Moines): "I got beaten in the mine and thrown in the guardhouse. They finally let me have a job in the zinc factory. I couldn't keep from stealing from the Japanese galley because they had good food there, and naturally I got beaten for that, too."

Machinist's Mate Lucian Boehm (Honolulu): "I broke this finger, and tried to break my whole hand, trying to evade underground work. Most of my weight was lost digging for Satahara, whom we called the Greyhound. The Greyhound began by hitting me with a rock, then with a dynamite tamping rod. I got four really serious beatings in six weeks. But the Greyhound was mild compared to the Pig, who would crack you on your bare back, while bent over, with a special flogging whip made from four expended dynamite fuses bound together."

Sergeant Robert Gwaltmy (Newville, Pennsylvania): "Coming up from the night shift we noticed a big white football-shaped cloud hanging over Nagasaki. Although we had no information about Hiroshima, we felt sure that something peculiar was going on."

Sergeant Wiley Smith (Coushatta, Louisiana): "We looked across the bay toward Nagasaki after emerging from the mine and saw black smoke starting up. The atomic bomb, falling ninety minutes before, had kindled Nagasaki. Our Japanese bosses kept pointing that way and chattering. It was better than Germany's surrender, which we had only heard about from Korean miners."

The camp's *First Sergeant, Joseph Lawson (Klamath Falls, Oregon):* "When you've waited so long for freedom, you find yourself beyond words to say what you feel."

"OMUTA FAREWELL"

With the arrival by train from Nagasaki of the first Army-Navy team for the evacuation of Kyushu's largest prisoner of war camp, the final *sinkes* (Japanese for roll calls) were sounding today over the grimy buildings and meagerly-clad G.I.s. This camp, 1,700 strong— 700 being Americans from Bataan and Corregidor—has been thinned already to 1,300 by impatient ex-prisoners, mostly Americans, who have hit the high road for the American airbase at Kanoya in southernmost Kyushu.

The camp commandant, dentist Major R. W. Schott of What Cheer, Iowa, found it difficult to keep discipline after the writer, arriving as the first visitor from the outside world, candidly admitted that scores of loaded transport planes were coming daily from Okinawa to Kyushu and returning empty to Okinawa. The first day only about a hundred men left. However, these glib ex-prisoners, on arriving in Kanoya, persuaded softhearted transport pilots to fly them back over Prison Camps #17 and #25. They dropped notes to friends still obeying the camps' bugles, with revolutionary slogans like *I'll be in Frisco in a week!* and *Don't wait, kid; take off!*

So profound is the prisoners' hatred of Baron Mitsui's coal mine, the Japanese military police, and the *aeso* or guardhouse where five Americans have found a violent death, that the entire camp would probably have been deserted had not the Army-Navy team arrived today. Hospitals filled with cases of malnutrition, diarrhea, beriberi, and mutilated men offer special problems.

Interviewed today as they were being broken down into groups for enshipment out of Nagasaki homeward, most prisoners commented either on the clouds formed by the two atomic bombs which some saw burst to the northeast over Hiroshima and to the southwest over Nagasaki, or on the miserable and dangerous conditions prevailing in the Mitsui mine where they labored for the equivalent of one cent daily and suffered repeated beatings.

Hardened bantam *Sergeant Jimmy Jordan,* with thirty-three years in the Marine Corps behind him, said, "Now I know what that mushroom cloud meant that we saw over Nagasaki. I don't call it an atomic but a 'tonic' bomb, because it brought the Japs to their senses."

Robert Williams (Tucson): "The atomic bomb looked like rings of white smoke rising in columns with red tint. I'm glad the bomb didn't hit our camp, because Crupper and I were firefighters and the Japs forced us to move the pump nearest their quarters."

Charles Crupper (Tyro, Kansas): "Hiroshima looked like a ring of fire under a cloud of white smoke, all suspended in the air. Nagasaki looked the same but bigger, being nearby."

Pharmacist Roy Lynch (Waynesboro, Tennessee): "I heard not a sound with the Nagasaki cloud, which resembled a thick white pencil rising and then turning inside out, with a reddish-orange flame. I felt the earth trembling."

Boatswain Jesse Lee (Binger, Oklahoma): "It was conical-shaped, something similar to a big cumulus, white and fleecy at first, then broadening until we saw red inside."

Gunner Clifford Sweet of Chulavista, California, captured at Fort Hughes: "I was working at our salt mill when I saw the Nagasaki cloud, which kept rolling up, turning inside out, and getting redder at the top."

Richard Steele (Dise, Montana): "It looked like white smoke piling up over Nagasaki."

Pharmacist Donald Tapocott (Mason City, Iowa): "The windows shook like a battleship gunnery and a big white cloud rose, with flashes of red."

Clarence Perkerson (Atlanta): "An ice cream cone in the sky."

Howard Ekre (Tacoma, Washington): "When the atomic cloud

spread over Nagasaki, I saw enormous heat waves spreading around it."

Floyd Walker (Port Young, Michigan): "I felt buildings in our camp nearly forty miles away tremble."

Sergeant Louis Goldbrum (Brooklyn): "I surrendered after serving a year with Major Walter Cushing as a guerrilla in northern Luzon. We had ambushed and killed their Colonel Hara in a car, and after that the Japs got tough and sent up a big force to wipe us out."

Physician Lieutenant Harold Proff of Olympia, Washington, captured at Little Baguio, Bataan: "More food, especially more meat, would have saved one-half to three-fourths of the men we've lost. The Japs could have got it; they're getting meat now for us, aren't they?"

Navy Cook Laurel Whitworth (Bourne, Texas): "Leaving Japan for me means not having to cook any more dogs to eat. One day I had to cook sixty-nine, another seventy-three, another fifty-five. I hate cooking dogs."

Louis Veros (Cleveland): "Cleaner and warmer quarters would have saved lives, because the Japs kept us often barefoot in heatless barracks and held back Red Cross clothing until the war ended."

Raymond Haynes (Spartanburg): "The Japs would always send us into the doubtful tunnels first, to see if the ceiling would hold."

John Norrile (Red Lodge, Montana): "A coal cavern fell on me when I was working in the mine and weighed 110. But I'm holding my own now."

Gilbert Morris (Brownfield, Texas): "I weigh 108, against my normal 200."

Pharmacist John Istock (Pittsburgh): "I got three lickings in eighteen weeks, mostly for not understanding Japanese. The mine people were so indifferent to our security that accidents were common, such as rock falling from overhead. Once we just touched a rotten timber in a dripping roof where we worked, and the entire tunnel settled four inches."

Jack Hargrove (Olivehill, Tennessee): "I got hit several times during April working in the coal mine, particularly by overmen called the Screamer, the Parrot, and the Pig."

Richard McCaffrey (San Francisco): "Last winter the guard we called the Pig beat me, and the camp commandant Fukuhara worked me over so thoroughly with a stove poker that I woke up in hospital."

Ernest Robinson (Kingman, Indiana): "In one month underground I never received a single beating."

Raymond Carrisales (Corsicana, Texas): "In the forty months of my imprisonment I've received one letter and one radiogram."

Pharmacist Frank Maxwell (Birmingham): "When I left Camp Bilibid in December for Japan, I weighed 172. On my arrival January 30th, I weighed 94. I now weigh 135."

Patrick Hilton (Montgomery, West Virginia): "I'm one of the healthiest men here because a shrapnel wound, sustained when American planes attacked our convoy, kept me outside the Mitsui mine working above ground."

Dark-skinned *Junius Navardos (Los Angeles):* "Pressure in the mine caused me to pass out once while working. When I came around in the hospital I found myself with burned patches all over my skin. The boys told me that the burns had been made by an American-educated interpreter, Yamamuchi, whom we called Riverside because he was brought up there. Asked whether he had done the burning, the interpreter told the doctor, 'Yes, I did this, because I thought he was feigning.'"

Pharmacist Albert Tybur (Fort Johnson, New York): "I got beaten with a coal shovel for not saluting the soldiers on the surface. They forced me to hold two buckets of water at arm's length, and whenever I lowered them they'd say 'America *tsuyoi*' which means 'America strong,' and crack me again."

Pharmacist Merrill Dodson (Chariton, Iowa): "In one month underground I escaped beating, but unfortunately caught one from an Army guard on the surface who saw me putting a cigarette stub in a can where I saved butt ends and assumed wrongly that I'd been smoking outside hours. The guard stood on a ledge in order to increase his height and reach, and made me stand with my arms locked behind me while he struck me ten times in the face with a bamboo pole."

Chief Pharmacist John Vernon (Fresno, California): "For crossing the street of the camp as a newcomer, not realizing it was forbidden, I got beaten along with Kusek by guards who struck us with fists and with two-by-fours."

Pharmacist John Luther (Orleans, Nebraska): "I got these shin ulcers from falling down in the mine due to weakness, not from beatings. Some Jap bosses saw that I was not well, and gave me a break."

Pharmacist William Derrick (Leesville, Louisiana): "The Korean straw bosses were decent to us except when the Japs were around, who frightened them."

Gene Letspech (Floydada, Texas): "Beriberi from undernourishment gave me heart trouble, but I'm gaining now."

Thomas Rayburn (Bogalusa, Louisiana): "I was beaten myself only twice, but I was section leader and often had to watch my men being beaten while sick."

Ivy Spears (Arvin, California): "It's no exaggeration to say I've been beaten twice weekly for the whole two years and five days I've worked in the Mitsui coal mine."

Leland Sims (Smackover, Arkansas): "Many guards could speak English. One who we called Long Beach, because he was educated there, caught me smoking and said, 'It's all right with me, but don't let the other guards catch you.' "

Clarence Griffiths (Fall River, Massachusetts): "In two years in the mine I've been beaten almost weekly. The guards we nicknamed the Mouse, the Pig, and the Screamer were toughest on me."

Dick Lavender (Lewiston, Idaho): "I gambled by hitting back the first Jap who hit me, and had peace that way for the first nine of my twenty-six months underground. Later a new boss called Smiley began beating me daily. I stood him for two weeks, then threatened to beat him back, and he stopped just like the first one."

Sergeant Floyd Johnson (Drumright, Oklahoma): "For nine months I've been getting easily two stick beatings a week, often by a young kid we called Pretty Boy."

Theodore Berez (Bay City, Texas): "For twenty-six months I was beaten daily by the guards we called Big Stoop and Gold Teeth."

Ronald Hutchison (Las Vegas, Nevada): "In two years I've been beaten often, but mostly brought punishment on myself by not hurrying when the Japs tried to drive me."

Harold Newton (Eldorado, Kansas): "In my five months in the coal mine I had only one real beating, but that was with a four-foot club and put me in my quarters for nine days."

An American Indian, *Henry Reed (Shawnee, Oklahoma):* "In two years, by working hard, I got beaten only once, by a Jap we called Wingy for his crumpled arm."

Tervald Thorpson (Wadena, Iowa): "I managed to go a whole year without being beaten. Americans worked hard in the mine, but some had difficulty learning Japanese, and misunderstanding commands got them beatings."

William McConnell (Arcata, California): "In two years I got two beatings, for losing or misplacing tags. Once I was beaten with a *naraki,* or five-foot pole, till I had to go to hospital. I got pneumonia and ended up spending a month there."

Corporal Louis Muller (Alexandria, Louisiana): "In seven months in the mine I got slapped around enough but got only one real beating, from the Fox. I couldn't understand what he wanted, and the Fox hit me with a shovel and kicked me when down."

Thomas Bohn (St. Louis): "For two years we've had a bunch of overmen who amused themselves underground by beating someone chosen at random each lunchtime."

Jesse Tomes (Liberty, Kentucky): "I caught bad luck only once, when an overman named Sikimato San, who we called Blinky, thought an Aussie and I were carrying a roof timber too slowly and socked me. It took three weeks for my wrist to recover."

Alf Buchanan (Geraldine, Montana): "I was never beaten much because the overmen saw I was too weak from diarrhea to work hard."

Sam Blank (Monticello, New York): "In twenty-two months I was careful and I got only one beating—for turning in my cap-lamp before roll call, instead of after. A soldier hit me across the back with a pick handle and I went down. It took me two days to recover."

Joseph Bayles (Little Rock, Arkansas): "I got a couple of beatings in five months underground. Once for using wire instead of rope to pull timbers through low tunnels. And once an overseer made an

Oklahoman named Dale Pope and me fight each other. When we failed to hit hard enough, he beat us both."

Redheaded *Ernest Arnaud (Great Falls, Montana):* "In two years underground, I used to make the coal conveyor belt break down in order to give my friends working in tunnels a little rest. Sometimes the conveyor broke itself. Either way, I got beaten."

Thomas Gurley (Milan, Tennessee): "I got about three bad beatings in twenty-two months, including once having an eye almost knocked out by an overman we called the Greyhound for going into another tunnel at lunchtime and staying too long."

Carlton Wilder (Manchester, New Hampshire): "In ten months I got only one severe beating from the Mule, because I was too weak to carry heavy things. I had to stop work for six days."

Corporal John Peterson (Big Timber, Montana): "For twelve of my sixteen months I worked for a sadist named Flangeface or Yotojisa, who beat me three times weekly with hammers, pliers, clubs, and his fists. You could not do anything in a way that would please him."

Edward Martel (Lynn, Massachusetts): "In eighteen weeks underground I got worked over so often by the Fox and the Screamer that I had phobia. We'd hold our breath at work assignments, fearing to draw those two."

Sydney Snow (Haynesville, Louisiana): "I escaped working underground through having lost one eye at Bataan. But I caught four beatings from soldiers on the surface: once for eating before rice time, once for not keeping my fingers straight at my sides, once for being too weak to lift a sledgehammer, and once for not understanding orders."

Earl Rose (Kansas City): "In six months I've been beaten half a dozen times, especially by the Pig and the Screamin' Demon."

Julian Court (Stafford, Texas): "I've been on the shovelling shift for two years and it's been tough working barefoot down there in the winter. I got one bad beating for not working, when the guards knocked me down with kicks and hit me with rifle butts. Another winter night a soldier who caught me going to the latrine only in my shorts kept me at attention for half an hour, slapping me in the face about forty times."

William Smith (Huntsville, Alabama): "I weighed 103 pounds on the day when I was incapacitated by an accident. But I hope someday to weigh 190 again like the old days."

Harry Staunton (Henderson, North Carolina): "I got heavy beatings, not including slappings, about twice monthly in the past two years because I was always too weak to carry out what they called *hayako*—that's a rush job."

Displaying a scalp wound with two stitches, *Luis Lopez of Espanola, New Mexico,* said: "I got that wound from a beating by the Rat."

John Yovetich (Butte, Montana): "In two years I've been beaten several times, especially by a two-striper called the Pig who uses a bamboo stick loaded with red clay."

Alfred Langley (Monette, Arkansas): "I worked six months in the mine until I lost a finger and the Japs let me come to the surface."

Cecile Parrott (Weiser, Idaho): "In three months here, I've been beaten only lightly. But in the Fukuoka camp I was hit fifteen times in the jaw by a guard who was later removed for killing a Dutch prisoner."

Harry Sater (Englewood, California): "I used mostly to get beaten for using pieces of old wire instead of rope in order to haul roof timbers."

Sheridan Prendergast (Sauk City, Wisconsin): "I had an overman with an explosive temper who used to attack us with a hatchet. One day a faulty ceiling fell and broke his back. In two years I've been beaten with everything from a pick and a shovel to a hatchet."

John Mason (Graham, Texas): "I've been a year underground with the Nips and all I can say is, they're funny people. They'll beat you one day and give you a cigarette the next. Screamin' Demon was the worst, for me."

Pharmacist Earl Gordon (Oakland): "I worked for nineteen days underground until a Jap we called the Sailor beat me with a six-foot club. After four blows I passed out, because he was hitting me too high in the small of the back. And now I have nephritis of the kidney."

John Hixon (Miami): "I spent twenty-two months in the mine, and my heavy punishments were often for the last thing you'd imagine. Once a soldier clubbed me in the face with his shoes, and I was often slapped for not understanding."

Louis Voros (Cleveland): "My clearest memory was seeing a lieutenant who worked on Commissioner Sayre's staff shot in his garden at Cabanatuan, without any reason, by a Japanese sentry. The first shot hit him in the chest, then the second killed him."

Sergeant James Palone (Minerva, Ohio): "When the guards and Colonel Fukuhara beat to death an American we called Mother for his kindheartedness, I saw Mother's eyes open glassy, and I am certain they beat him long after he was actually dead."

Harry Simms (Butte, Montana): "I was knocked cold several times by an overman called the Bull for his bullfrog voice. My weight then, due to malnutrition and dysentery, was 102. But I escaped, because the last time the Bull broke my glasses, so I could no longer see the coal face for work."

Sergeant William Glenn (Salinas, California): "In two years I only got kicks and slaps, except once when a whole Jap cable car company turned to me and beat me up because I had crowded them in a tunnel. Technically, they were justified."

Clifford Schamberger (North York, Pennsylvania): "In two years I've been knocked around but never really beaten. I used to cuss Japs right back and they passed around the word that I was crazy. I've watched them give the water punishment on Bataan: tie a chap's hands behind him, pour him full of water while lying on the ground, then jump on his stomach till he dies."

John Sullivan (Preston, Mississippi): "In eighteen months I was twice beaten up with a club by Toko-san or Billygoat for breaking one of their bum, patched-up drills. The second time I was sensible enough to fall, and he slacked off."

Virgil Darurs (Mena, Arkansas): "In eighteen months in the mine I was twice beaten heavily: once with a tamping rod by an overman who, when I failed to lift heavy things, made me do push-ups and hold two big lumps of coal at arm's length for ten minutes; and the second time by a soldier with a billy club, for slowing down."

Acting Chaplain Marvin Denny (Fort Worth): "Whenever Americans died, I read from First Corinthians, 15th chapter."

Billy Campbell (Vincennes, Indiana): "Since September 1943 I've been continually beaten by the Pig, the Devil, and the Turtle, with severe lickings about every three weeks."

Bruce Watson (Muscatine, Iowa): "A fellow we called Flutterbutt was my worst enemy. I got a double hernia from heavy lifting."

Aristotle Romero (Tinnie, New Mexico): "I had a leg and arm broken in a cave-in, but Captain Tom Hewlett did a beautiful job of skin grafting."

Henry Moore (Tyler, Texas): "For two years the Jap overmen, chiefly the Wolf, beat me across the face with a club due to my contradicting an order from another overman. I was also beaten by surface soldiers when, coming off my shift with swollen feet, I stopped to rest on a bench that was not authorized for sitting."

Sergeant Robert Aldrich (Capitan, New Mexico): "I was in the mine ever since it opened, but I was more fortunate than most because I learned Japanese, thus avoiding beatings due to misunderstanding."

Zachary Kush (Albert, West Virginia): "We saw the Hiroshima bomb cloud over the mine shed roof, and the Nagasaki cloud shaped like a white spinning top with many colors."

Sergeant Charles Basham (Louisville, Kentucky): "I got only a glimpse of the Nagasaki cloud, because we were marching out of the mine and the Jap guards kept pushing us. But what I saw seemed rosy and beautiful."

James Copenhaver (Salem, Illinois): "The atomic cloud looked like a thunderhead, and I argued that it would bring rain."

Allied Prison Camp #17, Omuta, Kyushu

Headed by flag-draped American, Dutch, Australian and British coffins, the first columns of released prisoners marched singing this morning to a train and to freedom from Kyushu's largest and most notorious prisoner of war camp. The British were in the van, followed by the Dutch, while the Americans were forming up this afternoon for departure. The Australians are slated to bring up the rear. A Navy medical party, headed by ex–Yale football coach Lieutenant Commander Mal Stevens, were in charge of approximately one hundred patients already waiting at the train. Many of the latter were emaciated to the point that they resembled inmates of Nazi prison camps.

The Dutch column was headed by gray-haired chaplain Captain J. Carl Hamel of the Dutch Reformed Church and the Netherlands Indies Army. Only four national coffins were carried, which bore within each one several rows of wooden boxes containing the ashes of a total of about 120 prisoners, most of whom had died from malnutrition, overwork or mine accidents. Included were the ashes of five Americans who were beaten or starved to death by the Mitsui Company's soldier guards.

The coffins were draped with homemade flags, sewn together from panels scissored from multicolored parachutes dropped by food-carrying B-29s. Hamel, who has accompanied Dutchmen through years of building the Thailand railroad, said services over three Americans and one Aussie who have died since Japan surrendered, too weak to await liberation. By noon tomorrow the last American Navy medicos will leave, and what was probably Japan's largest and most remote prison camp will be deserted. Most former overmen and camp commandants are temporarily lying low, though Baron Mitsui has agreed to produce them on demand by the American authorities. The Sixth Army is expected to reach here about ten days hence.

Of Camp #17's total roster of about 1,700 men (including 700 Americans), approximately 500 have made their way to the American airfield at Kanoya in small roving parties—about 300 of these being American and almost all the remainder Australian.

Omuta, Japan—Saturday, September 15, 1945
0900 hours

Allied Prison Camp #17, Omuta, Kyushu

Among 420 Aussies who marched to a train today from the horror camp of a Mitsui coal mine was one who had to be borne on piggyback by a willing comrade. It was Private David Ernest Runge of Miwillahbah, Queensland, and he could not walk because both legs had been amputated just below the knees on March 3rd by Captain Thomas Hewlett, a U.S. physician prisoner captured on Bataan.

Five Americans and one Aussie have been put to death by the Japanese here, and many Americans permanently mutilated by beatings from Mitsui's overmen and soldiers. But by common consent among 1,700 Dutch, English, Australian and American prisoners at this camp, Runge's case is the sheerest example of deliberate Japanese cruelty short of executions without trial.

Runge, captured at Singapore, was "an old Aussie," which means he arrived at the Mitsui camp and entered the coal mine in June 1944, joining the Bataan and Corregidor Americans who had already been toiling for nearly a year underground. By February 1945 Runge was instructing "new Aussies" in the use of a jackhammer. He was showing F. R. Willis and Robert Tideswell how to chip rock, the whole party being under an overman named Katu-san, when three cars carrying coal ran off the rails, causing Katu-san's temper to do likewise. Saying "Dummy dummy, that's no good," the Japanese promised that he would report Runge for *haitis savis,* meaning "military gifts"—that is, a beating.

Guards waiting for Runge at the mine's shafthead hustled him to the *aeso.* Five soldiers beat him with fists and heavy timbers, then muscled him to the camp guardhouse a half mile away. Runge and his two students remained ignorant of what the charge was, if any.

The day was bitter cold with sleet, and Runge wore cotton pants, a shirt, an overcoat and cracked Japanese-style rubber shoes which

104

fell from his feet as he obeyed the guards' first command: that he kneel on bamboo.

Runge's sworn affadavit says, "From four in the afternoon until noon the next day I was kept kneeling in this position with twelve rests of fifteen minutes each, standing at attention." He was allowed his first sleep from the following midnight until four in the morning of February 14th, two days after his arrest.

From four in the morning Runge was stood at attention all day in the freezing guardhouse, barefoot. His feet were already swollen so large that he would have been unable to replace his sneakers even if allowed. On the 16th and 17th he was also stood continuously at attention, barefoot, from four in the morning until nine at night.

From the first day of Runge's arrest the Australian commanding officer, Motor Transport Lieutenant Percival Howell, visited twice daily the camp commandant, Captain Fukuhara, and explained to him Runge's increasingly grave condition. Runge's feet were turning black and blue, and for the first three days he went foodless. Finally on the 17th he was no longer able to hold himself upright. Runge was then compelled to sign a form determined by Captain Fukuhara which was standard. The statement said that Runge must expect severer treatment if sent to the *aeso* again and that he must obey all orders by any Japanese, whether civilian or military.

Carried to the hospital by two American comrades, Runge underwent treatment by Dr. Hewlett and Captain Ian Duncan. After a week his feet were still numb and his toes cadaveric. In three weeks his toes began dropping off and gangrene was spreading. On the morning of March 9th Howell visited the young ex–banana plantation worker and told him that his feet must go.

That's why Davey Runge was carried instead of walking today as he departed for Nagasaki, where the American hospital ship *Haven* has a bed waiting for him.

"The Japanese Was a Strange Jailer"

Allied Prison Camp #17, Omuta, Kyushu

Though nobody cares much what the Japanese think about any more, the processes of the Japanese mind are still a cause of wonderment to those who were their prisoners. These men have the advantage, if it can be called that, of having known the Japanese both before and after surrender. They believe, many of them, that the Japanese are a bit crazy. The prisoners do not exclude the possibility they may have become crazy too, by association. But the Japanese seem to have been a little more so.

In Java, the prison enclosure at Bandoeng had two sets of captives: 5,000 men, Allied military, and 1,200 ducks, Javanese. By a system of ruses the Allied prisoners, who were always hungry, found a way of stealing the eggs laid in captivity by their fellow prisoners. Egg production went down 50%. The commandant blamed the ducks. He studied their lives and reached the conclusion that they were dissolute and frivolous. One day he ordered all the ducks to be driven off their ponds and arranged before him in as orderly a fashion as frightened ducks could be. Then, roaring at the top of his voice, he delivered them a lecture.

"Your egg production is down, do you understand?" he shouted. "And why has it fallen? It is not for lack of food. Do not tell me you are starving. You eat well. But you are not like Japanese ducks. You are lazy. You simply do not wish to lay. You are insubordinate ducks, obstructionist ducks. Well, I have a cure for that. For two days you will go on half rations." The commandant dismissed the ducks without seeing the abashed looks on the faces of the Allied prisoners who had overheard his lecture.

American culture has had a part in making the Japanese what they are today. In each camp the best guards were those who had lived in the United States and returned to Japan out of a sense of duty. The worst, the most ingrown and the most disoriented, were

Japanese who had been dunked in a Californian atmosphere and withdrawn before they were coated. Finally there was also a kind of Japanese who had been barely sideswiped by the American dream, recovered his balance but was still slightly askew.

One Japanese guard in a Mitsui coal mine on Kyushu had never visited the United States, but was as touched as if he had. He rarely raised a *narugi* or *kiboko* (stick or club) against his prisoners, as the other jailers regularly did. While his skinny Americans toiled in the narrow, hot tunnels, their thin shoulders bent under the sagging, rotten beams, he watched them through half-closed eyes, feeding a golden dream. When they gradually learned what this dream was, they nicknamed him "Tom Mix". In his own inward vision this little Japanese was a cowpuncher. He had seen every western movie that ever came to Japan, from William S. Hart to Roy Rogers. While his weary wards labored under the dripping black overhead, their hearts were already at home in the United States. His heart was at home too, but it was home on the range. He was riding the prairie, a black mustang dancing under him, his six-guns unlimbered and a lariat swinging loose on his finger.

Every now and then, swept away by his inner vision, this stubby Tom Mix would stand up in his stirrups as though forgetful where he was. He would give his lariat of air a few easy swirls around his flickering cap-lamp, and cast the imaginary lasso the length of the humid black tunnel toward an imaginary calf, pulling up sharply on his reins with his left hand. Easy in the saddle, he would push back his sombrero and haul in the reluctant animal.

Suddenly a suspicion would strike him. Was that a crooked sheriff, drawing bead on him from behind yonder cactus? In an instant he would make his lasso fast to his saddle horn—1,500 feet underground in a sweaty coal mine, its tunnels swishing with icy waters—twist in his coal car saddle, and let his six-guns split the dark with lightning. And then, while the thin, gaping prisoners from Bataan and Corregidor eased down their picks to watch him, he would dismount, swagger over and give the face-down sheriff (a discarded hand-drill) a kick full of contempt. Then he would swing up again on his pony. Watching the half-naked, sweating Americans through faraway eyes as they lugged nuggets to their cradle cars, he would roll and light himself a plainsman's cigarette.

To most prisoners Tom Mix was just a Japanese who happened to be crazy in a western manner. But among the New Mexicans of the 200th Coast Artillery, almost all taken on Corregidor and Bataan, he was outright popular. For these southwesterners Tom Mix came as near as any Japanese could to making up for undreaming sadists like Squeaky, Clark Gable, the Greyhound, the Greek, Pretty Boy Floyd, and Flangeface. (I saw a Brooklyn boy beat up Flangeface in a lineup of guards before the evacuation team reached this camp.) Each guard generally beat up an American once or twice a week.

Perhaps the Japanese least likely to be forgotten by those who knew him is First Lieutenant Y. Murao, who until his downfall held the post of physician in a prison coal mine near Omuta. Murao did not "strafe" (plunder) Red Cross prisoner packages nor beat prisoners. He was himself a prisoner, of his own weakness. His vice was one no American should have found hard to forgive: an overpowering devotion to baseball. At first he concealed his frailty. It was not until he had doctored for several weeks at the camp that he gradually revealed that baseball, played as he conceived it, could be a method of torturing prisoners comparable with the electric seat and the water cup.

The idea of the camp administrator, Captain Yuri, was that a prisoner's main and only job was to dig coal for the Japanese, and his only reward for twelve hours' daily labor should be his salary of three-quarters of a cent daily, plus a *yassamai* or rest day every ten days or so.

Lieutenant Murao, whose nickname was "The Grunt", had a view so opposite to this that it might almost be called dangerous. He believed that the Americans were in Japan simply to wait out the war. He felt that they should spend their time not digging coal but playing baseball. He had two reasons for this attitude: first, he argued that baseball was a healthy and natural conditioner for Americans; and second, he believed that he himself was a great coach. When he spoke of "playing baseball" he did not mean in any loose or sportive sense. "Play" was a euphemism. He meant play in the sense Knute Rockne did.

To see this Durocher *manqué* in the frame of his ambition it is necessary first to realize that all the prisoners in Camp #17, in hospital or out, were suffering from deficiency diseases. Living on three half-bowlfuls of rice a day, they had faded away till many looked like walking hat racks. Many had lost as much as fifty pounds. They had frequent fainting spells. They rarely understood anything not repeated twice. They found it nearly impossible to drag themselves to the top of the shaft when their shift was called. These miners were the fit. But the Grunt did not begin with the fit. He started with those who were worse off, who were confined to his hospital.

Murao entered baseball in a deceptively small way. Some of his patients had tuberculosis or pneumonia and could not even walk. He was forced to build his team around those who could arise from bed, a limitation he clearly resented. A few had broken arms or legs. Several had breaks they had caused themselves, or ulcers they had fed with cap-lamp acid. He was ready to excuse them from digging coal, but not from baseball. His infield was built around players who had diarrhea or dysentery. They were hardly able to swing a bat or walk to their positions with self-control. Running bases was to invite scenes of a very humiliating nature.

This impossible squad of listless misfits, on command, would follow the Grunt out of the hospital doors and dispose themselves about the diamond he had marked out. Then the ordeal of infield play or pepper practice would commence. The Grunt, as coach, would stand at home plate, rapping out the ball and calling the throws. The reactions of the players were slow. They could not even bend over quickly. Their straw sandals came off. A hard-hit ball would go through four or five skinny forks of legs, like croquet wickets. They reached for everything, but too late.

"We all had rice brain from under-nourishment," says a former member of this squad. "When the Grunt said, 'Two on and one out' and then cracked the ball at us, we never had time to figure things out. He would try to ginger us up, scolding us when our throws fell short, as they nearly always did. But if we made a good play, he was pleased."

Murao's ambition was to have his patients play a town team of Japanese 4-F civilians. The day seemed far away. The favorite hit in the inter-patient games was the bunt; it was one way of making sure that no matter how many errors were made you would not have to run beyond first on the hit itself, and might even be fortunate enough to arrive after the ball. A man unlucky enough to beat out a bunt in his shambling shuffle would arrive on first and beseech the man coaching behind the bag to get him a bedpan. Players whom the Grunt signaled to steal second would reach the midway bag in such condition they would have to lie down and use the base as a pillow. ("To die on base" is only an expression, but many of Murao's patients were nearer death after an enforced lope down to second than at any other time in their lives.)

The physician-coach was rather short, about thirty-two years old. He wore a baseball cap when coaching. Though a fireball as a manager, he never did any actual playing. During a game among the invalids he would sit on the mound of a bunker-style air raid shelter and make notes on the styles of his pathetic players. He also kept scorebooks and complete season records. On short notice he could tell anyone who was hitting better—a left fielder from the 26th Cavalry of Bataan whose legs were covered with ulcers of malnutrition, or a catcher from the Navy's Yangtze patrols with two throwing fingers amputated from being caught in Mitsui's outworn gears.

Captain Thomas Hewlett, a small, thoughtful physician who himself once operated outdoors on a prisoner's appendix with a razor blade for scalpel, was a frequent involuntary player. In the Philippines Hewlett had originally worn a beard, but when Murao found out that he was less than thirty years old, he made him cut it off. "You would walk up there to the plate, feebly supporting your bat," says Hewlett. "You wouldn't dare take any practice swings; they made you feel too weak. If the pitch was good you would swing so that Murao wouldn't give you hell. But you would pray not to hit it. You hoped to miss because if you had to run around those bases, you would not have strength enough to walk out to your place in the field when sides changed."

As the Grunt's obsession grew, the games got longer and longer. There was no regard for innings. When the last out of the ninth was played, and the gloves slipped limply from the hands of the players, the coach often ordered, "No stop—play extra innings."

Murao's teams were particularly weak because the rice ration descended for hospitalized men to one-half of the ration for the able-bodied, who went into the mine. Moreover, the military executives of the mine began taking away his stronger players to dig coal. He would hardly build up an infield of sound invalids than it would be ordered underground. He soon found a way to keep his squads normal, however. Whenever a miner pleaded illness, even though an obvious malingerer, the Grunt would ask, "You pray basebawr?" If he did, he went to the hospital. It was a game. The mine robbed the hospital and the hospital robbed the mine.

A time arrived when Murao considered that he had a first team capable of beating outsiders. He had already found a squad in a nearby town which he considered suitably unfit to meet his tottering Americans. Before bringing the visitors to the camp, he explained to them that all his players were "from the hospital". He apologized in advance for the poor game they would offer. It was his one act of frankness. Privately he was sure that his own cripples would clean up, because he had plugged the worst leaks in his infield with an able-bodied doctor and a mine corpsman.

The game was an unspeakable reversal of ordinary baseball, with the errors greatly outnumbering the chances accepted. In the ninth inning the physician-coach was confronted with a question of sporting ethics. He had a run on third—a potbellied skeleton with acute edema and a xylophone breast development—and he needed a clean hit to bring the near-cadaver home. His other players were lying on the sooty clay of the mine-yard, hollow-eyed, panting, and collapsed. He needed a pinch-hitter able to run at least as far as second, and the hospital rolls were exhausted.

But the Grunt had a card still unplayed. There was a prisoner who worked in the mine, who had once played semi-pro baseball around Denver, but whom the Grunt had never been able to make into a hospital patient because he refused to apply for treatment. He preferred slaving in the tunnels to participating in such a macabre parody of a game he loved. The card Murao held was that once, months before, this man had served as assistant in an emergency operation in the hospital.

He ordered the ex-player, who was off-shift and asleep, summoned. The game was stopped. At length the ringer arrived, yawning with sleep and dazed. Murao explained to him what was expected. When the visitors saw his practiced and relatively virile swing, they protested. The Grunt sweetly produced testimony that the pinch-hitter had actually been a hospital assistant.

The ringer hit a clean single, the skeleton galloped home with a gaunt giraffe-like step, and the game was won. The ringer went back to his cot and sleep immediately, and when he was roused by starlight for his shift in the mine, he remarked, "Funny what you dream in a camp. I dreamed Murao had me playing ball for him."

As the sharp Japanese autumn verged into winter, the prisoners nursed a hope that the doctor's passion would wear off. The patients were playing in thin cotton clothing, bare-legged and with straw sandals. The wind coming down from the mountains cut their lungs and set them coughing. The field was hard and icy, and sometimes snow fell.

Instead of halting, the coach intensified his training. "Pray harder, you keep warmer," he said. The patients played from the cold winter sunrise until the sorrowful sunset. A man tagged with a ball simply fell over as though clubbed. Murao, feeling that hardening exercises were called for, introduced a new training program. Under this system, patients were called from their wooden pallets at 5:30 in the morning, when it was dark and frosty, and given a half hour of calisthenics to toughen them for the winter baseball season.

At the same time, however, conditions were deteriorating in the mine. Cave-ins were frequent. Miners began to turn themselves into baseball players. The hospital doubled its patients, then doubled them again. Captain Yuri had gone and the new commander was

Captain Fukuhara, an unpliant personality. He was heard to complain to Lieutenant Murao that extending the influence of baseball was cutting down coal production by encouraging men to aim at avoiding the mine. "Hold more men above ground!" retorted the Grunt in Japanese rather wildly. "Hold five hundred! Hold a thousand! We'll have a baseball league—maybe two leagues!"

Murao eventually did overreach himself. He proposed that several new hospital buildings be built, and drew up plans. If carried out, his camp plans would have changed the entire coal mine into a gigantic hospital, completely girdled with ball fields. He also demanded more gloves, mitts, balls and bats. At this point the Army officers saw that they had an empire-builder on their hands, though of a peculiar order. They decided to get rid of him.

The Grunt was hustled out of camp without even a chance for a farewell speech to his squad. The same afternoon the new commandant went through the hospital swinging a large *narugi,* followed by several guards with *kibokos.* They cut the squad. Later Murao's diamond was dug up into air raid shelters, and just in time too, for the first B-29 raids were beginning.

An American officer of one of the prisoner-recovery teams, coming up from Nagasaki after the surrender, reminded the men in this camp that the World Series would begin soon back home. "They reacted a lot different in this camp from our boys on Honshu," he remarked, puzzled. "Instead of wanting to know all about who was playing and so forth, they looked at each other and gave a kind of shudder. I guess they must've had some experiences so terrible they just couldn't talk about them."

Izuka, Japan—Monday, September 17, 1945
1800 hours

Allied Prison Camp #7, Izuka, Kyushu

All names herewith exclusively obtained by myself, being the first correspondent to reach this camp.

Two Mitsui coal mines, Shinko and Honko—the scene of bitter toil by 186 American, 360 Dutch, and 2 British prisoners for the past year—limped along on Japanese labor today while eager prisoners, hungry for home, waited for a typhoon which has grounded transport planes to blow itself out.

Men were paid ten *sen* daily, non-coms fifteen; that's about seven-tenths of one American penny, and a cent and a quarter, for twelve hours' work. Beatings were frequent but, unlike the Mitsui mine at Omuta where five Americans were "executed" thus, none of the beatings were prolonged. However, one American weakened by malnutrition was beaten enough to bring about his death.

Fifty-four Dutch died, having passed away with pneumonia before camp physician Captain Sidney Vernon of Willimantic, Connecticut, arrived with the first sulfadiozene.

The Japanese here introduced two types of speed-up days or *odashis*. On big *odashi* days prisoners got worked one hour beyond the normal twelve, and received one potato as a bonus. On little *odashi* days they worked one hour extra and got nothing.

The camp is commanded by a Dutchman, Captain Willem Andrau, who before the war was the Dutch East Indies representative of the Universal Oil Products Company, a Chicago builder of international refineries.

Joseph Matheny of Zanesville, Illinois, a member of the 192nd Tanks, said that Maywood Company "was hit harder than any other and I cannot believe many are alive. I've been trying to find them among Kyushu's prison camps, without success. My best buddy, a Chicagoan, died in O'Donnell. [*Correspondent's note: Names are known here but cannot be released until confirmed by the War Department.*] Our company was one-quarter Chicago boys, and I cannot remember a single one who's still alive."

Pharmacist Kenneth Moffat of San Diego was more hopeful, saying: "I saw Chicagoan Steve Gados and the whole crew of his suicide tank alive at Cabanatuan between April and July of last year. I also saw the Japs force another Chicagoan, from a tank battalion, to hold his hands aloft while they beat him severely with bamboo sticks. They then had him lower his hands, and they beat his head until it was covered with swollen knobs."

Moffat gave a moving account of how five Americans (Emery of the Quartermaster Corps, Smith of the 200th Coast Artillery, Gustafson of the 31st Infantry, Adams of the Air Corps, and one other believed to be from the 192nd Tanks) were executed by a firing squad in August 1942 when the Japanese detached a bridge-building party to Calumpet in Bulagan, thirty miles from Manila. The Japanese at first refused to allow Moffat to give medical care to the party, but when all but ten of 120 were down, they permitted him to open an infirmary but denied him medicine. Four cases died from appendicitis within three months because the Japanese doctor who came every ten days from Manila refused Moffat's pleas to remove them in his empty truck. In the face of a death penalty for any absence from camp, Moffat used to swim nightly across Pampanga's river to receive gifts of medicine from Filipinos who "pledged us twenty percent of their wages for medicine but actually gave us nearer sixty percent."

The showdown came when "Adobe Citizen"—an American, Gottlieb Neigum of the 31st Infantry, who was living Philippine-style—escaped despite a warning from the Japanese lieutenant, Watanabe, that ten Americans would be killed if one departed. Watanabe lined up the Americans and informed them that because he was generous he had decided to shoot five instead ten. Neigum had been holder of camp number #120. Watanabe announced that under the presumption of having influenced or known about Neigum's escape, two numbers below and three above Neigum's—the holders of #118, #119, #121, #122, and #123—would be executed. Having been accidentally next to Neigum in the lineup, but otherwise not even acquainted with him, these five Americans were completely innocent of any complicity. Nevertheless, without any religious rites, the Americans were immediately led by an improvised firing squad of camp guards to a schoolhouse across Pampanga's river.

"Only one accepted a blindfold," said Moffat. "They're buried in unmarked graves which I visited. Three had been sick with malaria and diarrhea. The four whose names I know represented the 200th Coast Artillery, the 31st Infantry, the Air Corps, the Quartermaster Corps, and I think the fifth was from the 192nd Tanks. Just the day before, everybody had taken up a collection of sixty dollars for one of those executed who was low with malaria but without the money for black market quinine."

En route to Japan, Moffat had suffered a beating from a guard which deprived him of his hearing for several weeks. After about seventy-five blows on the head, the Japanese compelled him to kneel motionless on a hatch cover for two hours.

The above reprisal shooting is additional to the one which occurred at Lumban, Laguna, southwest of Manila, in June 1943, when the Japanese exacted a full toll of ten American lives, a massacre celebrated by the prison camp bard Raymond Russel of Pittsburg, Texas, in a long homespun ballad famous among prisoners.

Sergeant William Snyder (Cairo, West Virginia): "I was with the Philippine guerrilla bands under Lieutenant Arnold in northern Luzon for about a year as one among about thirty Americans who'd formerly run an air raid system. We had to break up into separate bands because of a lack of food. One day we destroyed nine Japanese truckloads of equipment and three field guns, killing around two hundred Japs. After that it became too hot and I had to give in."

Administrative officer of the camp, here by way of Bataan, *Captain Roscoe Price (Lasalle, Colorado):* "The Japanese never recognize officer status. I was forced to work in the garden, to clean the latrine. Once all the officers were lined up and slapped because we allowed the men to get up five minutes later than the fixed rising time."

Medical Officer Vernon said that the camp developed two new diseases: colon malnutrition, evidenced by a burning sensation in the feet which failed to respond to thiamin chloride but only to more food and which affected at its peak one-tenth of the camp; and what he calls "pseudo-adolescent mastitis" which involved thirty percent of the camp and "resembles transient breast enlargment at puberty."

Addressing this writer in the camp's infirmary, Corregidor *Marine Corporal Harry Douthit of Dalles, Oregon,* said: "That oily smiling Jap doctor right across from you sent me back to work with my calf swollen enormously from this infected ulcer." The Marine showed me fifty old scars.

Prisoners from *Tyler, Texas, Sergeant Robert Coley* and *Lloyd Durbin,* are both Corregidor veterans. Said Coley: "The Japs wouldn't recognize that losing sweat deprives the body of salt and causes weakness. I got caught taking salt from cattle on the farm, and our former Japanese commander stood me up and beat me uninterruptedly for forty-five minutes." Said Durbin: "I was beaten, sometimes daily, sometimes weekly. They seemed to be reacting to outside events rather than anything we did, and it was noticeably worse just before the surrender."

Corregidor *Corporal Fred Patrick (Sherman, Texas):* "We lived on thin soup, rice, occasionally a little fish, wheat, soybeans. It seemed the Japs were trying to starve us to death."

Marine First Sergeant John Coe of Saltyville, Virginia, also out of Corregidor: "I weighed 210 prewar and fell to 103 working in the mine. But pneumonia and the onset of dysentery gave me three months in the infirmary, which saved my life."

Nick Page (Los Angeles): "I'd been in bed for nine weeks with pneumonia. I wasn't supposed to get up. The Jap doctor refused to see me unless I came to the infirmary, so two corpsmen supported me to get there. On returning I collapsed on their shoulders from sheer weakness, and this Jap administrator we called Napoleon overtook me in the corridor and gave me a thorough kicking from behind."

Tall Marine drum major captured at Corregidor, *Jackson Rauh of Mission Beach, California:* "I'm closing out the war very short of teeth, because I lost my uppers en route to Japan in a packed ship's hold where the Japs jammed us, and my gold-filled lowers disappeared during a Japanese shakedown of prisoners' bunks."

Fireman Leo Hughes of Dayton, Washington, captured at Fort Hughes: "I'll never forget July 17th, 1944, when the Japanese put 1568 men in a hold forty by fifty feet, four levels of bunks deep, for the trip from Manila to Japan in the *Nissyo Maru.* When men passed out they simply carried them on deck, then put them below again."

Radioman William Laplante (Grafton, North Dakota): "The boat ride here knocked my weight from 140 to 100 due to weakness, and I've never recovered."

The average weight of an American laboring for the Mitsuis in the coal mine, computed according to age/height charts, should be just under 153 pounds, but for the entire camp period it is 123½.

Corregidor *Marine Corporal James DeNixon (New Orleans):* "I started out yapping back at the Jap straw bosses regardless of how much they beat me. It was tough going, but finally I convinced them I was crazy."

Marine Corporal from Corregidor, *Edward Howe (Beverly Hills):* "Many Americans burned themselves with battery acid or anything else handy in order to escape underground work. On the surface the Japs were halfway human, but underneath they became beasts."

Machinist Albert Roberts (Brookfield, Illinois): "I've done all sorts of work. They had Americans doing airport building, farmwork, a coal mine. I've been beaten in the mine with a pick handle, an axe handle, a saw, a timber. I've been kicked in the shins, spat on in the face, and had coal thrown at me."

Sergeant Glenn Wayman of Paola, Kansas, captured on Bataan: "In nine months underground I never got anything more serious than cuffs and slaps. Then I was beaten above ground for protesting about the day guard making noise while the American night shift slept."

Donald Versam (Bloomington, Nebraska): "I got only two cuffs, for not extinguishing my cigarette when the Japs rang their bell. I was wise enough to take my blows without flinching, as the Japanese demand. But Chester Williams of Fresno, who erred by turning his head, was made to kneel on cement while they burned him with bamboo."

Corregidor *Marine Corporal Franklin Boyer (Philadelphia):* "I got slapped around so much in the mine that I began keeping my ulcers open in order to keep above ground. But the Japanese caught on."

Monford Charlton (Denbo, Pennsylvania): "I went from 145 to 102. So I dropped a rock on my hand, mashed it, and got eighty-nine days of sick rest. When that was gone, I spilled acid on this scarred foot and got forty-nine days more. Guys would plead for someone to do a fracture job for them. Chicagoan Albert Roberts obliged four fellows that way, but the best deal he could get was three rations of rice for a breakage fee when he wanted the same done to himself."

Raised in Fort Dodge, Iowa, a resident of Long Beach, California, the longest-term prisoner is *Chief Pharmacist Fred Roepke:* forty-four months in Japanese hands since Guam fell on the third day of the war. "We had sixty self-inflicted wounds in one year among 190 Americans. They took turns fracturing bones and pouring acid. I've seen a Jap walk through a hospital and slap every man. My worst job was when the whole Guam medical team was summoned by Japs from the Zentsuji model prison camp in Shikoku Island to care for an arriving Allied ship. It proved to be the *Shonan Maru* from Singapore, with 250 Englishmen of whom, despite all our efforts, 127 died in six weeks from dysentery and malnutrition."

Corregidor *Marine Sergeant Potter Sillman (Burr, Nebraska):* "My normal weight of 185 hit 85 on Bataan from malaria, and 90 in Japan from malnutrition."

Seaman Edward Walaszek (Holyoke, Massachusetts), captured at Fort Hughes: "I got my only beating when I tried to prevent a guard from making off with my shirt. I finally was forced to donate it anyway, then got beaten by another Japanese who accused me of black market trading."

The Mitsui coal mine had its own gallery of thugs whom the American prisoner miners named the Beast, the Pig, Tom Mix, and the Dripper, so-called because he was personally so filthy. *Sergeant Hubert Barber of Williamsfield, Illinois:* "For eight months in the mine I was the pet peeve of a straw boss we called the Cobra. He would throw coal at me too close for me to duck, sometimes within three feet of my face. Once he wrestled and threw me down because I was so weak." Medico Vernon described Barber as having "a severe case of malnutrition, beriberi, and edema."

Pharmacist Thomas Locklear (Powderlee, Alabama): "We called our bossman the Gorilla because of the way he would jump around, clawing at us, trying to get us to fight him."

William White (Kingsbury, Indiana): "What was toughest for me was being sent back to the mine by the Jap doctor after a cave-in injured my shoulder. My inability to work put a heavier burden on my buddies."

Sergeant Forest Swartz (Sacramento): "When my weight reached 103, the Japs allowed me to work in the kitchen instead of the mine."

A Marine from Corregidor, *Sergeant Charles Eckstein (San Francisco):* "There was an old camp commander we called Emma or Dreamy Eyes. When three prisoner rooms were in disarray, he lined up seventeen room-heads and punched each personally in the jaw. I believe the Japs are the lowest people on earth, and I would rather have spent my three years on Alcatraz."

Corregidor *Marine Herbert Klingbeil (Minneapolis):* "I was lucky enough to make the same camp as my brother Arthur, who's already en route home. When Arthur tried to ease his heavy burden of mine timbers in a rising tunnel and was beaten with a saw handle across his arms and face, the overseer found me resting in my bunk with my sandals on and beat me twenty-three times across my face until it swelled up."

Bataan prisoner *Freddie Ray (Erico, Oklahoma):* "My worst experience was on the Bataan death march, when I had to go seven days without food and water. With my own eyes I saw at least fifty men shot, and forty to fifty bayoneted. I saw men drink water from ditches where dead Americans and Filipinos lay. When the Japs caught you asking for water, they'd throw a bucketful in your face."

Corregidor *Gunner George Beuris (Hazard, Kentucky):* "My worst time was from May 7th until May 22nd, when the Japs kept us in the broiling sun on Corregidor all day." Beuris has a mangled finger which was operated on without anesthesia by a Japanese doctor.

Captain James Corrigan (Wichita): "Just for pausing a moment in order to watch a Japanese beating up a Dutchman, I got a punch in the jaw."

Corregidor *Marine Corporal Clarence Thompson (Commerce, Texas):* "I got several slappings—though no beatings—for no apparent reason other than the disagreeable Japanese temperament."

Woodrow Wilson (Poplar Bluffs, Mississippi): "Lots of my friends have been seriously beaten, but I've had only casual blows."

Sergeant Hubert Seal (Rupert, Idaho): "In eight months I've been beaten quite a lot, but starvation was what really hardened my heart toward the Japanese people. Before the war my weight was 175. At the surrender I weighed 112."

Sergeant Joseph Fragale (Buffalo): "The Japs would beat us for putting our hands in our pockets anytime, and they were harder on Americans than on the Dutch. I got the worst beating of my career as a prisoner for taking some squash seeds out of the garden because I was very hungry and didn't realize it was forbidden. They beat me until I could no longer hear, and until I had a big boil on my back. I'll never forget the day of that beating. It was August 15th—the day the war ended."

Izuka, Japan—Tuesday, September 18, 1945
0900 hours

Allied Prison Camp #7, Izuka, Kyushu

Unflaggingly bold as a prisoner of war, just as when he was a jungle sniper on Bataan, Chicago's Captain Arthur Wermuth, the one-time "one-man army," remains in the history of the Pacific War another man to whom the same aphorism is applied as to MacArthur: "Some like him, some don't like him, but even those who don't like him respect him."

His rough and tough tactics of personal leadership gained him the respect of the Japanese, for the Nipponese admire daring and cunning above all other characteristics. Friends of his with whom the writer has talked say that American estimates giving the stocky Chicagoan over a hundred Japanese scalps were exaggerated, but that the number certainly was at least sixty. They add however that much credit should be given to the Filipino scouts who went everywhere with the Chicagoan and who "got the Jap who would have got Wermuth, while the one-man army was getting his."

How Wermuth gained the admiration of enlisted men even during his prison days was explained by Navy Pharmacist T. E. Locklear of Powderlee, Alabama, who recounted a clash at Camp Cabanatuan between the one-man army and a vicious Japanese sentry called Laughing Boy.

The Japanese forced ailing amoebic dysentery patients in groups of four to carry loads of 600 pounds of manure. When Laughing Boy refused to lighten the loads, Wermuth cursed him openly, took a spade, and fell to, saying, "I'll lighten their loads myself."

For this defiance, Laughing Boy began his punishment by kicking Wermuth's shins and making him kneel. Then Laughing Boy, with two other Japanese, beat Wermuth's face and buttocks, leaving him with blackened eyes and a visage covered with bruises—but more popular than ever with G.I.s for having attempted to defend the prisoners' cause.

Gene Riding of Whitehall, Illinois remembers "seeing Captain Wermuth after having been kicked and beaten in the face at Cabanatuan. Three of his ribs were supposed to be fractured. Ordinarily he did everything himself, but this time he asked me to carry a bucket of water which he was unable to lift."

Wermuth later saved many lives by his coolness aboard a bombed Japanese freighter carrying American prisoners. The bomb fell in the forward hold, full of ailing Americans, while the Japan-bound freighter was in Takau* harbor, Formosa, on January 6th of this year. Approximately 371 Americans were killed, including many officers who had served both at Corregidor and Bataan.

After the bodies had lain untouched by the Japanese, who refused to allow them to be moved from the hold, Wermuth seized the situation below decks. Despite light shrapnel wounds in both legs, he was able to organize a burial detail for the bodies piled under a hatch. Wermuth also smuggled a note asking for medicine up through hatches guarded by the Japanese and, with the aid of former Los Angeles newspaperman Theodore Lewin, was able to get medicine from the crew in return for keepsakes of the men killed.

His insistence on reestablishing cleanliness in the body-strewn forward hold of the freighter saved many lives after the Japanese allowed the bodies to be taken ashore and cremated.

* Also spelled Takao. Present-day Kao-hsiung on Taiwan. See "The Death Cruise."

Izuka, Japan—Wednesday, September 19, 1945

Allied Prison Camp #23, Izuka, Kyushu

The miracle of a Japanese prison camp where nobody was beaten to death, and cuffs and slaps took the place of the usual torture, was revealed here when Camp #23, with all American prisoners, was liberated today. It is another worn-out coal mine in the Mitsui chain that was abandoned till U.S. prisoners arrived. By American standards, Camp #23 was one where the treatment of prisoners would call for stern investigation with blue-ribbon juries and special committees. But by the standards which Americans learned from the Japanese on Bataan's death march, it was almost comfortable. Stick beatings were relatively rare. While one Japanese doctor withheld medicine provided by the Red Cross from medical officer Major Kenneth Hagen of Fresno, another physician named Shigata secretly opened the forbidden boxes and sneaked him drugs. Hagen himself was beaten up "two or three times" by a Japanese who called him contemptuously "Bamboo Doctor."

Hagen told the Japanese camp physician, "Unless these men get help they'll die," and the latter replied, "Sick men die, okay okay." Patients were often slapped for being too weak to be able to descend in the mine, but never were deliberately starved to death in confinement as they were by the notorious Captain Fukuhara at Omuta. Sometimes the mine authorities gave extra portions of rice to supplement the thin gruel of ordinary fare. Yet Americans from Bataan and Corregidor whom this writer interviewed, like pharmacist Dudley DeGroat of South Bend and Thomas Boyle of Mason City, Iowa, showed marks of malnutrition, Boyle having fallen from 216 pounds to 109 pounds at his worst. Beatings were common enough for the Japanese clubs to gain the name " 'vitamin sticks', because when you're weak they pep you up."

The fact that only 5 out of 200 Americans at Izuka have died is proof enough of the Japanese government's direct responsibility for the much higher death rolls elsewhere. This Mitsui mine is extremely dangerous like all the others in Kyushu, which had been dropped as economically unprofitable until the Americans came with their one-cent-daily labor. It is a "wet mine", with roofs mushy and constantly falling. The American prisoners were actually chipping at the coal pillars which alone supported the ceiling in this stripped mine. And yet here the death roll was lower, due to the absence of constant beatings, than in other mines even though the same dangerous conditions prevailed and the food was almost the same. Here the Americans were provided with overcoats, which lessened the toll from pneumonia even though most worked in winter in straw sandals or rubber split-toe sneakers. Elsewhere many were forced to work barefoot. Here only about two percent of the prisoners' injuries were caused by the Americans voluntarily breaking their own limbs or pouring acid on themselves to escape going underground, whereas in Camp #7, about five miles away, conditions were so cruel that one-third of the Americans broke their feet or arms, put their hands in conveyor machines, or poured acid on themselves to get relief from the mine tunnels.

The Japanese camp commander at today's parting from Captain Marvin Lucas of Albuquerque voluntarily presented him with a four-hundred-year-old samurai sword. Of the ex-commander, *Captain Frank Turner of Gallup, New Mexico,* said, "Nakamura was all right, and although the guards were often rough, all our Japanese commanders have been generally just."

Through the bitter winter in the Japanese coal mountains, the only heat provided was in the dispensary. It was freezing from December to May but the Americans were unable to use the coal which they provided by the tons for the Mitsui chain. *Lieutenant Joe Allen of Santa Fe* said, "That green soup made from grass gathered around the camp, with a bowlful of rice, was hardly enough to satisfy a man after twelve hours' labor in the mine." Officers were not allowed to go below in the mine and share or even witness the conditions prevailing there.

Sergeant Gilbert Soifer (Philadelphia): "The worst thing was expecting us to do heavy physical labor on two bowls of rice in the morning, a small box of rice with a pickle at noon, and rice with a bowl of thin green soup at night. But if you were hospitalized you got one-third less food."

Taking their cue from the tough camp physician, the medicos were Camp #23's hardiest Americans. After being beaten, *Erwin Kilburn of Lake Placid, New York,* was forced to stand up at attention all day. He became paralyzed and now has "drop foot" making it impossible for him to move without crutches.

Chicagoan Robert Oliver: "Physical treatment by the Japanese has been reasonably good by their standards, but the food has been very skimpy, and the mine was very dangerous. Several men have been permanently injured by cave-ins."

Earl Burchard (Janesville, Wisconsin): "I twice got real beatings for simply not understanding."

Robert Bartz (Beloit, Wisconsin): "Living conditions were good, but working was rough, with abusive treatment and long hours."

Sergeant William Wright (Niantic, Illinois): "Outside of the food, I've got no particular complaint—the Nip who was my boss acted pretty decent."

Edward Urbaschak (Roxbury, Massachusetts): "We sometimes averaged fifteen hours a day underground."

Corporal Peter Jumonville (Baton Rouge): "I was beaten twice for sore feet. Once the guards lined us up for fun and ordered us to slap each other. When we refused, they went to work on us with clubs."

Antonio Tafolla (San Angelo, Texas): "Due to the bullets in my shoulder I worked in the mess hall. The Japanese beat me for not being able to lift more."

Ruel Lott (Alma, Georgia): "I've seen lots of men beaten, and not more than one-tenth deserved it."

Buren Jonston (Clovis, New Mexico): "I got along without beatings or slaps for nearly a year."

Garley Silverio (Belen, New Mexico): "I've been treated pretty fair."

Corporal Oscar Look (Addison, Maine): "My normal weight is 180 and the Japanese beat me for weakness when I weighed only a little over 100."

Franklin Ivins (Red Bank, New Jersey): "We used to call going underground 'getting the axe.' But I got dry beriberi even above ground."

Sergeant Ray Tow (Silver City, New Mexico): "Even well-fed American workmen have cradles to hold a jackhammer above their heads for ceiling work. Despite my weakness, I had to hold my jackhammer up with my arms. In the United States we use water in order to keep digging a hole dry; here they use dust blowers, which saturated our lungs."

Logan Kay (Clearlake Park, California): "Coal dust blown back in our faces while we were forced to work invited silicosis."

Machinist Laverne Dunning (Centralia, Washington): "The Japanese were unable to repair their own mine machinery."

Edward Gorda (Fresno): "My main complaint is the way the Japanese hoarded our medical supplies while men sank."

Handsome Bataan soldier *William Johnston of Mountain Grove, Missouri,* with his left leg amputated, described how the continual failure of lights in defective mine equipment cost him his leg. "I was working 'in the loose'—that's where a cave-in is possible at any minute—when the lights failed and my leg was pinned between two cars."

Robert Harrison (Wheatland, California): "I lost half my sight. My left eye was buried during a cave-in, when I was picking coal down in these dangerous tunnels. The Japanese made me keep working in the mine anyhow."

Corporal Sanford Doucette (Graniteville, Massachusetts): "I pulled Harrison out from his cave-in, but got hurt myself and began to dwindle away. The Japanese still had me working with that fifty-pound jackhammer in August when I weighed only 90 myself. The war's end saved my life."

Izuka, Japan—Thursday, September 20, 1945
0130 hours

Allied Prison Camp #23, Izuka, Kyushu

How the Dutch police head in the East Indies died under Japanese torture, rather than reveal how guerrillas were communicating by radio with the refugee Dutch government, was recounted here by an RAF officer now commanding a Japanese prison camp.

After Java fell in March 1942, Dutch secret police who stayed behind managed to keep a radio set going, but their chief died and the second-in-command, named De Kuyper, succeeded him. Natives who cooperated with the enemy betrayed him. De Kuyper for over two weeks was subjected to the most refined tortures known to the Japanese, who did not realize they were now dealing with the top man because they were ignorant that De Kuyper's superior was dead. They demanded both the latter's location and the radio.

The Japanese denied him water, fed him salted meat, and drank ice water in front of him. They denied him sleep. They gave him beatings of many different kinds. When these failed they pierced his eardrums with pencils. Next they brought in his fifty-three year-old sister and caused her to be raped by a half-witted Javanese before De Kuyper's eyes. At this point De Kuyper's reason gave way. Finally they gave him the "water cure" of forced feeding, then jumping on his belly until his entrails cracked.

When De Kuyper's periods of consciousness became so brief and his insanity so evident that further questioning was useless, he was thrown into prison where the RAF officer, who was a surgeon, treated him. De Kuyper had fleeting moments of sanity before death, when he explained what had been done to him.

"Perhaps we might have saved his life, but knowing the Japs would only resume working on him we considered it more merciful to let him go," the RAF officer told this correspondent. "In order to keep the Japs appeased, we put 'pneumonia' on the death certificate."

IV

Return to Nagasaki

(September 20-25, 1945)

Weller returned to Nagasaki from the POW camps for a week (September 20–25) and found that the U.S. military, including much-needed medical staff—the Navy, not the Army—had finally arrived en masse, five weeks after the Japanese surrender and six weeks after the dropping of the atomic bomb. No longer impersonating a colonel, he wrote more material about the effects of radiation, hoping to be able to get the Navy to transmit all his dispatches and bypass MacArthur's censors. He was blocked in this hope as well, though they did let through three brief hometown POW stories. Then, trying to catch a medicine ball aboard a hospital ship in the harbor, he injured himself and was put in plaster. Utterly thwarted, Weller decided to leave Nagasaki.

Nagasaki, Japan—Thursday, September 20, 1945

The gulf separating American and Japanese ideas of humanity is both deep and wide, according to Navy Chief Quartermaster Clarence Sosviale of Auburn, Massachusetts. Since his capture while serving aboard one of the "bait boats" for Bulkeley's PT boats of Bataan, Sosviale spent most of the time working underground in Baron Mitsui's worn-out coal mine at Omuta in central Kyushu. Sosviale is now forty years old and once took fifty-two blows with a stick from a Japanese guard before losing his senses on Kyushu.

"On my shift there was a Solomon Schwartz of New York City, whose hand was mangled in their defective machinery. For one hour I was refused permission to take him above ground while he bled. When permission came, Schwartz lay on the Mitsui Company's operating table for another hour waiting for the Japanese physician to arrive. Finally the physician operated but without anesthesia although he possessed plenty, and put the man's mangled hand back together amateurishly, with little regard to the bones or tendons."

Japanese reluctance to allow any Americans to leave the mine with less than twelve hours' daily labor—for which they were paid less than one cent daily—also contributed to the permanent mutilation of John E. Garner of Nacogdoches, Texas. Garner stepped backward into a post and was blocked when trying to escape one of the defective mine's recurrent cave-ins. Dug out by friends, Garner was found to have a compound fracture of his leg. Yet it was impossible for one whole hour to move him to the surface due to the Japanese obstructing his rescue. In the mine dispensary the Japanese doctor refused to give Garner anesthesia and simply put his leg in a cast without setting the bones, with the result that Garner spent the next six months in hospital in traction trying to straighten his limb.

In contrast is the operation performed by Major Thomas Hewlett of New Albany, Indiana, who was confronted with the problem of saving a man with a ruptured appendix on a prison ship where the

Japanese refused all aid. Hewlett made himself a bent needle with pliers and, using an old razor blade for a scalpel and a ship's hatch cover as an operating table, saved the American prisoner's life. Hewlett is today a recuperative patient aboard the Navy hospital ship *Haven* in Nagasaki harbor.

Nagasaki, Japan—Saturday, September 22, 1945
1200 hours

New cases of atomic bomb poisoning with an approximate fifty percent death rate are still appearing at Nagasaki's hospital six weeks
after the blow fell, but United States Navy physicians who have examined them report that the death rate is falling off.

Under the authority of Rear Admiral F. G. Fahrion, commanding
the rescue task force now anchored in Nagasaki's bottle-shaped harbor, doctors from both the flagship cruiser *Wichita* and the hospital
ship *Haven* have conducted an informal study of deaths from radium
burns in this sixty-percent-flattened but uncratered city where, according to Japanese figures, about 21,000 persons died. These inves-
tigations support unqualifiedly the statement that the ground has
no signs of saturation with dangerous radium rays—as first revealed in the *Chicago Daily News'* original series from here a fort-
night ago.

The investigation has been under Commander Joseph Timmes,
the flagship's physician, a Georgetown and Fordham graduate.
Earth gathered from the bombed area was scattered on the spotless
floor of the *Haven*'s X-ray laboratory for a test of its radioactivity.
Commander Norman Birkbeck, a graduate of the Universities of
Wisconsin and Michigan and the *Haven*'s chief roentgenologist,
found that the scorched earth was radioactively lifeless. Moreover,
sensitive film found accidentally in the Mitsubishi torpedo plant
where hundreds of Allied prisoners worked was revealed to be un-
affected.

Whereas formerly twenty patients a day with dwindling hair and
their bone marrow affected were coming to Japanese hospitals, the
rate is now fallen to about ten. Deaths, which at the time of the
writer's first series of dispatches were eight daily, are now about five
or less.

Nagasaki's medical center, with virtually all its staff, was wiped
out by the same blast which laid a heavy hand on the Mitsubishi

133

torpedo plants, diesel motor plants, and shipbuilding yards. This circumstance plus the lack of medicines has slowed any comparison between Nagasaki's shock deaths, ordinary burn deaths, radium
deaths, and disease deaths of which astonishingly few have appeared. What happens in so-called atomic bomb poisoning is now
definitely known to be that the bone marrow is paralyzed. Human
blood has three solid substances: red cells, white cells, and platelets.
Red cells, normally numbered at five million in density, drop to two
million or even one. White cells, which are disease fighters, fall from
about eight thousand to fifteen hundred and in one case to four hundred. But the effect on the platelets, which are organisms giving
blood the power to clot, is not merely to diminish them but to para-
lyze and apparently kill them.

Ordinarily platelets enable the blood to clot by itself in three to
four minutes. The blood of persons exposed to the atomic bomb's
rays, which are mainly of the gamma variety, requires thirty minutes to two hours to clot and sometimes as long as three to four
hours. Autopsies have shown the bone marrow's effort to recover,
and its failure.

In the first on-the-spot interviews with Japanese doctors, this
writer reported that certain organs, especially the intestine, were affected by hemorrhages. Timmes said today: "Which organ is affected
has no particular significance. Hemorrhages may occur anywhere—
lungs, kidneys, duodenum. What really happens is that the nature of
the entire bloodstream alters and aplastic anemia develops without
particular regard for location. These late cases mostly have no exter-
nal burns, but do have headache, fever, diarrhea, bleeding gums,
loose teeth, falling hair, and often throat sores or lip sores."

Without attempting any large-scale therapy—impossible because
Admiral Fahrion's main task is rescuing Allied prisoners in Kyushu's
prison camps—the Navy is trying to ease somewhat the Japanese
doctors' task by providing modest amounts of those medicines whose
expiration date would soon make them unusable anyway. Penicillin
has been provided, and given some help in strengthening those cases
where infection is present and the patient can be saved simply by
strengthening the scavenger white cells. Penicillin is restricted to

cases where pneumonia, abscesses, and mouth or throat infections are present.

To meet ravages on the bone marrow by deadly gamma shortwaves, the Navy is providing a marrow-building drug, pentnucleotide, in experimental quantities. Its effects are still inconclusive. Pentnucleotide has been used in the United States to revive flagging bone marrow. Pentnucleotide is okay for agranulous cytosis—white cell diminishment—but nearly no help for aplastic anemia.

Loosely summarized, it may be said that Nagasakians suffer from what used be known as "X-ray poisoning." 21,000 died, however, not because the atomic bomb's ray is deadly, but because with American planes in full view overhead, the population failed go into air raid shelters and ignored earlier warnings. Mitsubishi plant workers—including Allied prisoners whose camp was in the plant's heart—were killed when their empty shelters would have saved them, simply because the Mitsubishis chose to keep the war work going with enemy planes overhead. And Japanese doctors are in agreement that losses from an atomic bomb can be more sharply cut by concrete shelters than by any drug.

How the two largest American prisoner of war camps in the Philippines were able to pierce Japan's blackout on overseas news with tiny secret listening sets operating within the camps was related here today aboard hospital ship *Haven* by a liberated inventor. The sets were developed independently in barbed wire enclosures at Davao in southern Mindanao and at Cabanatuan outside Manila, in defiance of the death penalty.

Not only was each camp ignorant that the other possessed a set, but only a close inner circle comprising the American commandant and inventor in each camp knew that any set existed. The secret was kept from Americans by Americans themselves.

Each inventor thought he alone had outwitted the Japanese. Yet when Davao's inventor—Bataan death march veteran Captain Russell J. Hutchison of Albuquerque—was transferred by a Japanese troopship hundreds of miles northward to Cabanatuan, he smuggled along parts of his set in corned beef cans and cakes of soap. After working his way into Cabanatuan's prisoner engineering aristocracy, he discovered that a set built inside a water canteen was already functioning there. What made the hair stand up on his scalp was the unbelievable coincidence that the Cabanatuan inventor was also named Hutchison—Lieutenant Howard Hutchison, formerly a civil engineer in Manila.

The odds against such a coincidence of names, spelled exactly the same but without any known family relationship, defy mathematical calculation. But Davao Hutchison was already heavily under suspicion as an operator of the Davao set, and feared that some leak would occur, imperiling the life of Manila Hutchison as well as his own. The inventor therefore caused the Davao radio set, brought under peril of death from Mindanao to Manila and already secretly operating in Cabanatuan's Catholic chapel, to be dismantled. It was eventually buried in a latrine at Cabanatuan by the former Davao commandant, Lieutenant Colonel "Oley" Olson. Cabanatuan's canteen set has disappeared somewhere in the maelstrom of war.

The two radio sets were similar, each being a single-tube affair, but otherwise different because Davao Hutchison depended on a plug-in electric light socket while Cabanatuan Hutchison used batteries. Both sets were used principally at night with an elaborate split-second system of American guards and plausible diversions to keep the Japanese lulled. Davao Hutchison had rehearsed his raid warning system until it was down to fifty-five seconds for a complete dismantling.

Hutchison's listening post was a watch repair shop run by Air Corps Warrant Officer Jack Day. The guards were two New Mexican Coast artillery captains captured on Bataan: Charles Brown of Deming and Clyde Ely of Silver City. (Ely was afterward one among the passengers on the death cruise from Bilibid to Japan, whose arrival has not been reported.) When Ely whispered, "The Japs are coming," Hutchison would detach the headphones and pitch them through the window to Brown who would walk to the nearby latrine before the Japanese guard hove into view. He would thus be able to simulate emerging from the latrine when the Japanese arrived.

Once, when Hutchison had stolen a new tube and was entering the camp gate with it concealed in his armpit, the Japanese commandant Major Mayeda brought him to a trembling halt. It developed that all Mayeda wanted was to ask the inventor to make him a souvenir cigarette case.

"Our first big news—that Mussolini had chucked in the towel— nearly wrecked us," Hutchison said today. "Everybody was told the news under a strict pledge of secrecy to his best friend and soon the Japs smelled trouble. I'd been given four months' jail after Major Dyess [author of the revelations of the Bataan death march] escaped. The Japs were now certain I was listening abroad. I bluffed them, however, by playing injured innocent and threatening to refuse to repair their own sets if accused again. Actually, their sets were furnishing parts for mine."

It was necessary to suppress most news received from abroad

because any gossip invited Japanese investigation. The set had been built not to pick up news but in order get some advance warning of when MacArthur was approaching. "We felt the Japs would be sure to massacre all the Americans in Davao and in nearby Lasang camp as soon as landing parties came ashore. We hoped to break out from the camp beforehand and evade a massacre by hiding in the hills. The news from Mindanao that a hundred and fifty skulls had been found there confirms our fears and we dread the possibility that many may be our friends. I used to smuggle out intelligence reports to our contact man in Lasang, Lieutenant Johnny Morrett."

The demounted set was smuggled from Davao to Manila and Cabanatuan in three sealed-up cans of corned beef, and the tube in a can of cocoa. The potentiometer, too big to be hidden in cans, was buried in medicine by the camp physician Lieutenant Colonel Dwight Deter. When an unknown hand opened the food cans and found the parts, Hutchison obtained four bars of laundry soap and buried them in those.

At Cabanatuan, finding a plug-in current in a safe place was a stickler for some time until it occurred to Davao Hutchison that the altar of the Catholic chapel was rarely observed by Japanese guards. He fixed the set so that it could be plugged in from the chapel's chandelier and hidden among lacy altar cloths. This Hutchison's "devotions" gained him a brief reputation for piety until the inventor found that Cabanatuan Hutchison had a canteen set already working, and dismantled his.

Nagasaki, Japan—Monday, September 24, 1945

Allied Prison Camp #18, Sasebo, Kyushu

Marines and other forces under Kreuger's Sixth Army, landing this weekend at Sasebo, the famous Japanese naval base, saw a big (75 feet tall) concrete irrigation dam nearby, but few knew that it was built with American blood. Japan owes the USA more than fifty lives for building this dam, the lives of American civilians captured at Wake Island who were literally starved and worked to death at notorious Camp #18. An imposing array of Japanese admirals and vice admirals who greeted the vanguard of American landing forces said nothing regarding the death camp, of which all traces have now been removed. But in an obscure plot of land on a hill overlooking the dam lie row on row of graves of the Americans who died from starvation, disease and pneumonia that Japan might be strong. Such is Sasebo's *horio haka,* or prisoner graveyard, of Camp #18.

265 Americans captured on Wake Island while working for the Pacific Naval Airbase Company, many of whom had gallantly served on guns in helping Marines to defend the island to the last, were brought to Sasebo on October 13, 1942. They were the less prepared for what the Japanese Navy was to do to them because their treatment by Japanese jailers on Wake itself during the first ten months of their captivity had been reasonable. The only execution was of Julius Hofmeister of San Francisco, who was publicly beheaded before all the other prisoners on May 10, 1942, as an incorrigible troublemaker. Other treatment, however, was relatively mild, and leftover American stores maintained the prisoners' health for the first months.

American workmen at Sasebo, mostly past military age, came under a Japanese Navy sadist named Egawa Haso who specialized in what Americans bitterly called "floor shows." The "floor show" meant arousing men from a dead sleep—which followed twelve hours' daily work on the dam—and lining them up, kneeling with their buttocks exposed. The men were then collectively beaten until their flanks purpled with clotted blood, they vomited and finally fainted. This punishment was applied to all prisoners when any single one was caught "garbaging", that is attempting to buy the offal rice left uneaten by Korean coolies. "They'd simply race up and down, clubbing us until we fell over," said Harry Forsberg of Clayton, Washington. When his weight fell to 100, Forsberg was still compelled to carry 110-pound cement sacks.

When G. W. Huntley of Billings, Montana, was reeling with pneumonia, the Japanese forced him at gunpoint to continue shoveling sand for the dam's concrete. On the following day Huntley died. Lester Meyer of San Francisco became unbalanced under continuous Japanese mistreatment and lost his eyeglasses, on which his vision was dependent. One day Meyer walked past a guard the prisoners had nicknamed Frisco Sailor, failing to salute the Japanese because he never saw him. Meyer was beaten for three days straight: knocked down with fists, clubbed with rifles in the head, finally kicked into unconsciousness and eventually death.

Both Huntley and Meyer were thirty-one years old and survived relatively long. Forty-six-year-old "Captain" Gehman of Boise, Idaho—in bed with pneumonia aggravated by starvation from January 19–21, 1944—was finally kicked from his bunk by the Japanese. "We had to help him to his feet so he could walk," said Logan Kay of Clearlake Park, California. "The next day he was unable even to walk, and at eleven o'clock he died."

Gehman was particularly *persona non grata* with Japanese naval wardens because when the higher Navy officers inspected the camp, all the sick prisoners had been taken up the hill near the present graveyard and there confined in order that their condition not become known. In some way Gehman, crazed with fever, managed to escape and descend the hill, tottered into the bunkhouse and fell to the floor before the inspector. In two hours he was dead.

All punishment was collective at Sasebo Dam. Earl Wilson of Olympia, Oregon, said: "We had no soap for the first year and then finally one-quarter of a bar each. I felt so filthy I stole a piece of Japanese soap. We had almost no medical treatment but the Japs announced that it would be totally abolished unless the thief gave himself up. I stepped forward and they had me hold buckets full of water at arm's length, and beat me whenever my arms lowered. Finally they beat me with their heavy fencing sticks for two and a half hours."

The men were housed in an old cement shed whose floor, usually flooded with water, accounted for their lung diseases complicated by malnutrition. They slept on boards covered with rice sacks, and in the winter got straw underneath. None were allowed to lie down and rest during the day if sick, unless absolutely unable to hold themselves erect.

The camp's good samaritan was Robert Neylan of Oakland, California, who connived with guards at the risk of his life to get medicine and save elderly men stricken with stomach diseases or beatings.

Twenty-six-year-old Robert Harrison of Wheatland, California, said: "We had old men who could not learn Japanese, and they received terrible beatings simply for not understanding. The Japs also had one or two stooges whom they'd offer extra cigarettes for giving them the numbers of the men who loafed whenever the guards' backs were turned. At parade drill their numbers would be called out and the men were beaten without a hearing."

Three night guards required that a prisoner report before going to the latrine, and be fully dressed.

Walter "Red" Thompson of Boise, Idaho, a former world's champion cowboy, was totally unable to learn Japanese. For misunderstanding an order Thompson was beaten with a split-toed *tabi*—a Japanese work sneaker—till he was "a mass of bloodshot beef." Unable to endure the pain any longer, Thompson tried to attack the guard but was restrained by his comrades.

Fifty-one-year-old Claude "Curly" Howes of Portland, Oregon, devised an electric cigarette lighter. The Japanese discovered it in a shakedown raid and claimed it would have interfered with the camp's lighting system if used, then summoned all the prisoners and gave them a general beating.

Frank Burns of Spokane, Washington, was among those prisoners most frequently beaten for stealing food to supplement the three bowls daily of rice, "fluffed in, not packed down", which were the prisoners' fare.

When the camp was one year less three days old—October 10th, 1943—the Japanese Army took it over from the Navy, providing their own sadist, Lieutenant Ikagami. The prisoners had passed their first bitter winter with the meagerest of clothing. Weakening with cold, E. H. Knox of Cuba City, Wisconsin, made himself a shirt from a camp blanket. Ikagami had him thrown into a freezing jail with nothing on but the shirt, then regularly drenched him with water. Prisoner squad leaders plucked up courage and went in as a body to see Ikagami and said that Knox was dying. Ikagami said, "Let him freeze to death and die." When Ikagami visited the suffering prisoner in the guardhouse he said to Knox, "You are going to stay here until your mind freezes numb." Forty-two-year-old Knox died on January 15th.

C. A. Scott of Sacramento, California, was jailed with Knox in his last hours for having picked up an orange peel, which constituted "garbaging". Scott had been beaten until his eyes were swollen almost closed. The Japanese, seeing that Knox was going die from pneumonia, gave him one blanket. Knox told Scott, "When I go, you take my blanket." A little while later he was dead.

The Japanese insisted that American workmen stand at attention while being beaten. Tom Gillen of Portland, Oregon, "broke a finger trying to ward off the blows."

Fifty-six-year-old Walter Gell of Wadena, Iowa—both his pipe-stem legs swathed in bandages from foot to thigh—said: "If one man fouled up, everybody got it, with anything from a broomstick to an axe handle." Another prisoner told about carrying Gell unconscious from the line after the collective chastisement of all for some single infraction.

George Dillon of Metaline Falls, Washington, was beaten by a snooping elderly Japanese whom the prisoners called "Grammo" for grandma. Dillon returned to work but sagged, and drew another beating. This time he struck back. All 250 men were called off work and given a mass beating. Dillon was removed and tried; he is believed to have died.

Sasebo's roster was 210 when the dam was finished in April 1944 and the prisoners were scattered among other camps. (The death list for eighteen months' work on the dam comprises twenty percent of the men who participated.) The burial details were headed by Ora Johnson of Boise City, a preacher. They were rewarded by extra rice balls, which the Japanese enjoyed tossing at will among them in order to watch the ensuing scramble.

Aboard hospital ship <u>Haven</u>

Puzzled service psychiatrists rearranged their theories about mental complexes among prisoners of war as this new Navy hospital ship bore homeward the last load of liberated POWs from Japan. Less than three percent of patients aboard showed any serious psychoneurotic effect from an experience which in many cases had seriously harmed their physical health. Their mental attitude, far from requiring coddling or understanding, was found to be self-confident, normal and fully sane. The paradox that Japanese prison life is turning out men unafraid of the post-war world is explained in their common phrase: "If there's anything tougher ahead than three years in a camp under the Japanese after Bataan and Corregidor, we cannot imagine what that might be."

Psychiatrists say that acute collective normalcy among ex-prisoners is due to the fact that psychoneurotics waned away and died and are returning home cremated in boxes of ashes, and that others who harbored such inclinations in the United States, where they gain sympathy, threw them off in Japan. In the prison camps all were really alike, and therefore it was useless for an individual to develop his "social protest" because nobody was any better off, and nobody would listen. So that's how Japanese wardens cured decadent America, but lost the war—or so it says here in fine print.

V

The Two Robinson Crusoes
of Wake Island

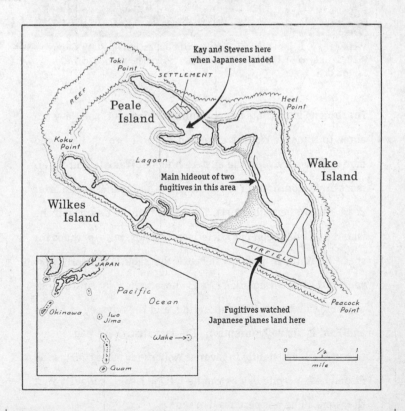

Kay and Stevens here
when Japanese landed

Toki
Point

SETTLEMENT

REEF

Heel
Point

Peale
Island

Koku
Point

Lagoon

Main hideout of two
fugitives in this area

Wake
Island

Wilkes
Island

AIRFIELD

Peacock
Point

Fugitives watched
Japanese planes land here

JAPAN

Pacific
Ocean

Okinawa

Iwo
Jima

Wake →

Guam

0   ½   1
mile

Weller (l.) & Logan "Scotty" Kay at the liberation of POW Camp #23, Izuka, Sept 19, 1945. The helmet bears the names of Wake Island dead.

For reasons impossible to determine at this point, the Navy did agree to transmit Weller's extended story of two civilians who managed to survive in the austere brush of Wake Island for almost three months after it was taken by the Japanese soon after Pearl Harbor, December 1941. The gallant, futile defense of the island itself has been chronicled many times, but—perhaps for space limitations, perhaps because the saga was nearly four years old—the *Chicago Daily News* chose to heavily cut this improbable tale of survival and hiding, and the odyssey of Scotty and Fred is virtually unknown. The fact that these pages were transmitted, apparently in favor of Weller's far more timely POW dispatches and one day before he left Nagasaki, suggests that they were all he was permitted to send.

Nagasaki, Japan—Tuesday, September 25, 1945

"The Two Robinson Crusoes of Wake Island"

Opening the doors to Prison Camp #23 at Izuka in central Kyushu has revealed the unbelievable story of how two middle-aged American construction men lived in Robinson Crusoe style for seventy-seven days on tiny Wake Island after the coral speck fell to the Japanese. Though other Americans have lived on large islands like Guam while they were held by the Japanese, none ever succeeded under such hairs' breadth terms as "Wake Island Scotty", who is fifty-five-year-old Logan Kay of Clearlake Park, California, and his pal Fred J. Stevens, forty-nine, of Sioux City, Iowa.

Wake Island is only four miles long and less than a third of a mile across. It is so flat that seas sometimes wash over its beaches, being only twenty-one feet at its highest point. There are no caves and no coconut groves. Yet Wake Island Scotty and his pal, by creeping from one rabbit's nest to another in bushy thickets, managed to keep the Japanese outwitted from December 8th, 1941, when the Japanese first bombed Wake, until March 9th, 1942. They lived on the hopes of seeing American warships steam in and recover Wake and set them free—dreams never realized until after six months' labor on Wake and nearly two years of bitter servitude in Japan, including a period at Death Camp #18, building the dam at Sasebo where twenty percent of 265 Wake Island Americans died.

Wake Island Scotty has survived to return to his beloved wife Fritzi and his soldier son Howard in California, and Stevens is en route to join his wife and three children. But their days of being hunted while hiding literally in a Japanese backyard on Wake live again in the diary kept by Wake Island Scotty and made available by him to a *Chicago Daily News* correspondent. This diary—written while the two men were ill, thin, afraid and on the run—has been

147

buried and redug many times. It has been searched for by dozens of Japanese sentries in camps where merely possessing any writing materials was a capital crime. Yet it has prevailed with its full record of hope, disappointment and faith, together with the human will to live and even some sparks of humor.

Wake Island looks like the open jaw of an alligator, with a lagoon as the inside of its mouth which, before the war, was intended by the United States as a submarine base. The ends of both the upper and lower jaw are broken off into separate islets, the upper being Peale and the lower Wilkes. Scotty and Stevens both served on the guns with Marines on Peale before becoming fugitives. Their hideout eventually was in skimpy thickets which lie on the inner side of the upper jaw along the lagoon, but by night they wandered in other parts of the island searching for food and water. From their thicket hideout looking southward across the lagoon, they were able to watch Japanese planes take off and land on the single American-built airfield on the southern or lower half of the jaw a mile away. Scotty noted down all such movements in hopes of aiding the naval rescue party which never came.

Stevens had served on Wake for nine months and Scotty for only five weeks when Japan struck. They were two of eleven hundred men hired by the Morrison Knudsen Company of Boise City, Idaho, one of six contracting firms joined to build the government airfield and the submarine entrance under the name of the Pacific Naval Air-bases Company, with its main offices in Alameda, California. Salaries averaged two hundred dollars monthly, with up to ninety dollars' bonus for prolonged service. The Panair Company already had Clipper service, with buildings on Peale Island, while the government had a single Marine flying field on the lower jaw of Wake. The Wake workmen first knew something was amiss when a Clipper—after taking off for Guam at seven in the morning—returned, jettisoned some gas, took Panair personnel aboard, and departed for Honolulu.

[Wake Island Scotty's journal is given here with brief interpolations in brackets by Weller in order to explain the captives' situation more fully.]

Scotty's diary:

Dec. 8 1941
We were bombed at 11.55 AM by eighteen planes which we heard came
from Marshall Islands 600 miles south of Wake. 27 killed, 130 injured.
Panair buildings on Peale entirely demolished and seven marine
planes. Clipper left one hour after bombing for Honolulu with white
personnel.

Dec. 9
Eleven planes bombed company hospital and new warehouse on
Wake. They also set afire six of our barracks. [These buildings were
on Peale, the northern or upper jaw.] *Ground batteries got one plane;*
scouts got one plane. [That day Scotty found Stevens sick with stomach poisoning and hid him in a dredge pipe against the bombings.
Scotty made his way to the demolished Panair hospital and found an
untouched bottle of physic in the ruins, returned to the dredge pipe
and treated Stevens.]

Dec. 10
10.40 AM—one hour earlier than yesterday—planes came in high and
got our powder storage on Wilkes Island. [This powder was being used
to blast a new mouth through the eastern end of Wilkes, 500 feet long
and 30 feet deep, to permit submarines after entering the fringing
coral reef to pass through Wilkes Island to the deeper, northwestern
end of Wake's central lagoon. It was two-thirds done when taken by
Japan.] *Planes and land batteries claimed two bombers down.*

Dec. 11
Were shelled from ocean at 5.45 AM by destroyers. American subs and
land planes got four or five boats and transports. [The estimate was
later raised to eleven enemy.] *One was sunk by a direct hit from our*
five-inch guns in powder magazine. Planes got one and sub got the
rest, all sunk. [That day civilian workmen abandoned all their

smashed new buildings on the northern jaw, carrying their wounded
around a bend in Wake's horseshoe to the eastern end of the Marine
airfield. There they improvised a hospital in the abandoned concrete
ammunition magazines.] *Planes came at 9.50 but did no damage as
batteries kept them away.*

Dec. 12

*I helped move guns last night as bombers had our old positions spot-
ted.* [Scotty and other workmen took the anti-aircraft battery which
had been in the middle of Peale and moved it to the northeastern end,
then camouflaged the old position to resemble guns and try to draw
Japanese bombs. The dredge pipe where Scotty lived with the invalid
Stevens was located on Peale about a quarter-mile from the inlet separating Peale and Wilkes.]

Dec. 13

*Quiet all day no bombers. One observation plane shot down by our
scouts at 5.30 AM. Buried forty-two of our boys today.* [About thirty-
five were civilian workmen, the remainder Marines and Navy sailors.
Stevens, now recovered, was serving on the same anti-aircraft gun
with Scotty.]

Dec. 14

Bombed at 10.45 by twenty-seven German Heinkels [as they appeared
to Marine fighters]. *Lots of damage and some dead. Built bomb shelters for air crews. One of our three last planes cracked up taking off.
Now have two left which will fly.*

Dec. 15

Had breakfast and moved back to barracks [from the dredge pipe on
Peale where he had been living with Stevens]. *Japs came at 6 PM. No
great damage and no casualties.*

Dec. 16

Eighteen bombers came at 1 PM got old camp one [at the western end
of the airfield, on Wake's southern jaw] *and oil storage.*

Dec. 17
Planes came at 5.50 PM—dropped a few bombs and machine-gunned camp. We went inside concrete pipe. Panair was given another dose of bombs.

Dec. 18
Went over to Panair and got medical supplies [from the ruins] *for our doctor* [Dr. L. Shank of San Diego].

Dec. 19
Bombers came at 10.30 AM. Not much damage, burned a small amount of fuel.

Dec. 20
Rain all day. No bombers today. PBY [a PBY Catalina, i.e. a flying boat] *came in with brass hat aboard. Looks like we may get some help.*

Dec. 21
Dive bombers came in flocks at 9 AM and gave us hell, just about ruined us. PBY left just before raid and took our commanding officer with him to Honolulu. Twelve o'clock high bombers came and bombed our barracks so we moved back to Panair. Dive bombers got one of our range finders and crippled gun [where Scotty was serving as ammunition loader]. *Our first sergeant was killed on range finder.* [Scotty never knew his name but says, "He was a very brave boy."]*

Dec. 21
They came in today and stayed a half hour. Leisurely bombed and gunned our camp. Got our last little plane. We have no range finder left, and are now practically down to rifles, one for each two men on island. All they have to do now is land and take over whenever they want to. Got small piece shrapnel in back of right shoulder. Doctor says will get it out in day or two. Does not hurt more than sliver so will not

---

* The PBY brought the news that a relief force was en route and would arrive on the 24th, when 350 civilian workers would be taken off Wake. Meanwhile, Major Walter Bayler, commanding officer, was ordered to leave on the PBY.

worry about it. They bombed for an hour in getting our range finder,
also both our last planes. We are now sure out of luck.

Dec. 23
Jap fleet moved in and after many signals opened up on our batteries
[only three remained on Peale] *making a direct hit on the first emplace-*
ment, blasting it out, then ceased firing. At dawn dozens of planes started
bombing and things were in a panic in camp, and Pat [Patrick Herndon
of Fox Park, Wyoming] *deserted our dredge pipe. Fred and I found a hole*
right in the middle of camp and crawled in. [Marine officers who that
day came to the construction camp notified the homeless among the
ruins that the Japanese were about to land, and warned them to avoid
being caught with rifles because the Japanese would shoot any thus captured. Fear grew in the trapped men, who saw themselves unable to
fight any longer to hold Wake.] *Later the bombing stopped and every-*
thing got quiet except enemy planes flying low all over island. At 11.30 I
looked out carefully and will never forget the sight. About five hundred of
our company men were being herded past stripped down to nothing but
shorts and being headed towards Peale. Looked like brick wall [a firing
squad] *for these men. Fred and I sat tight.*

Christmas Eve
Jap sentry almost found us last night. Was within five feet but missed
us. We hope to escape tonight if there is a chance. We had a close call
but something attracted sentry's attention. If we can hold for two hours
more until darkness we will move out of here and hide in brush. We
will not give up without a fight as we think the other boys were stripped
for firing squad. Japs working frantically everywhere to set up guns. If
we can make the brush [from their dugout in the center of the camp's
ruins] *we can live until we are found. As food is scattered all over is-*
land water is our problem once out of the woods. Getting dark now—
we are waiting for cloud to cover moon.

Dec. 25 Christmas
We made it on hands and knees, lying in depressions when clouds went
off the moon. Went to beach and south [east] *along beach in edge of*

breakers. Got wet but got around sentries and made the brush. Ran into one big gun where twenty Japs were sleeping but did not wake up and went another way lying by road in brush till moon got out and clouds came and then crossed over to large brush patch. If I were not so ill [Scotty was suffering with severe diarrhea] *I would enjoy the trip as I got a kick out of every close call and this trip was full of them. I am getting better today. We found dugout at 11 PM and got a bed for night. Am all in. Woke at daybreak and wished Fred Merry Christmas. We believe there is a Santa Claus. Spent the day in brush lying low—and how low!—but feel better tonight.*

Dec. 26

Found another bed last night and crawled back in brush this AM. Foliage is thick and ground is wet, and flies about bad as Japs. We are getting set for months here. Found water enough last night to last us a month. U.S. should have this place back by then. We will try be here when they do. Jap sentries patrol constantly on lookout. Trucks are working fast all day and night. Am getting much better. Made the lagoon last night and found some clean clothes. Japs will soon have all camps looted and then will be easier for us. They loot through everything and throw it out on ground just like monkeys. Found a dollar bill and some silver they threw away. They tore the bill into bits first. [These camps were in patches of brush where company men had hidden during the day in order to avoid being strafed by Japanese planes. There are only about one hundred acres of such brush in Wake's entire area of twenty-four-hundred acres. These hundred acres were Scotty's and Stevens' hideout for the coming weeks, during which the Japanese continually looted and relooted.] *Lots of food everywhere and we are burying some each night, but not too much so it won't show or be missed.*

Dec. 27

Slept in deserted camp last night. Buried much canned food and four gallons water in glass jars, forgot two containers and will get them tonight. Did a little looting behind the Japs. Sat by lagoon and watched lights signalling at sea. [The fugitives used to watch a

Japanese submarine surface in what had been planned as an American base, and wink signal lights to warships on the surface.] *Rose at 5 AM and moved back into the jungle and had apricot juice for breakfast and then a can boneless chicken each. Camouflaged our hideout but must move soon as it is getting too wilted. We are as snug as two rabbits with four thousand hounds after us. We are not afraid; just careful. We have coffee for breakfast, tea for lunch, beer for dinner—all from the same canteen. It's now 3 PM—we will set out again in about 2½ hours.*

Dec. 28
Heard Japs looting all around last evening between 4 and 5, talking and breaking open trunks, the brush being full of loot. Over 500 men carried their stuff out here and there are probably one half that many foxholes to be looked into and torn apart. We found one $2.50 gold piece they overlooked and 81¢ in silver. I carry a hatchet and knife, Fred a hammer and knife. Wish we had revolvers. At 2.15 today Sunday three Japs walked right over the edge of our nest, one carrying a suitcase over his shoulder on a stick, two following behind him. They were off the trail looking for more camps to loot and walked right onto our doorstep. Fred and I sat tight and they did not see us though were less than ten feet away. They were close, too close. I just sat still and crossed my fingers. Fred did the same.

Dec. 29
(I found a fountain pen and here we go from pencil to ink.) Now 2.15 PM and we are hugging turf. Have heard Japs two times today within a hundred feet of our apartment. Thought we heard siren short while ago but birds do so much screaming one is not certain. Seaplane just took off and passed over at low altitude going very fast. We were looking for Japs starting to pick up all food around camps soon so we hide some each night. Did not venture out until 11.30 last night and came in at 5 this AM but crawled under a bush and slept three hours. What a life! We stayed in bed for breakfast this AM, had the morning paper first, then coffee and ham and eggs. Coffee was weak. It will be tea for

supper, all out of the same water canister. Laundryman has not called today; must change laundry.

Dec. 30
Well, here we are at 2.15 again and going strong. [Scotty often wrote at this hour because the Japanese were resting in the heat after luncheon, instead of scouring the brush.] *Found more water last night and brought in one big can chili beans, sardines, and cheese crackers. Also found drafts and cashier's checks for $400, $200, $100 and $18 cash. Total for night $718.11. Put it in kitty. Getting so can smell money in dark. Brought in a can of powdered milk and milk our own cow now. One more day of this year left, and soon Congress will come back from their vacation and do some more talking about fighting. What a bunch of boys we have been paying all these years. We two do not know what is going on in the world, but we can bet that in Washington it is mostly talk.*

Dec. 31
Last day of 1941 and what a year. Enough happenings to make some people a lifetime. No Japs within alarming limits today. Rained and we had to take cover in adjacent dugout. Maybe safe while raining, but in sunshine looters are often snooping.

Jan. 1
Happy New Year everybody. Started out lucky for me for found check for $150 and 20¢ cash. Check was wet but will put it by to dry. [Scotty is very Scottish, though born at Bridgeville, California.] *This swells our potential pot to more than $800. Went to dugout to escape rain and Fred heard Japs coming. They missed us by inches. Our closest call to date. Moving today to drier hideout.*

Jan. 2
Fixed up dry shelter further away from camp. Spent day undisturbed there but once heard Japs looting camp. We will only be found by accident here if they search for us, but we now can tell there are probably

three thousand on this little island and only about hundred acres of brush [for hiding]. When not busy the Japs often prowl through it to kill birds and look for new camps to loot—well, here's hoping.

Jan. 3
Day passed quickly. We fixed one brush fence to keep Japs out of trails near camp. Ate salad and shrimp with mayonnaise. We have half gallon of this stuff left. Now getting sundown and moon will be right up. Going out at dusk to get some exercise.

Jan. 4
Found a real food cache last night. Got ten cans sausage and six chipped beef also twelve tuna and gal cranberries and one gal Bartlett pears. Good food ahead except crackers or bread. But will make cereals do. We do not dare light a fire; maybe later when it gets stormy. Cloudy tonight, will set paper [tarpaper roofing] to catch rainwater. Stayed quiet but heard looters frequently.

Jan. 5
Found 6 gals water. Fourteenth day since we became fugitives from monkey gang. We slept at Palace Hotel last night because of rain. Two Japs went by very near but not so close as before. Have blocked most of near trails with dead trees but they must have climbed over. I think they were lost. Would like to know what the U.S. is doing about getting back this place. Guess they know by now that we are at war. Christmas holidays are over and Congress must have about finished its bicarbonate of soda. The Japs here are working every minute to make it harder and cost more lives to take back Wake but our navy don't seem to be showing up yet. We know they can't let the Japs keep this place as it would be a base to bomb shipping and the Pacific must be kept open for supplies if we are to win this war. Seems we are not so ready as Knox says we are. We need a revision of our whole defense setup with some young brains. Weather is broken today into some sunshine and a little rain. Spring looking in on us. Quails are mating around us and little lizards hatching out. Birds are nesting and days getting noticeably longer. Jap trucks are very busy strengthening positions. All buildings

are being mined no doubt and will be destroyed as soon as looks like the island would be retaken. Fred and I are sitting tight but days are getting awful long and flies are very bad. Am better but not well yet. Very weak and dizzy and do not have the right food, also very thin. Some days the stomach is fairly normal but next day not so good. I cannot get over seeing the other boys stripped to their shorts by Japs and wonder if they were put on boat or was it a brick wall for them. We will probably find out some day if we are not caught. If caught we will surely find out.

Jan. 6
Got up early and camouflaged camp. This is our first work at daybreak each AM. One scout and three bombers went out northeast at 6. Scout returned twice and bombers returned about 3–4 in afternoon. Four alarms from sirens seem to have the Jap boys on their toes. We hope Uncle Sam starts knocking at the door soon. Eleven-inch guns will be music to us.

Jan. 7
Up at 5.30 and more camou. Read a story in <u>Reader's Digest</u> and started a novel. Went back to old camp and found it had been looted yesterday—another close call. We are still one move ahead of the Japs. Sat a long time on our front porch und finally to bed with lima beans for lunch and plums for dessert.

Jan. 8
Went to Chinese labor camp and brought in some cornflakes. Bomber #13 just passed over on way out. . . . a large four-motored job. #20 followed going south. Little scout plane left at 6.15. Third bomber now going out. Lunch was new potatoes, corn, sardines, seedless grapes (good).

Jan. 9
Slid out at 4.30 AM and lone wolfed for sugar and books while Fred camouflaged camp. Near visit from one Jap who at 11.30 came within thirty feet of camp. We are going to screen some getaway so that we can

*crawl off unseen if they climb in on us. All three bombers went out
today as usual.*

Jan. 10

*Mary's birthday . . . happy birthday, sister. Arose at 3.30 AM and went
out for food—moon was light as day. Camouflaged at 5. At 11.30 a Jap
knocked on the door. Thought we were finally caught. He looked right
at us then turned and walked away. Must have had his eyes on something nearer to him. We moved into deeper brush and lay low the rest of
the day thinking perhaps Jap had gone for help. Now about dark think
we will move camp.*

Jan. 11

*35 days since war started. About 20 since island was captured. Japs
came back raided us and we lost what few trinkets we had gathered.
But we are still at large thanks to our lucky star. We have moved a half
mile southeast along edge lagoon. By one o'clock four Japs have already passed near. There are just too many people on Wake for so small
a spot. Probably 3,500 Japs or more. They are very nervous today.
Think they expect U.S. soon. It's about time, we think.*

Jan. 12

*Yesterday was a nightmare from noon on. Japs all afternoon almost
stepping on us. Seems we picked a group of trees that reached to the
lagoon's edge. At high tide Japs could not get by on the lagoon side
so they either went around us or crawled through. At least three were
twenty feet from us in brush and five more passed nearby just
outside. This is not good for our nerves—we moved back near the
old camp.*

Jan. 13

Slept at Waldorf Astoria. Had good bed and overslept until it was too
late for safe traveling. Am jittery and wish uncle would start knocking*

---

* Scotty and Fred nicknamed their hideouts after prominent hotels: the Waldorf Astoria, the Mark Hopkins.

on the door with some eleven-inch guns. That will be sweet music to us and we will find a hole while it is going on.

Jan. 14
Well, we got by the 13th just by a hair and hope for better as we are getting jittery. We slept on coral. Wish we had some outside news and knew how our folks are and when uncle is coming to get us.

Jan. 15
It is now approaching midafternoon when looting is heaviest. We may get by with little or no alarm as the near camps have been pretty well combed over and hence Japs work farther away. But by the same token they creep into all likely trails looking for more loot. We have camouflaged trails to our camp as much as possible. We expect American help about Sunday if not before.

Jan. 16
We almost had callers—missed us by fifteen feet. They were probably lost while looting and trying to find road. They did it, but almost stepped on us doing it. Guess we will have to put up signs. Private property, keep out. Lots of noise today, trucks and tractors going all day. We were out two hours last night and got a little exercise. We really need it. Have been lying down so long we get dizzy when we stand up, and are very weak. Made another day by the grace of God and fifteen feet of brush. Something is sure taking care of us as we couldn't be this lucky.

Jan. 17
Son's birthday—25 years old. Well, it doesn't matter much what happens to me. I have the comfort of knowing that my son will carry on and that our little mother will be provided for and this makes it easier to face the hazard of each succeeding day. We have been within the Valley of the Shadow now for 41 days and we have had a lot of close calls. But we are being as careful as we know how to be. If I don't get back I will have had what few folks have had—25 years with two of the best scouts on earth. Nips were busy at big gun practice all day.

Jan. 18
*Went out early and found a two by six tongue-and-groove to make body
of a crossbow. Will hunt some nails for ammunition tonight.* [Scotty
made the bent part of the bow from cocowood and eventually was able
to kill rats at twenty yards.] *Flies are terrible today—about twenty on
my hands as I write.*

Jan. 19
*Japs are collecting all mattresses in camps around us. They were
here today at 11.30 and got truckload. Now is zero hour. Japs moving
all around us. Some talk English to each other.* [Scotty later learned
that the voices talking English belonged to parties of American prisoners whom the Japanese brought back under guard to reveal hidden supplies.]

Jan. 20
*One alarm at 10.30 when three Japs walked past back of our camp. We
could see them but they could not see us. Tractor working near us
makes a lot of noise. I slept out at Mark Hopkins last night and Fred
stayed in camp. I had the bridal suite but no blanket and no rat trap
but I slept better—no snoring by Fred to listen to. Another alarm this
afternoon but the trail drew them away.*

Jan. 21
*Up at 5.30 and looked for new home. More we looked the better we liked
what we have. Morning passed without alarm except for some rocks
thrown at birds by Japs. Only one plane took off this morning. I guess
Japs have given up expecting Uncle Sam to try to take back Wake.*

Jan. 22
*We went out last night and looked after our water supply and found
two gallons missing. We feel there may be some other Americans still
on the island. Although we are not sure we keep close to our dugouts.
Found four company contracts and am picking up all I can.*

Jan. 23

Bad news last night Japs found two-thirds of all our food supply and took it away. Now we are crowded for thirty days supply food even if we cut down on eats. We caught no water last night as we had only one shower and it was too light. We are moving all our food to what we hope are safer places but these Japs are regular bloodhounds.

Jan. 24

We caught eleven gallons water last night, enough for three weeks. We also buried twenty cans of food that we brought in from another cache where the Japs are combing the brush harder. Today is 48 days since war started and 32 days we have been in brush dodging Japs. They should soon get tired.

Jan. 25

Two mild alarms this morning but they went by. Some news of home folks would be welcome but we don't dwell too much on that because it gets us down. We do wonder why uncle doesn't get going but guess he just wasn't ready when this thing started. If he had seen as much of the navy as we have here on Wake he would know he wasn't ready.

Jan. 26

Jap construction dragline moved up to our place at nine this morning and there has been heavy blasting at times so near that small rocks fell around us. These boys have a lot of efficiency and don't seem to mess around. We would do well to send some of our boys to their school especially Knox who was telling the world he was ready months ago. Fifty days since war started and we are not ready yet.

Jan. 27

Blasting today. We got rocked at noon but not hit. We have looked for new hotel but can't find one so well hid, so will stay here. Our jitters are better.

Jan. 28
Just at twelve we heard brush crack and looked up to see three Japs
going by the trail just fifty feet from camp. Suddenly one turned back
and then started in over the brush directly toward us. When he got
within twenty feet we faded out the other way making as little noise as
possible. We crawled on hands and knees for seven hundred feet and
ran across a road and dived into brush on the other side. Went into
camp and crawled into a place right under doormat and stayed all
night and day without food and water then went back to see if could
salvage anything and found camp intact. God is still looking after us
but why I don't know.

Jan. 29
Spent day in hideout #4: no light no food no flies no room no air but no
Japs. Felt lucky we were alive. These Japs have done more actual work
on this island in 37 days than the U.S. did in nine months, work that
we should have been doing and we would not have lost Wake. Of course
there was no war on when we started but everything for the service
should be built first, not for beauty. Came home at 10 last night and
found hideout #3 okay, our gift from God. Arrived on island three
months ago—my $30 bonus will start Sunday.

Jan. 30
Fred discovered this morning that the last Jap who went after us had
found his little bag of treasures and that is evidently why he stopped
and did not find the camp as he was all excited about the bag. Planes
patrolling all day and trucks busy. Gosh but we are glad to be in this
home again after thinking we had lost it. I have been very weak of late
and get so tired—no starch food and not enough exercise. Am losing
weight but putting on whiskers. I begin to look like Christ.

Jan. 31
Feel better today but still weak and tired. Three planes overhead all afternoon. I am burying this book tonight and will start a new one, so as
not to lose my record if anything slips.

Feb. 1

I went for a walk and ran into two Japs but they turned away in time. Hard rain came and Fred had uncovered our bed before he left and it got wet through. We feel the Japs may get out a detail to hunt us down soon. We will have to be on the watch for sentries at night on the trails. My $30 monthly bonus from the company begins today my fourth month on Wake.

Feb. 2

We are two groundhogs and today is groundhog day. Planes up at 6.30 seem to be expecting company I hope it's uncle. Sun is shining so guess we will stay in our holes for six weeks more unless Japs smoke us out. There's a cold northeast wind and we have nothing to wear except shirt, shorts and pants—no undershirts, sox or coats. It's hard to keep warm. Planes have been lazy; not much doing in war business. Good-night, dear mother and son.

Feb. 3

Showers and cold, breakers rolling high. We took stock and can go about three weeks on food we have; then we must raid the main camp. However, if we get the right kind of windy dark night in the next week or two we will go in to ease our worries. It's like pulling a tooth; we will get it over.

Feb. 4

Fred has a hunch help is coming soon—first time he has been optimistic about it. With planes up all morning half the day is licked, which is something to us as we are living from hour to hour now. Little lizards crawl over us catching flies. They are so tame now we have to brush them off while writing. Their heads and bodies are just 2 in. long and tails about 3 in., dark brown with three gold stripes from end to end of body. There are six on me as I write and I love them. One has a purple tail and one little fellow is speckled and has no stripes— I guess he's just a private.

Feb. 5
According to my figures it should take Uncle Sam about sixty days to get organized, equipped and supplied to start steaming up the Pacific. So he should be on his way here any day now with plenty of planes, boats & subs to take care of the situation. One Jap plane is still out. We can only speculate as we are in the dark, on the underside of the war. We only know that for uncle to control the Pacific he has to occupy all the islands that can be used as bombing bases and that includes Wake. Yesterday I think would have been Grandpa Kay's birthday—am hoping soon to hear some sweet music like 1000 lb. bombs dropping on our roof.

Feb. 6
Put a layer under our bed on the ground raising it up from dampness two inches which is too much altitude for safety. I guess we'll get used to it as the new leaves are coming to help our camouflage. We now lie down all day and are really getting soft. You should see our hair and whiskers. Japs are putting in crops around us as though they intend to stay. Soon they may move out families and maybe even dogs. Then we will have real trouble.

Feb. 7
Time going past today more slowly than ever before. Birds are sitting in trees along our back trail and sun beating down very hot. We are getting soft we can hardly get around after lying flat so much.

Feb. 8
Now two months since war on Wake started and we are still okay but with our fingers crossed. Have not tasted bread for six weeks and won't, I guess. I read most of the day. My eyes are okay. Lost my glasses with my bag when the Japs landed but found a good enough pair.

Feb. 9
Fred and I wish nights were longer, they are so restful. When one has to be alert every minute of the day it is very fatiguing. Fred and I agree that we are more tired after a day of watching than after a day of hard

work. Try lying flat just one day watching constantly for Japs with guns who are looking for you and probably will shoot you on sight.

Feb. 10
Went to old barracks to see if any food was still there. Found the place boarded up and it looks as though Japs are using it for a warehouse. Coming back I ran into a trap in the dark but luckily I was going very slowly and found it before making any alarm. We detoured and got no food. I'm getting corns on my seat from lying down so much. The Japs have a large garden right near us with a well but their water is too brackish to drink and so we will have to continue to catch ours from the rain. We have been going very light on food—about half what we should have. I feel very weak and tired but a few good events will cure that.

Feb. 11
Morning moon is just a sickle and two patrol planes were up at 6. We figure we can get by three weeks more by being careful with our food and if we don't get help then it will be tough. We hope it rains bombs soon. How sweet they will sound on our roof. Each one that lands will be as welcome as money dropping in the cash register. Fifty days since occupation and sixty-six since bombing; uncle must be on his way by now.

Feb. 12
Lincoln's birthday. Well, Abe, we found ten days supply of food this morning. I got up early and took a crawl through the brush for exercise and found a sack with seven cans artichokes five cans milk and gallon can lima beans also one gal water. We are safe now for four or five weeks if we get rain for water. My corns on my seat from lying down are getting larger and my whiskers are sixty days long.

Feb. 13
I breakfasted off lima beans and feel full for the first time in months. I feel bloated, just right. You got us through this day, Fritzi, sweetheart.
[Fritzi is Scotty's wife.]

Feb. 14
Valentine's greetings to my wife and pal. Well, Fred and I have it all
fixed for uncle to be here about tomorrow the 15th and if he doesn't come
we will still think he should. We set roofing paper last night for water
but only a small shower fell and we got only one quart. This is the hard-
est 53 days Fred and I can remember in our lifetimes, we agree. Am
about fifteen pounds lighter and waistline is 24 inches by measure.

Feb. 15
Daylight falls on Logan Crusoe and Fred Friday or the other way
around and we feel and look like the original pictures of Robinson C.
This is the day we picked and we still stick to it that help is on the way
to us somewhere in the Pacific. [Actually this was the day that Singapore fell to the Japanese.] *We are getting along much better than a*
month ago as there is less traffic in the woods. I keep planning what I
am going to do when I get back to the States, so I must be going to get
back okay. Had bad Jap dreams, tho. A large four-motor bomber came
over and circled the island about 11 and the little scout went up high at
once. The Japs fired at the bomber which we think was one of ours tak-
ing observations. Maybe our hunch is right and today is the day.

Feb. 16
Birds being disturbed indicates Japs coming through trail en route to
work in garden. Water shortage still haunts us. Japs seem to be getting
ready for something. Much machine gun practice. After sixty days the
American fleet must surely be provisioned and equipped to go into ac-
tion. The fleet should now be working on the Marshall Islands,
Palmyra and Johnson and Midway.

Feb. 17
All work has been stopped from 11 until 2 these last two days. We think
the Japs may be afraid of air raids at these hours and stop work to use
listening device.

Feb. 18
The Japs seem to have ants in their pants this morning. Planes took off
at sunrise and went up high instead of going outward. We are ready for

our part and hope it won't be long now. I dreamed of Aunt Renée so she must have been thinking of me. Am hoping to get home soon now so that Fritzi can stop worrying.

Feb. 19
I got up at midnight. You can feel excitement in the wind. Planes are coming and going, only staying out one hour. I can almost feel help is on the way. We are all set to hear the Star-Spangled Banner played on fourteen-inch guns; we will stand up and cheer or even climb a tree as soon as they start.

Feb. 20
Things seem to be shaping up. No machinery moving except trucks. No tractors draglines or heavy equipment like yesterday. Ants gave me hell all night. I keep planning on all the things I'll do at the ranch when I get back.

Feb. 21
Planes were up early. I can't get my stomach to behave because of having no starch but one quarter ounce of cornflakes each day. Fred is whittling a stick this morning to pass time as yesterday dragged on him and he snored all night and I did not sleep. When we get out of here I am going to move clear to the other end of the island at night and try to get some rest.

Feb. 22
Washington's birthday. Happy Birthday, George. We have a new bomber in the air this morning and possibly two. I told Fred when we moved in here we would be here at least two months, now we have food for only two days more and that is skimpy. We have both had not more than half enough food to date. Both of us are very light and weak and have had no hot food or fire for seventy-seven days. Heavy calluses on the bottoms of my feet but actually they are as soft as my hands. No action yet from the U.S. though they must be near us from the way the Japs are acting. It can't be long now. Will get by fine for two weeks and we know help should be here by then.

Feb. 23

From the viewpoint of two gophers something seems to be cooking on Wake. The Japs should know that if our fleet comes they cannot hold the island so it would be the part of wisdom for them to grab everything and go as they have sacrificed but few lives getting Wake. They could probably load out five million dollars worth of stuff in a week.

Feb. 24

[The day of the American counterattack.] Shooting started all over the island at 5.30 and continued until 7. We went into the dugout at 6 when shells from the fleet began dropping all over the brush. Four of our planes went over and the Japs opened on them with machine guns but held fire with their anti-aircraft batteries. Our planes shot down two little Jap scouts first thing. Now we are probably getting our pictures developed and if the Japs don't surrender we will lay it on. The music this morning is the sweetest symphony I have ever heard. Our shells whistle in and seem to burst like a Roman candle and steel flies in all directions. Then fragments start exploding like firecrackers in an alley in Chinatown. Fred and I spend one-third of our time in a tree, one-third climbing up or down and one-third in a dugout. We are sure like two little boys with toy red boats. We assume our planes got pictures of such gun positions as opened up and anytime from now on we expect action to start and not stop until the island is occupied. We hope Wake doesn't cost too many lives to retake but these boys have had it now too long to suit us. The Japs are going right ahead working on the garden today just like they thought the war was all over and they had won it. Nothing to worry about, they think. Whatever was dropped in shells was new to us as they still seem to be exploding in small pieces like firecrackers for five minutes after the main shell, and it seems to burst with a series like a machine gun rather than just one explosion. I suppose they use different shells after they locate the targets to blast the guns out. We moved back to our camp which is 100 yards from the dugout and is well hidden and we will remain here. When anti-aircraft starts barking and singing into our neck of the woods we'll go into our holes. We would give our left arms for a good old Springfield apiece and plenty of ammunition. We would move out into the brush

and get in the game. Maybe we can pick a gun off some casualty if things get going good. The biggest anti-aircraft gun is about 1000 feet from us but there is a machine gun very near, probably about 500 feet. Wish my family were here, they would get a kick out of this. Myself I would not miss it for anything. Son, better hurry and get me some grandchildren because I am going to have some good stories to tell them. Boy, how our big shells whistle before they land—and do our little planes sound sweet when they dive! When Japs dive on our guns they shut off their motors and drift down, but our boys step on the gas when they dive and come in like wasps. Soon they will come in flocks. 4.30 in the afternoon patrol planes are up but it is quiet. Uncle Sam seems to have left his calling card and departed as though the war is over. But we expected this as uncle was just getting pictures today. We will dust off the furniture and air out the spare bedroom and get ready to welcome him before the week is out and maybe tomorrow morning. We will probably be too happy to sleep much tonight, but we hope to get corns off our knees and elbows and walk upright again soon.

Feb. 25
A squadron of nine Heinkel bombers came in after dark last night and Fred heard some more come in while I was asleep. These are two-motored jobs with landing gear that does not retract. From what we saw of them when they first bombed us on Dec. 8–23 they are slow. They are probably going out to work on our fleet but if our scouts see them first it is just too bad for them. We don't think our boats will arrive for two or three days and by that time we hope that the surf will be quiet enough. It is lots too rough today to try a landing. Japanese work is going right ahead on the island as though nothing were going to happen, but we know better. One of Fred's boys is a gunner on Idaho and Fred hopes Idaho is with the fleet so that he may get to see him. But the fleet may not lay here more than a couple of days and then push on to take Guam back. [Guam was actually recovered three years later.] I found a crippled booby bird from yesterday's bombing and I skinned him to see what he had in the way of meat. He has about the same as a duck, we could do nicely on them. We can catch them at night on the low bushes. [Scotty eventually made a net hook from a

piece of cable and wove several bird nets.] *But cooking is a problem. We have had no hot food for eighty days today and been hiding for sixty-four. Again at one o'clock a Jap came and looked straight at us through the brush for fifteen seconds. Fred was right out in the open and I was crouched behind a log. We are anxious to see the fireworks start as we are going to see some show. Our dugout is okay except for a direct hit and if that should happen we won't suffer any but we will be okay, and have had a wonderful adventure along with some hardships and excitement.*

Feb. 26
Four of eight Heinkels which left this morning did not come back. That could mean they could have found our navy or that they flew to Mid-way—but we assume Midway is ours by now.

Feb. 27
Eight bombers that went out yesterday are still out. Jap patrols did not go out last night. Either they are getting careless or they are getting cautious. Uncle Sam has two more days to arrive on March 1st as I predicted.

Feb. 28
I watched from a tree while a Jap scout took off then I took a walk in the woods and found where one of our shells lit and got some frag-ments as souvenirs. Breakers are dashing high over the brush in the northern shore of the island. We wonder if the storm is delaying an at-tack by our fleet. I feel good today for a change but am still very weak. Am putting this book away and starting another so as not to lose my records if possible.

March 1
The bush near us has taken an awful beating in the past weeks—looks as though the whole Japanese army has been hunting us. Had a good night's sleep and am feeling better but what we need is a wheelbarrow to help us walk upright again. After closing our February book I tied it up in a package with some tools in a neat bundle and took them to our

hollow cache tree, fifty feet northeast of our camp where we had about six more packages hid. I slid them into the tree through a hole about six feet from the ground and heard them fall down into the hollow stump with the others. My plan is to come and get them when uncle arrives and meantime they're safe and dry. At ten o'clock a big tractor with bulldozer came through the brush like an elephant and pushed the tree down right towards our camp. Then he backed up and got some more trees and piled them up. Our other diaries were buried six feet under the earth. We saw the bulldozer moving near us and heard words in English and assumed some Americans were still at work.

March 2
If God will only send rain we will catch it for ourselves. I looked at my broken cache tree sticking out from the ground and debris buried four feet. We made a special two-day cache for leaving if shelling broke out suddenly. We still think help is only a matter of waiting for sea to calm down.

March 3
We caught three gallons rainwater which should help us over hump. We went and watched with envy a Jap building going up in sight of our dugout with eight of our carpenters working on it. One is Davis and another is Dick Meyers, also a good friend. I may slip them a note if I get a chance. They seemed to have only one guard and he doesn't seem to rush them. Everybody seems good and well fed but I think still we'll string out luck as long as she lasts.

March 4
Building progressing fine 200 feet from us and we know several workmen well but shall not make effort contact them yet. Fred wants to go join them. I'm afraid he will stay with me until food is all eaten and then join them.

March 5
Hammer goes on nearby while I read Hilton's <u>Random Harvest.</u> I've been getting a little exercise but am very tired.

March 6
Japs nearly stepped on us. I've lost terror I had of them at first now that I see so many our boys working around them. Japs used decoy trail I'd made a half hour after I'd finished with it. Am very weak growing more so each day. I am not sick but very thin legs and arms only one half normal size and my knees won't control. I just stumble along wherever we want to go. Still when I sit or lie down I am perfectly comfortable and not really ill.

March 7
I am thinking of all the food I am going to have when I get home, chicken rabbit turkey. I will build a new canning house on the ranch in the shade under the trees. Lots of hammering on the building nearby— we had to build new trail to shunt visitors still further away.

March 8
In garden ate two raw seed potatoes placed by Japs and helped our vegetable diet in starches this way. We are going to catch booby birds tonight and cook only breast liver heart and fat.

March 9
Ate three booby birds entrails for breakfast—our first hot food in 77 days. We found our first egg last night but Fred broke it. He is impatient and lefthanded, like Pinkey Gibson. I have no fear of Japs even if they catch us now, seeing how other boys been treated. Last night was so weak and tired could hardly get back to camp. Just heard voices near so will hug ground awhile.

March 10
Ten more days till your birthday Fritzi and I want somehow to get word to you so that you can enjoy it more. Booby birds are starting to lay and frigates hatching. Trees are getting flowers, spring is almost here.

Scotty's diary ends at this moment, but his adventures in captivity had hardly begun.

That same afternoon while foraging for food, he walked almost into the arms of sixty-seven-year-old Ted F. Hensel of Burbank, Washington, a carpenter who was working for the Japanese. Aghast at the bearded, dirty, rag-clad fugitives who stood tottering before him, Hensel cried, "You can't be living men. You're already identified as dead and buried."

Finally convinced that Stevens and Scotty were living men rather than ghosts, Hensel said, "You two look terrible. Better give yourselves up. The Japs won't hurt you. They're treating us fine. Better come in with me." The two hungry, thin scarecrows held a war council and Scotty finally said to Fred, "If you want to go in now, I'm with you."

So the two gave themselves up together, having been, as Scotty says, "without ever serious quarrel, just like brothers to the end." The Japanese naval officers were inclined to treat the fugitives as had been predicted by Hensel. Ironically, Hensel himself was to die May 1st, 1943, at Sasebo, the horror camp in Japan where the naval jailers were as merciless as those on Wake were tolerant.

An official interpreter named Katsumai, however, claimed that the two men were spies planted by the Americans. They were stripped and their identification marks checked with company lists. Then they were taken out into brush camps and told to dig up their radio or be shot. "Go ahead and shoot," said Scotty. Katsumai persuaded the Navy to throw both into jail and informed them that they would be shot in five days. Scotty had to give an exhibition with his crossbow, shooting rats, to prove it was not a secret weapon. Each day they were reminded of the number of days they had left. They were kept apart and fed only bread and water. Their last day came and they were allowed to be together and given a hearty meal. Scotty said, "I guess this is the payoff, Fred," and Fred responded, "I can't believe it."

At nightfall their diet was suddenly returned to bread and water. Katsumai came and informed them that their shooting sentence had been postponed because Tokyo had failed to give its approval. Both were released and told that if they returned to the brush they would be shot.

On March 20th—his wife's birthday—Scotty returned to the brush, found his cache tree, and dug out his diary.

Two months later the fugitives saw what they had missed when the Japanese executed Julius Hofmeister of San Francisco for stealing liquor and being a troublemaker. As Scotty saw it, "A grave was dug, two feet wide by five feet long. The Japs made Hofmeister crouch on his hands and knees. A Jap officer took his sword, laid the blade once against the American's neck, brought it back like a golf club and then down on his neck, severing his head with a single blow. His arteries spurted blood into the trench and the body was placed there and covered."

Still inseparable, Scotty and Fred were taken in September 1942 to Sasebo camp, where 53 Americans out of 265 from Wake died in eighteen months of hard labor and starvation, with many cases of pneumonia and beating. They survived, and were found in Camp #23 in central Kyushu by this *Chicago Daily News* correspondent accompanying prisoner recovery teams.

VI

The Death Cruise:
Seven Weeks in Hell

(September-October 1945)

Immobilized, having abandoned Nagasaki, still under the control of MacArthur's censors, Weller left by Navy ship for Okinawa, Saipan, and Guam, which he reached around October 20. En route he seems to have devoted most of his time to drawing up an eyewitness narrative of the 1944–1945 Death Cruise—one of the last and very worst of the two-hundred-plus Japanese "hellship" voyages—that bore some of the U.S. prisoners he had just interviewed to POW camps on Kyushu. This unique historical account was sent to the *Chicago Daily News* from Guam, where Weller was now accredited to Admiral Nimitz, and soon appeared in the newspaper, heavily sanitized, and in San Francisco, St. Louis, and elsewhere. It has never appeared complete until now.

Railroad tracks at the city's heart (p. 30). In the distance (*center*) is the Medical Institute Hospital, 700 meters south of where the bomb exploded. Nagasaki, September 7, 1945.

One of two *torii* (gates) still standing after their shrine was destroyed, 700 meters south of the atomic blast. The Medical Institute Hospital is in the background. Nagasaki, September 7, 1945.

The exact "hypocenter" beneath where the bomb burst; the district is Matsuyama-cho. The Catholic cathedral is in the background (p. 37). Nagasaki, September 7, 1945.

The Medical Institute Hospital (p. 31) 700 meters south of the bomb hypocenter. In the distance (*center*) is a prison; on the hill (*right*) a medical school. Nagasaki, September 7, 1945.

Passersby covering their noses from the lingering stench of the dead near the demolished Nagasaki Steel Company, approximately 700 meters from the blast. Nagasaki, September 7, 1945.

Presumably a Mitsubishi factory. Nagasaki, September 7, 1945.

A Mitsubishi weapons complex about 500 meters from the blast, destroyed except for two concrete walls. In the background is a middle school. This man may be Weller's interpreter. Nagasaki, September 7, 1945.

In the concrete Mitsubishi headquarters, surviving employees set up an altar of little boxes containing the ashes of unknown colleagues (p. 280). Nagasaki, September 7, 1945.

Just-liberated Allied prisoners, probably U.S. servicemen. Camp #17, Omuta, September 12 to 14, 1945.

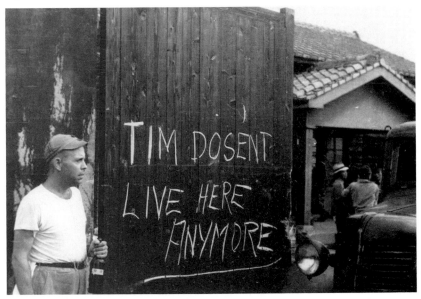

POW Sgt. Wallace Timmons of Chicago, presumably nicknamed "Tim" (see p. 50). Camp #17, September 12 to 14, 1945.

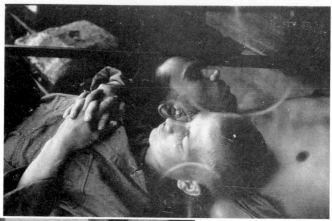

Sleeping just-liberated prisoners. Camp #17, September 12 to 14, 1945.

George Weller (*above right*), probably with members of a prisoner recovery team. Camp #17, September 12 to 14, 1945.

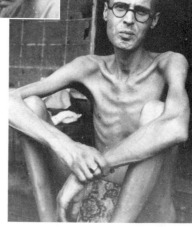

A just-liberated prisoner. Camp #17, September 12 to 14, 1945.

George Weller (*left*) at Camp #17 with ex-prisoner U.S. Marine Sgt. Major James J. Jordan, who also survived the Death Cruise (see pp. 93 and 230). September 12 to 14, 1945.

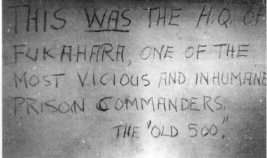

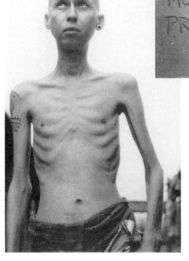

Graffiti done by U.S. POWs upon liberation. The "old 500" were the first five hundred prisoners at the camp (pp. 295–296). Camp #17, September 12 to 14, 1945.

A just-liberated prisoner. Camp #17, September 12 to 14, 1945.

Camp #17, September 12 to 14, 1945.

One final funeral, led by members of a recovery team, as ex-prisoners say farewell to a comrade. Camp #17, September 12 to 14, 1945.

The *Chicago Daily News* Foreign Service presents herewith the first attempt to recount historically one of the great American tragedies of the Pacific War: how more than 1,600 American officers and enlisted men, prisoners of the Japanese and survivors of the defenses of Bataan, Corregidor, and Mindanao, were reduced to about 300 survivors alive today. These Americans, having lived through nearly three years of Japanese prison camps, died in the course of a broken journey seven weeks long from Bilibid Prison in Manila to a chain of prison camps in Kyushu, southern Japan. They died of Japanese bullets and American bombs, of suffocation, dehydration, disease, starvation and murder. Some went insane.

This series is based on interviews obtained by George Weller of the *Chicago Daily News* during a period of eight weeks' investigation in the prison camps of Kyushu, in American rest camps, aboard hospital ships in bomb-torn Nagasaki, at Okinawa and Saipan and Guam.

Because an official record of the death cruise cannot be prepared for many weeks, this account must be regarded as a preliminary one in a historical sense. Survivors' stories conflict in minor details; absolutely reliable lists are not obtainable in the Pacific; in spelling some names phonetic methods had to be used because of the uncertainty of the survivors.

This tragic odyssey was the fourth and last part of the general tragedy of the Philippines, which began with the fall of Bataan and Corregidor, entered its crescendo with the death march of prisoners to Camp O'Donnell, passed its midpoint with their three years of imprisonment, and closed with the death cruise to Japan.

> *Omuta—Nagasaki—Okinawa—Saipan—Guam*
> *November 1, 1945*

THIN from nearly three years' confinement, guarded by bayoneted Japanese, a column of American prisoners numbering somewhere above 1,600 men shuffled in ranks of four through Manila's dusty streets on the morning of December 13, 1944, on their way from Bilibid Prison to what in pre-war days had been known as "The Million Dollar Pier."

They shuffled rather than marched because the sun was hot and many of them were ill. The ragged streetboys of Manila made them furtive *V-for-Victory* signs. In the lace-curtained parlors of the poor Philippine homes the cheap radios were turned on full blast as they approached, then tuned down after they left: an indirect salute of the underground.

Nearly all the prisoners were veterans of the defense of Bataan, Corregidor and Mindanao. About half were officers. They represented about 90 per cent of the field, staff and medical officers who had sustained the defense of the Philippines for six months totally without help from the United States. The officers ranked from Navy commanders and lieutenant colonels of the Army and Marines down through lieutenants and ensigns. Some were civilians who had been commissioned hastily after Japan struck south. Others were civilians who had helped in the defense of Bataan and Corregidor without ever having formally entered the armed forces. There were also 37 British prisoners.

The 1,600 prisoners (the exact number is given by various survivors as 1,615, 1,619, and 1,635) marched slowly through Manila not only because of heat and illness, but because rumor had already spread that they were being sent to Japan. If true, this report meant that their long-sustained hope of being rescued and freed by MacArthur's forces was ended.

The prisoners thought their journey by sea to Japan might take as much as a week or ten days. Had they realized what lay ahead of them—that some would die of suffocation even before the next dawn—many undoubtedly would have chosen immediate death on the bayonets of the Japanese guards who flanked them.

Many of the prisoners were survivors of the death march from Bataan to Camp O'Donnell, where the willful denial of water and food by the Japanese cost the lives of hundreds of Americans—a trip which for deliberate butchery and needless sacrifice would take its place with the Alamo and the Boston Massacre. These men, including everything from highly trained West Point and Annapolis graduates to hastily registered missionary chaplains, had no inkling that they were setting forth on a journey no less cruel and far more extended.

Instead of lasting ten days, as the prisoners expected, their journey to Japan would last seven weeks. Instead of going the whole distance on the ship waiting for them at the Million Dollar Pier, the prisoners would use four ships, besides motor trucks, railroad freightcars and their own naked feet. And instead of arriving in Japan with 1,600 survivors, they would reach there with slightly over 400 still alive, most of whom would be so far sunken that more than 100 would die soon after being turned over to prison authorities ashore.

About 1,880 prisoners were crammed into Bilibid military prison in downtown Manila when the Japanese decided to move them to Japan. Many, like Commander Warner Portz, the sharp-nosed, kindly former senior officer of the Davao prison camp, and Lieutenant Colonel Kenneth Olson who had been commandant there, had been moved northward to Manila on June 6th, leaving in Mindanao a residue of 175 officers of junior grade and about 600 enlisted men in the camps at Davao and nearby Lasang. Even today the fate of these men is only partly known, and the reported finding of large caches of American skeletons in Mindanao leaves it still unclarified.

The prisoners were thin and weak. Their sustaining dish in Bilibid was *lugau*—watered rice made into a thin, gluey substance. So unnourishing is *lugau* that many prisoners descending from the second floor of the Bilibid Prison for their morning dishful on the ground floor found themselves still too weak to climb the stairs to their pallets again. They would remain in the prison yard to await the evening bowlful in order to husband their strength for that ascent of the single flight of stairs.

Against this liability of their own weakness the column of prisoners had an asset: a dedicated group of doctors, both Army and Navy, poor in medicine but rich in spirit. In one of the camps—Cabanatuan—there had existed a group of irresponsible men who lived in part by manufacturing spurious sulfathiozole tablets, stamped with a mold made from a cartridge, and selling them to the Japanese guards. But the Bilibid doctors were superior to that ilk. From May 30, 1942, three weeks after the fall of Corregidor, to October, 1943, the naval medical unit at Bilibid had been under Commander L. B. Sartin of Mississippi, who was then succeeded by Commander Thomas H. Hayes of Norfolk, Virginia. Hayes was marching through the Manila streets now with the column, marching toward the death that was waiting for him in Formosa.

The Japanese had made plans for evacuating the Americans sooner, but Manila was under almost constant air bombardment. They had not dared to bring in ships of large enough tonnage to carry so many men. From the upper levels of Bilibid the Americans had watched the American carrier planes dive bombing the harbor. Their hopes rose that the American dive bombers would be able to keep the harbor clear of shipping long enough so that the Japanese would not attempt to evacuate them.

For some reason, however, the American air attacks stopped suddenly on November 28th, giving the Japanese their chance to sneak their freighters into Manila. As with dragging feet the prisoners marched their last miles on American soil, they feared that for them MacArthur would come too late.

The Japanese had divided them into three groups. Group One, which numbered about 500 superior officers, included ranks from Navy commander and Army or Marine lieutenant colonel down through major and Navy senior lieutenant. Group Two had a few majors, all the rest of the junior officers, and some Navy medical corpsmen attached to their respective doctors, and numbered about 600. Group Three included all non-commissioned officers and enlisted men, a few medical officers, about 50 American civilians, plus the 37 British. This last group, comprising some 520 men, was in the charge of Chief Boatswain Clarence Taylor of Cloverdale, Virginia, and Long Beach, California, who had been executive of the naval receiving station at Cavite. In marching toward the pier the prisoners were further broken down into sections of 200 men, and provided with a small ration of soap and some toilet paper.

Sympathetic Filipinos were frequently rapped back with rifle butts for getting too close to the prisoners. The column reached the Million Dollar Pier at about 2 p.m. The pier was crowded with Japanese civilians by the hundreds, all well dressed, with wives, babies, luggage and often large casks of sugar to take with them. At the pier was the *Oryoku Maru,* a passenger and freight ship of 9,000–10,000 tons, built in Nagasaki in 1939.*

On hand to supervise the prisoners were several Japanese whom the prisoners knew. There was General Koa, who was in charge of all prisoners in the Philippines, and also Lieutenant N. Nogi, director of the Bilibid hospital—a former Seattle physician who customarily had been kind to Americans. The prisoners mounted by single file the gangplank to the ship. The Japanese sentries all had *narugis,* clubs. The Americans were already showing signs of straggling from weakness and frequently had to be touched up with a blow of the *narugi.*

The Japanese elected to fill the aft hold first, and to put aboard the highest ranking officers before the others. It was this circumstance which was to make the death toll heaviest the first night among the top officers, men who had commanded regiments and battalions in the hopeless struggle for Bataan and Corregidor. The aft hold's hatch was cut off from free circulation of air by bulkheads fore and aft of it. A long slanting wooden staircase descended some 35 feet through the hatch, down which the prisoners weakly crept.

When the first officers reached the bottom of the ladder they were met by a Sergeant Dau, well known at Davao, who wore a sword and had several privates under him armed with brooms. Dau used the sword to direct the privates, and the privates used their brooms to beat the American officers back as far as possible into the dim bays of the hold.

---

* Actually 7,362 tons. The cargo included General MacArthur's Packard.

"We had to scamper back in there," one officer describes it, "or get a crack from the brooms or Dau's sword. There was a platform about five feet high built over the hatch above, and so the little light that came down in mid-afternoon was deflected. Long before the hold was filled the air was foul and breathing was difficult. But the Japanese kept driving more men down the ladder from the deck, and Dau and his men kept pushing the first-comers farther back into the airless dark."

This hold's dimensions none of the prisoners could then estimate, because it was already too dark, at three in the afternoon, to see its limits. The loading in this hold alone took 1½ hours. The first officers who had descended were sitting down in bays, a double tier system of wooden stalls something like a Pullman car. The lower bays were three feet high. A man could neither stand up nor extend his legs sitting down in them.

Each bay was about nine feet from passageway to rear wall. The Japanese insisted that the Americans could sit in rows four deep, each man's back against his neighbor's knees, in this nine-foot depth. The elder officers who were forced back in the rear almost immediately began to faint. Instead of making more space in the center under the fading light of the hatch, the Japanese insisted that the men in the center should not even sit down, but should be left standing, packed together vertically.

When the Japanese on deck looked down through the hatch they saw a pit of living men staring upward, their chests and shoulders heaving as they struggled for air and wriggled for better space. "The first fights," says one officer, "started when men began to pass out. We knew then that only the front men in each bay would be able to get enough air."

While the early struggles were beginning in the aft hold, the Japanese were herding the endless line of embarking prisoners forward to the bow hold. Here they managed to force down the ladder about 600 others against the 800 already under decks. The air here, too, was foul. Finally the last party to board, approximately 250 enlisted men and civilians, got the only fully ventilated hold of the *Oryoku Maru,* the second hold forward.

About 5 o'clock the *Oryoku Maru* cast off, and headed down the bay. Now the prisoners discovered into whose hands their lives had been committed. Their guards were mixed, some Japanese but mostly Formosans, or as they were taught to call them, "Taiwanis." The whole party was in the charge of Lieutenant Toshino, a Japanese officer of somewhat Western and Prussian aspect, with short clipped hair, spectacles and a severe manner.

Though Toshino was nominally in command, the real control fell, as it often did in Philippine prisons, in the hands of the interpreter. In the prisons of Luzon and Mindanao, as everywhere from Japan to Java, the treatment depended on the interpreter more than on the commanding officer. Toshino left as much as possible to the interpreter, and his interpreter was a Japanese no survivor will ever forget.

Mr. Wada was a hunchback. He hated the straight-backed world, and all his hatred had turned itself on the Americans. He had been an interpreter at Mindanao, and already laid up for himself an unusual record as spy and stool pigeon. The blood of the Americans who were to die needlessly between Manila and Moji is on the hands of all Japanese into whose care they were committed. But if you believe what the survivors say, the man whose hands are most ineradicably smeared is Mr. Wada. (There was something about him that made him always be called "Mr." Wada.)

The *Oryoku Maru,* as it moved down the harbor, became part of a convoy of five merchant ships, protected by a cruiser and several destroyers and lighter craft. They moved without lights, their holds vomiting forth the hoarse shouts of the Americans. Discipline had begun to slip in the struggling pits of the No. 3 and No. 1 holds. As air grew scarcer, the pleas for air grew louder and more raucous. Before long the Japanese threatened to board down the hatches and cut off all air.

As the cries of struggling men persisted, the Japanese lowered down into the complete darkness of the pit a series of wooden buckets filled with fried rice, cabbage and fried seaweed. In the stifling darkness, filled with moans and wild shouts, the buckets were handed around. The officers who had mess kits scooped in the buckets; the others simply grabbed blindly in the darkness, palming what they could. Some ate, but those in the rear ranks—if conscious—got as little as if they had fainted.

Fear was already working its way on the bowels and kidneys of the men. Asked for slop buckets, the Japanese sent them down. These buckets circulated in the utter darkness far less readily than the similar food buckets. A man could not tell what was being passed to him, food or excrement. In their increasingly crazed condition, men would tell their neighbors that the one bucket was the other, and consider it uproarious if a hand was dipped in the toilet bucket, or the food bucket was befouled by a man who had no way of knowing what he was doing.

Mr. Wada was very dissatisfied with the clamor issuing from the struggling pits of Americans. "You are disturbing the Japanese women and children," he called down from the top of the hatch to Commander Frank Bridget, who was shouting himself hoarse trying to keep order among the suffocating men. "Stop your noise, or the hatches will be closed."

The noise of the crazed men could not be stopped and the hatches were closed. That was at about 10 o'clock. Then some of the men crept up the ladder and parted the planks slightly, so that a little air could get through. Mr. Wada came again to the edge of the pit. "Unless you are quiet I shall give the guards the order to fire down into the hold."

A kind of relative quiet had settled on the hold—the quiet of exhaustion and death. The floor was covered with excrement and urine. Almost all the officers had stripped their bodies, so that the pores would have a chance to breathe what the lungs could not.

Occasionally an American would awaken from a stupor out of his mind. One began calling, around midnight, "Lieutenant Toshino, Lieutenant Toshino!" The others, fearful of Japanese repercussions, shouted, "Knife him, knife that son-of-a-bitch!" Someone said, "Denny, you get him!" There was movement, a struggle, and a scream in the darkness. Then somebody else called: "Get Denny, he did it, get him!" and there was another struggle.

Then came foreboding quiet, with all who had heard wondering what had happened. Men who owned jackknives unclasped the big blade, prepared to fight if they were attacked.

Around midnight the convoy ran into difficulties. American planes were sparing Manila Bay by day, but their submarines were still patrolling by night. The night attack, a specialty of the American underseas fleet, was at its high point of the war. Prisoners who crept up the ladder to open the planks for air reported that an enormous floating fire had broken out on the horizon at the point where the Japanese cruiser had been.

The *Oryoku Maru* crept through the mouth of Manila Bay and turned northward in the darkness, hugging closely the Luzon shore so that the remaining vessels in the convoy could protect her. Meantime death strode through the fetid, slippery bays, taking impartially soldiers old and new. Major James Bradley of Shanghai's famous 4th Marines passed away. Lieutenant Colonel John Bennett of the 31st Infantry was suffocated. So was Lieutenant Colonel Jasper Brady of the same outfit. The Army Lieutenant Colonel Norman Simmonds, who had the curious record of once having been middleweight boxing champion at Annapolis, went down and did not arise. Major Houston B. Houser, an outstandingly capable figure who had organized M.P.s of a sort to keep order in the darkness, who busied himself running up the ladder to plead with the Japanese and cleaning up excreta in the darkness, was felled with exhaustion and later took the short way home. He had been [General Jonathan] Wainwright's adjutant during part of the battle for Bataan. Major Maynard Snell, a veterinarian who had been a professor at Louisiana State University, also did not last till morning.

But in the darkness few knew that these men had died. It is even possible that some of them did not actually pass away till the next evening. "Once you passed out, you were gone," as an officer says, "but only those near you could tell that you were dead. The temperature down there must have been 130 degrees at least, and it took a long time for a body to grow cold."

Major Howard Cavender, Dollar Line representative in Manila and manager of the Manila Hotel, was among those who succumbed but were not recognized till light came.

"The worst thing," according to a major of the 26th Cavalry, "was the men who had gone mad but would not sit still. One kept pestering me, pushing a mess kit against my sweaty chest and saying, 'Have some of this chow? It's good.' I smelled of it and smelled what it was. It was not chow. 'All right,' he said, 'if you don't want it I'm going to eat it.' And a little while later I heard him eating it, right beside me."

There was a tendency on the part of men near the border of madness to get up and wander around, as though to get assurance where they were. "You would meet one of these men. He would seem to talk perfectly normally. But all the time he would keep putting out his hands, placing them on your shoulders in the darkness, running them up and down your arms as though trying to make sure that you and he were alive, and that you both were real. If you stepped away, he would follow you, pawing and trying to put his face close to yours, to make sure you were there."

After the hatches were closed the Japanese refused to allow any more *benjos,* or slop buckets, to be handed up the ladder. Overfull as they were, the buckets still circulated. A man would be heard saying, "Someone take this thing, for God's sake. I can't hold it and I have no place to put it." He would be ignored, because nobody would be willing to give up space in order to take the *benjo.* If angered or irrational, the badgered and weary man might simply overturn the mobile toilet on his neighbors.

As the first faint light crept down through the parted planks of the hatches, the men in three holds looked about them. Some men were in a stupor, a few were dead, a few were mad. The first step was to get the insane under control. In the pit of the aft hold, which was the worst affected, there were two decks and a bottom hatch, leading into the bilge. The most violent of those who were mad were lowered into this sub-hold.

It was hot. The labored working of hundreds of lungs had expelled moisture which clung to the sides of the bulkheads in great drops. Men tried to scrape off this moisture and drink it. Naked, sitting like galley slaves between each other's legs, they looked at their hands. Their fingers seemed long and thin and the ends were wrinkled as though they had been soaked a long time in hot water. But their throats were sandpaper-dry. They were in the first stages of weakening through dehydration, aggravated by the loss of body salts, the sparks of energy.

DAWN came slowly and at first almost no light filtered back into the rear bays, where most of the dead lay. Chief Warrant Officer Walter C. Smith of San Diego had found himself a tiny shelf beyond the last tiers of the suffocated. "I was jammed all the way up against the rudder. I could hardly see daylight at first."

Again the gray-haired, indefatigable Commander Bridget took charge. Under medium size, about one hundred fifty pounds, he had a fighting build, with a thin face and marked bow legs. To the few who were not naked—some had kept on their clothes even in the dripping heat, as protection against being pawed by the wandering insane men—he said: "Take off all the clothes you can. Don't move around. You use up extra oxygen that way and you sweat more. Use your shorts to fan each other."

He showed them how the little air that came down the hatch could be fanned with easy motions back into the rear bays. Some of the officers in the rear bays, lying in a stupor between suffocation and life, came slowly alive. Others did not stir. The Japanese lowered a little rice, and it was distributed by Warrant Officer Clifford Sweet of the U.S.S. *Tanager*. Water there was none.

Smith surveyed his tiny post on the vibrating counter of the ship. In a 10-foot circle around him were five officers. They sat, naked and doubled up, like white-skinned fakirs praying. But they were cold and dead. He wondered particularly what had happened to one big man who kept walking around all night, stepping indifferently on bodies and followed by a train of curses. For a time he had stopped by the rudder and insisted on sitting across Smith's stomach. This vagabond kept getting into fights wherever he roamed in the fetid dark. In the faint light Smith could see the big man, crumpled on the filthy deck, now dead.

He recognized another young man whom he knew, went to him, felt his heart and got no answer.

Bridget was a fountain of hope. He climbed to the top of the ladder into the very muzzle of the Formosan guard. He talked to the Japanese and persuaded them to allow three or four of the unconscious elder officers to be carried up the ladder and laid out on the deck. None of the dead were allowed to be removed. As soon as the unconscious men revived they had to go down the ladder again to make way for others.

Lieutenant Toshino, in charge of the prisoners, and Mr. Wada, the hunchbacked interpreter, learned what was happening in the pits of the holds.

In the growing light, with the unbalanced men out of the way and the dead no longer taking their share of air, and with everyone sitting down and none wandering around, it was possible for the officers to take cognizance of where they were.

"The whole space in the aft hold," according to Major John Fowler of Boston and Los Angeles, a 26th Cavalryman taken at Bataan, "looked about a hundred feet long by about forty feet wide. There were thirteen bays or little compartments on each side, and two across. Each bay was double, above and below, and the average was about eight feet by eleven and a half feet."

The *Oryoku Maru* coasted slowly and uncertainly along the edge of Luzon. In the morning, summoned perhaps by the submarines which had attacked the convoy during the night, American planes appeared overhead. Soon they began their attacks.

Bridget, completely cool, sat at the top of the ladder. Like an announcer in a press box, he called the plays. "I can see two planes going for a freighter off our starboard side," he would say. "Now two more are detached from the formation. I think they may be coming for us. They are! They're diving! Duck, everybody!"

The Japanese gun crews opened fire, and a wild cacophony of gun dialogue went back and forth. *Thump,* went the shock as the bombs hit the water. The bulkheads shook. The naked men lay flat on the filth-smeared planks, trembling.

Lieutenant Colonel Elvin Barr, executive of the 60th Coast Artillery on Corregidor, who had fought his guns magnificently until silenced by the crossfire of Japanese artillery and dive bombing, stumbled up to Fowler. Fowler was on the cargo deck; Barr had been in the well-deck.

"There's a hole knocked in the bulkheads down there," Barr said. He had a wound in his side that ran from armpit to hip. "Between thirty and forty majors and lieutenant colonels have already died down where I came from," he added. Though neither of them then knew it, Barr himself was to die from this wound, and from disease and neglect, before reaching Japan.

Out of bombs but not out of gas or bullets, the planes returned and began to strafe the ships. "It sounded like a riveting machine, running the whole length," recalled a survivor. These attacks could not sink the ship, but they raised havoc with its gun crews. First one crew was spattered to death, then another. There was nothing wanting in Japanese courage. An artillery officer says: "They were magnificent. As soon as a crew would be wiped out, another would take its place."

The half darkness that still reigned below decks gave a strange phenomenon. Bridget would announce a dive bomber, "Here comes one now!" and the prisoners would hear the scream of wings. Then, lying flat but with faces turned sideways, they would hear the crunch of the striking bomb. And suddenly the whole side of the bulkheads was alive with sparks. The bomb's concussion, causing the plates to scrape together, would throw off such will-o'-the-wisp flickers, by which blue glow they could see each others' faces and the dead around them.

Though the American flyers brought terror to the prisoners, they also brought two gifts: light and air. In the shock and disorder, the hatch planks had become disarrayed. Each party of United States Medical Corps men, when allowed to take up an officer who had fainted, made use of the confusion to open the planks more. At length Lieutenant Toshino and Mr. Wada gave permission for some of the suffocated who were dead to be brought up on deck.

Bridget's cool example, plus air and light, brought an improvement in morale and partial recovery of discipline. The situation was not altogether hopeless. If it grew better, they would live. If it grew worse, and the attacks continued, the Japanese could not send them to Japan, and they would be rescued by MacArthur after all.

Bridget and Commander Warner Portz, who as senior officer was nominally in charge of the whole party, took advantage of the slight lift in hope to order a roll call. Some sobering discoveries were made. The madness induced mainly by lack of air, and partly by lack of water, had caused men to pair off by twos in the night and go marauding. If they could not have water, they would have blood to drink; if not blood, then urine. There were slashed wrists. And "Cal" Coolidge, a large, fat former Navy petty officer who had been proprietor of the Luzon Bar in Manila, was found choked to death. There had been murder, then; the prisoners accepted that, too, with what distaste they could muster, but it seemed a natural part of the whole.

A food detail that was allowed to go up the ladder and forward to the galley reported that a big ship was burning in the convoy, and that the course was turning back toward Subic Bay. The Japanese captain sent word that if they were badly stricken in another attack, he would give Bridget and Portz the word when to bring up the prisoners, which side of the ship they should go over, and how far it was to nearest land. Through Lieutenant Colonel E. Carl Engelhart, the American interpreter, the Japanese sent down this warning: "If anyone other than an officer in charge so much as touches the hatch ladder, he will be instantly shot."

Among the 2,000 Japanese civilians there was terror and confusion. From the forward hold, where Lieutenant Colonel Curtis Beecher was in charge, the Army physicians Lieutenant Colonel William North and Lieutenant Colonel Jack W. Schwartz, along with several doctors and corpsmen, were summoned on deck to take care of the Japanese wounded.

Especially in the aft hold, blood seeped down through the hatch planks and gave the naked, panting men a spotted appearance.

In the middle hold, where approximately 250 men were under Commander Maurice Joses of Santa Monica, there was plenty of room and enough air to maintain discipline. This group even had resourcefulness enough to keep back the wooden buckets that the

Japanese sent down with food. By retaining one each time, they were able to accumulate enough toilet buckets for themselves. By now, in other holds, men were using their mess kits and their hats for *benjos*, being denied buckets by the Japanese.

Men in Hold No. 2 who got a peep over their hatch reported seeing "a tall lighthouse" on the shore. "That's Subic," said the Navy men with relief.

Between three and four in the afternoon the *Oryoku Maru* edged close to shore. The captain sent down word that he was going to disembark all passengers. The American prisoners would be disembarked too, as soon as guards were arranged on shore to keep them from escaping.

Suddenly there was a sandy, grating sound. The liner had run aground. Immediately the ban against going on deck was strictly enforced. For the next three or four hours, until well beyond sunset and the fall of gloom into the holds, there was a scraping of chains and spitting of winches as the captain strove to free the *Oryoku Maru*. It was foul, filthy and airless in the forward and aft holds; again discipline began to crack.

About 8 p.m. the *Oryoku Maru* floated free once more, moved in toward the American naval base at Olongapo, and at about ten began to discharge her Japanese passengers. Now the Japanese, knowing the conditions in the prisoners' holds by the number of dead already stacked on the decks, were fearful that a break for shore would take place. Below decks the sane prisoners were almost equally fearful that the unbalanced would unite against them and rush the ladder; they posted guards.

There were approximately sixteen chaplains in the three holds, and most of them carried Bibles or breviaries. A few other men had prayer books or religious works. Some read them aloud. A Navy Lieutenant O'Rourke, who had been on the Chinese river patrol, took out his prayer book and read a few words to those around him in the cargo hold in the stern. Suddenly he stopped and began tearing pages out of the book and scattering them. Then without warning he made a dash for the vertical iron ladder beside the wooden stairs, and began to climb up. A big chief boatswain, Jesse Earl Lee of San Diego, pulled him back before the guard above could draw a bead on him. They tied him to the ladder until he quieted down.

During the first night his fellow pharmacist mates had taken care of Chips Bowlin, who had become unmanageable. They saved him from being forced into the bilges with the miserable wretches whom no one could handle, but this second night he managed to creep away from them, made a furtive dash for the ladder and climbed up it before he was missed. They heard a sentry scream something, then three shots and finally Bowlin's voice: "The only thing I ask of the Japs is that they give me a decent burial." They never saw him again.

Bridget never left his post on the wooden ladder. His voice was hoarse, now, from continual shouting. He was relieved occasionally by an officer of the 4th Marines, Major Andrew J. Mathiesen of Los Angeles. Mathiesen had a cool smile that never came off; even in the darkness, hearing his unruffled voice, the prisoners imagined that they could see that smile. "Not going to Japan, boys," he would say. "Still right off old Subic. Not going to Japan."

"For God's sake, boys," Bridget would rasp, "keep fanning. Don't leave your place. Every move you make generates heat. There are men in the back bays who are going to die unless you sit still and keep fanning."

Some obeyed Bridget and Mathiesen, but not all. Some could hear, or imagined they heard, men plotting against them in the darkness. They unclasped their knives. Chief Pharmacist's Mate D. A. Hensen worked his way across through the foul and steaming aisles to a little cluster of chief warrant officers. "Look," he said, "I've lost my nerve. The fellows over in my bay are plotting against me. They are going to kill me." His friends allowed him to stay until he felt better, told him he was talking nonsense and that he must follow the general order and go back to his bay. In an hour he was back again, full of the same fear of murder. Again they told him it was a hallucination, and sent him back. In the morning he was found dead, his belly slit open.

There was Lieutenant Bill Williams, an Army engineer, who took the same line in talking aloud as Bridget and Mathiesen: if not sunk, they would get away; if sunk, they would land on Luzon and the Japanese would never again be able to get together enough ships to take them to Manila.

But there were also nuisances like the doctor who kept imagining he had to see someone in the next bay. He spent the whole night crawling back and forth, and could not be dissuaded from his empty errand.

Some who were visited by illusions seem to have been protected rather than harmed by them. One seaman medico says: "All that second night it seemed to me that I was not on a ship, but in a big hotel. I could hear people talking in the lobby. Right near me was a man who had suffocated, tangled with another who was also gone. Other people kept trying to move them toward the ladder to be carried up. I knew this and saw this and it still seemed to me that I was in a hotel. . . ."

Captain James McMinn of Carlsbad, who was to survive and reach Japan, had the idea that he was still in Bilibid Prison and kept visiting a friend, suggesting a game of cards.

After the *Oryoku Maru* dropped anchor almost no air came down the hatches, which were about 14 × 14 feet. There were no ventilators; animals could not have been shipped under such conditions and lived. Besides thirst and lack of air, the prisoners were suffering from something known to Christmas shoppers in a mild form—crowd poisoning. Crowd poisoning takes two common forms: the body may burst out in excessive heat, causing a swoon, or it may turn to a cold sweat, with dizziness and vomiting.

A medical aideman had received a back full of shrapnel on the open deck during the strafing. He had lead in his lungs. "Two fellows began to follow me around in the darkness. I knew they were out to get me, because I had turned one of them in for selling narcotics in Bilibid. I overheard them planning to knock me out with a metal canteen full of urine. I began wandering around trying to shake them off. Once I had to relieve myself and could not look for a bucket because they were following me. So I relieved myself right where I was. I felt wild and yet I knew what I was doing. I scooped up the excrement and threw it over the men around me. They raised hell. So just to show them, I scooped up some myself and rubbed it in my hair. Then I started fleeing again, trying to shake off my two enemies. When they got near me they would gouge at the wounds in my back. Finally I shook them off. I ended up against a bulkhead that was sweating. I collapsed at the bottom and it was cooler there and I enjoyed the drops from the bulkhead falling on my face."

In the last hours of darkness on the second night the Japanese sent down a new word to Portz, the leader of the Americans, and the three commanders of the different holds. In the aft hold Bridget announced: "Good news, boys! We're going to be put ashore here. The Japanese civilians who are still alive have all been put ashore, and our turn is next."

THE *Oryoku Maru*'s steering gear had been broken by the persistent strafing, and she had become unmanageable. But the Japanese did not forget to make special stipulations before releasing the Americans from the ship where nearly a hundred had already died. The prisoners might take their pants and shirts, but they could not take their haversacks, except for mess kit and canteen. And they were to wear no shoes; the Japanese were sure that barefooted Americans could not go far if they attempted to escape. Mr. Wada stopped at the middle hold and told Commander Maurice Joses to instruct the men there to leave the ship in 25-man groups.

The *Oryoku Maru* was almost dead in the water, about 300 yards off Olongapo Point. At Joses' order, Chief Boatswain Clarence M. Taylor took the first twenty-five men up past the Japanese guns and out of the hold. He lined them up at the accommodation ladder over the side. The Japanese signed that the American prisoners were to be used as oarsmen. Taylor took six men and himself as the first boat crew, and ordered the other nineteen prisoners to follow as crews in the next lifeboats. There were eight Japanese in the first boat with him.

"As we got in," says Taylor, "I heard the sound of airplane motors. I looked up and saw twelve fighter-bombers, in four flights of three each. They were American and they were circling for their dive."

Lieutenant Toshino, in charge of the prisoners, signalled from the rail for the boat to shove off. Taylor did so. The first wave of planes dived and dropped their bombs, small ones. The *Oryoku Maru* began to list. She still had four lifeboats swinging from davits on her starboard side. But the list was to port, and she was so far heeled over that the lifeboats, if released, would have bottomed on her deck, rather than in the water.

Another plane came around and selected Taylor's lifeboat for a strafing job. "What happened was the most lace-edged example of selective strafing I ever saw," says Taylor. "Of the eight Japs, six were killed. We looked straight into the faces of those machine guns, firing just 18 inches apart. And as I sat in the stern the Jap on my right was hit in the face and his whole head simply disintegrated, and the Jap on my left was hit in the chest and body and died instantly. Some day I'm going to find out who that pilot was and tell him he did the fanciest trick shooting since Wild Bill Hickok."

The oarsmen, who included three pharmacist's mates 2nd class— John Istock of Pittsburgh, Lester Tappy of Niagara, Wisconsin, and Roy Lynch of Waynesboro, Tennessee—were unharmed. But the lifeboat had turned over and two of the Americans were non-swimmers. The Japanese had provided lifebelts for themselves, but none for their prisoners. The prisoners therefore stripped the dead Japanese in the water and put their lifebelts on the non-swimmers.

As Taylor lay on his back, striving to rest before starting for shore, the next wave of American planes dove on their target. "I saw the whole thing, the bomb fall and hit near the stern hatch, the debris go flying up into the air. It looked as though it would fall in the water near us. I dove below the surface as far as I could go."

This bomb caught the aft hold just when the bodies of those who had suffocated in the second night were being removed. They included the Lieutenant O'Rourke who earlier had tried to escape from the hold; Lieutenant Commander Adolph Hede, former executive officer of the U.S.S. *Canopus;* and Lieutenant Williams, former executive of the *Mindanao* in the Chinese river patrol.

The bomb, striking barely aft of the hatch, rained splinters into the hold full of naked men. The iron girder supporting the hatch planks turned into a thousand pieces of shrapnel. The heavy 14-foot hatch planks blew into the hold, felling and braining several men. There was a wild, uncontrollable rush for the ladder.

"I saw the first man get it," says Major F. Langwith Berry of Burlingame, California, taken on Bataan with the 86th Field Artillery. "He had just put his feet on the bottom of the ladder. If he hadn't been there, I would have got it. He fell back dead in my arms. I did not know who he was. I put him down and jumped back into the dark bays, out of reach of Japanese fire. There I reached out and touched the two men on each side of me, who seemed to be asleep. They were cold. Both were dead, suffocated."

The deck above the prisoners was perforated with many holes; light was plentiful now. But suddenly a yellowish haze began to appear in the bays, and a smell of smoke. "She's on fire," yelled someone. "The coal dust has caught. Let us out of here! We'd rather be shot than suffocate!"

"I was standing right under the hatch," says Chief Boatswain Jesse Lee, "and I saw the plane go into its dive. I had been talking to an Army lieutenant, and he was saying how thirsty he was. Then the bomb hit. I was hit by one of the hatch planks, but I got up. I remember the big yellow flash and the hot blast of the explosion. I looked for the lieutenant. He was so full of holes that he looked like a pepper shaker, and he was quite dead. I'll never forget the way the hold looked. There were at least a dozen people lying under planks. The *benjo* buckets we had not yet had time to empty were burst and there was human slop all over the bodies."

In the aft hold under the hatch was always the most favored position, being the lightest and airiest, and some of the healthiest men had been gathered there. Captain Charles Brown of Deming, New Mexico, was one of the few who survived, and he was bleeding at the nose and mouth from a concussion. Seeing him, another member of the 200th Coast Artillery, Captain Ted Parker of Albuquerque, made a wild rush for the ladder, which was now sagging and splintered. A sentry shot him from above three times, twice through the body and once through the head.

Another 200th officer, Captain Gerald Greeman of Deming, who had been sitting at the foot of the ladder, was sought by his brother officers McMinn and Lieutenant Russell Hutchison. They could find no trace of him. In Hutchison's words: "We looked up and saw that after they shot Captain Parker the Japanese sentries had gone away from the edge of the hatch. Everywhere around us were bodies, bodies with faces blackened and lips purple. The guns had stopped and there was a kind of terrible silence. We took hold of the shaky ladder and climbed up through the smoke. We found the deck covered with Japanese and American bodies. Our men were scooping up sugar from the luggage and eating what they could before they jumped over. We had a hard time finding lifebelts. Only when we got over the side, in that clean cool water, we felt better. There were bloody men hanging to timbers, but they seemed encouraged. Their bodies were taking in water through their pores, and they felt cool as they struck out for the beach."

The last American shot by the Japanese while still on the decks of the *Oryoku Maru,* according to George L. Curtis, a 53-year-old native of New Bedford, Massachusetts, who had been the Packard agent in Manila, was his friend "Scotty" Lees, a Philippine mining engineer whose wife was a schoolteacher in Freeport, Illinois. "When I got on deck and felt the boat sinking, I saw Scotty a little way off," says Curtis. "I was just starting to go toward him, and turned away for a moment to see something. When I turned back he was staggering and I saw he was shot, for he was bleeding heavily in front." Dazed from being struck by the hatchway's beams, Curtis barely made his way ashore.

Some 57 civilians were in the party when it left as prisoners, and less than a dozen are believed to have arrived. More civilians perished from the bomb in the stern of the *Oryoku Maru* than any other cause.

Somehow one of the lifeboats had been lowered and Lieutenant Toshino, in full formal uniform, and Mr. Wada had made their way ashore. The water was full of swimming men, but the Japanese captain still remained at his post on the bridge. He knew a few limping words of English, and warned the last prisoners to leave quickly.

Small fires were breaking out in various places. The ship's increasing list had put out the coal dust fire in the hold and the yellow smoke ceased pouring through the hatches. But suddenly, beside the stern anti-aircraft gun littered with the bodies of the several successive crews killed by strafing United States planes, and with the suffocated American dead piled nearby, the ammunition boxes caught fire. They began to explode. Abruptly the looting of the decks ceased, and all scattered. Some prisoners ran forward to look for life preservers in the cabins of the dead Japanese passengers. Except for the captain's immediate circle, all the Japanese—soldiers, passengers, crew—were already gone by lifeboat.

The prisoners pushed open the stateroom doors. Looking in, they saw that theirs were not the only dead of the *Oryoku Maru*. Huddled together thickly as they huddle in foxholes and cities, the Japanese had died in their staterooms and been left there during the night by those who were already safe on shore.

Chief Boatswain Smith saw his friend James Terry, a Navy machinist also of San Diego, lying under a ladder with his chest torn open, quiet in death. Then a hand touched him. It was Navy Paymaster O. A. "Mike" Carmichael, another friend and San Diegan. "I can't see," said Carmichael. "I seem to be blind." Smith tried to lead him to the ladder, but Carmichael refused to go until he got his jacket. He said his collection of recipes was in the pocket of the jacket. As an escape from talking about food, prisoners in the Japanese camps often made collections of imaginary recipes, which they swapped and shared like boys trading postage stamps. The recipe book was each prison camp's equivalent of theaters, concerts and museums.

Smith persuaded Carmichael to mount the ladder, told him he was going to find drinking water and a lifejacket, and left him leaning blindly against the rail. He came back with a lifejacket, put it on Carmichael, and told him to remain while he went away to find water. All the water taps on the ship had stopped functioning, but in a tiny, secluded tearoom he finally found a leaky tap. He filled the canteen and started back for his friend. Carmichael had disappeared. "I searched everywhere from bow to stern, but Mike was nowhere." He never saw him again.

The ammunition ceased exploding. There were now only a dozen or so wounded men alive on the decks. A man in the water yelled, "Hey, throw us down some shoes." Smith threw him down four pairs, which the swimmer tied around his neck before setting off for the beach. For himself he found another pair of shoes, an officer's cap, two spoons, a canteen and some Japanese cigarettes. He filled himself up on water, put the cigarettes in the empty canteen, and went to the rail.

The planes began to come back, and for a moment he thought that the men in the water were going to be strafed. But they waved energetically to the planes. The pilots came down low, throttled back to see who it was in the water. They must have seen that it was Americans, for they swooped up over the small party that was gathering on the Olongapo beach, and they did not strafe the shore. . . . Smith let himself down over the side and struck out for the beach.

Possibly as many as thirty men died trying to reach shore. There would have been many more lost but for the fact that cool water followed by a nearby footing on land, with the ever-reviving hope that they would not go to Japan, brought up the morale of the prisoners with a bound. Men began to help each other. Lieutenant Colonel William Craig was far gone from heat exhaustion and dehydration; the physician North tied him to a board and swam him ashore. Naval Warrant Officer Jeremiah Crews of San Diego, a big man and a good swimmer, went into the water with a lifejacket strapped on over his clothes and was able to bring ashore two weaker men who clung to his shoulders.

A last effort had been made by the men who left the aft hold, including Major John Fowler, to pile the bodies in rice sacks, two to a sack. As the *Oryoku Maru* began to burn, the corpses on deck could still be seen. Some men who were wounded got a shot of morphine, before they went over the rail, from Lieutenant Commander Clyde Welsh.

A few men had cut loose rafts and planks on the offshore or starboard side, which was high. They set out to swim toward the

Zambales Mountains and a distant lighthouse, thinking to reach the beach there and escape into the bush. The Japanese, however, sent out a motorboat from shore with a machine gun and snipers. One by one the prisoners were hunted down. Lieutenant Gerald Darling of Deming, New Mexico, set forth on a raft with three others; they slipped off into the water and were not seen again. He was picked off by the Japanese.

A Major Peterson, who had been in the forward hold and claimed he left it straight through the side of the ship rather than through the hatch, reached the beach. He said that he had heard men groaning and believed that some were still alive on board.

The first men to reach shore found that there was no true beach at all, but ankle-deep water below an 8-foot seawall. A few mounted the seawall to lie exhausted in the sun. They had hardly fallen flat when a machine gun opened up on them. The shore was in the hands of the well-known JNLPs—the Japanese Naval Landing Party—a kind of shock marines. In a clump of bushes about 200 yards from the seawall they had mounted a machine gun.

Lieutenant Colonel Beecher of Chicago and Saratoga, California, a vigorous, gray-haired Marine "who looked like Victor McLaglen," as one prisoner said, took quick command of the seawall situation. He ordered the best swimmers to plunge in again and help those who were struggling. He dived in himself and brought back about a half dozen. Each time he would say, "Come on; let's help the men who are failing out there." Chief Boatswain Taylor and he, clad alike in nothing but shorts, brought in man after man.

One or two prisoners had afterthoughts about the wreck, swam all the way out again, filled up on brown sugar, and swam back.

It was difficult to persuade the newcomers, once they reached the seawall, to squat down in its cover in the shallow water. Not having heard the Japanese fire while they were thrashing toward shore, they refused to believe that there was already a machine gun set up against them. Several impetuously climbed up anyway, but when one was wounded they floundered back into the water again, and crouched in the lee of the bullet-swept seawall.

The American planes returned again. Beecher gave orders for the strongest men to run up and down in the water, waving their clothes. They ran and waved, and the leading pilot seemed to get the idea. He waggled his wings and flew off.

The Japanese set up systematic foxholes in the bushes, with snipers to cover the seawall. The Americans were then allowed, after a parley, to climb up and rest in the sun, under the eyes of Japanese rifles. Two Marine officers, Major Andrew Mathiesen and Lieutenant Keene, a graduate of South Carolina's Citadel, approached the JNLPs and explained that the Americans had been without water for two days. There was a small faucet near the Japanese positions. The Japanese allowed them to go to it in five-man details.

Around noon, after the half-naked men had lain in the open sun for about two hours, the Japanese gave orders to them to break camp and prepare to move. The small aid station which had been set up on the seawall by Commander Thomas Hayes was immediately packed into the mess kits and canteens which remained. When the barefoot, sunburned marchers were ready, with two men to help each of the wounded, the Japanese formed a line to guide them. With bayoneted rifles and clubs the JNLPs were placed at intervals of about 30 yards along a crooked line of march a half-mile long to a tennis court about 500 yards back from the seawall.

The long file of men straggled on slowly and weakly. Occasionally the Japanese batted them along, but there were no outright beatings. By about three in the afternoon the last of the bearded and bandaged prisoners were hobbling through the gate of the tennis court which was to be their prison.

It was a concrete court not far from an old Marine barracks, and undoubtedly some of the elder officers had played there in the happy days when service life had been a country club. There was only one court. It was, of course, without shade or shelter of any kind. It had the usual wire fencing strung around, with an unpainted wall about 6 feet high at the bottom. At the side was a tall referee's platform, and a small water faucet.

This court was to be the new prison for some 1,300 hungry, thirsty, battle-shocked, ill and in some cases wounded men who remained of the approximately 1,615 who had left Bilibid.

THEY stacked their dead at the entrance to the court. They moved the tall referee's platform to the middle of the court, where it be-came a kind of lookout and command post. Commander Portz was still nominally senior officer, but so exhausting had been the experi-ence he underwent in the aft hold that both he and Bridget were de-pleted as well as wounded. Leadership was passing into the hands of Lieutenant Colonel Beecher, whose forward hold had suffered greatly, but relatively not so much.

"We saw that Bridget and Portz were fading," says one Army lieutenant. "Their throats were almost gone from shouting orders; you could hardly hear them. Both had body wounds, and Portz was wounded in the head, too. I had never seen bravery and leadership in my life like that of Bridget when men began dying in the hold. As for Portz, I had come to think of him as I would of my own father."

Beecher, sitting aloft in the referee's chair, had great difficulty es-tablishing quiet and order, even in making himself heard. How could more than 1,300 men be arranged in a single tennis court? It was the problem of the ship holds all over again.

Finally it was managed—the Japanese paid no attention to this, leaving each impossible situation they created to the Americans—that the prisoners would be seated in rows of 52 men. This meant a row of 26 men in each court from the service baseline to where the net ordinarily would be, plus 26 in the same line in the opposite court. They sat as they had in the bays or shelves of the *Oryoku Maru,* with their knees drawn up to their chins. The only possible variant was sitting spread-eagle, with each man's haunches in the fork of his neighbor's legs.

The prisoners had barely got seated when they had reason to jump to their feet. A wave of three American planes came over the court. The prisoners crouched again a moment, not knowing whether they would be strafed. But the first plane's target was the Japanese anti-aircraft gun on a knoll beyond the tennis court. The guns spoke, the plane roared down and silenced the gun, and as it swung up again a tinkle of empty .50-caliber cartridge cases came hurtling down and struck the court's concrete and a few sunburned shoulders. The second plane hit the *Oryoku Maru,* apparently with a bomb, for a flame leaped up, and the third plane dropped another bomb about 1,500 feet off.

The prisoners, standing tiptoe, supporting each other, saw it all. The *Oryoku Maru,* which had lain all day lifeless in the water, negligently smoking, now burst into flames all over. There was no sign of life on her decks. The ammunition began to go off. She burned and burned, and in two hours she sank. (At the time of Japan's surrender she was still lying in the same place off Olongapo, with some fifteen feet of water over the tip of her mast.)

"When we saw those Jap *nipa* huts around their guns go up in smoke we liked it even more than seeing the ship go down," says one Navy man. "We enjoyed the whole scene immensely."

On the 15-foot wide strip of space beyond one baseline the prisoners established their "hospital." Hayes was now exhausted and another doctor, Lieutenant Commander Clyde Welsh of Chicago, took over. His next rank, with a similar name, Lieutenant Commander Cecil Welch of South Dakota, had disappeared, reportedly suffocated aboard the ship. The other doctors on the Navy side of the "hospital" were Lieutenant Bruce Langdon of North Carolina and Lieutenant Arthur Barrett of Louisiana.

The "hospital" consisted of two sheets and a couple of raincoats stretched to give protection from the sun. Otherwise it was no different from the tennis court. The Japanese furnished no medical supplies and naturally the half-clothed Americans had none. The first major operation was the amputation of the arm of a Marine corporal named Specht by Lieutenant Colonel Jack Schwartz, the surgeon of the famous Hospital No. 2 on Bataan, who—with another Army lieutenant colonel, James McG. Sullivan of San Francisco—sustained much of the medical burden all the way to Japan. The arm of the Marine corporal was in a poisoned condition, but the doctors had neither anesthesia nor scalpel. Finally they cauterized a razor blade and Schwartz amputated the arm without anesthesia. (The Marine lived for five days afterward on the exposed tennis court, fighting sturdily for life, but he died when the column moved.)

204 FIRST INTO NAGASAKI

The overpoweringly prevalent disease was diarrhea and dysentery, and there was no drug to check it, nor even food. "The Japs tell us," the officers announced from the referee's chair, "that they have no food or clothing for us. We will have to wait until they send to Manila." The men were now at the stage of nutritional diarrhea when the stomach can hold nothing, even if it is palatable and nutritious. Those who had saved some brown sugar from the wreck found that their bodies could not retain it. There was an unending procession through the court gate to the latrines outside and back again.

There were odd wounds, too. Captain Harold A. Jimerson, a University of Kansas man who was teaching mechanical engineering at the University of Arizona, received a cut from one of the American .50-calibers. Captain William Miner, a midwesterner who had commanded infantry in the Visayan group, got his fingers ripped by an American ricochet.

By now, after a full day's exposure to the sun, the prisoners were in desperate condition from thirst. They could easily have absorbed four or five quarts of water per man. But the Japanese denied them any water other than the faucet. Only an uncertain trickle came from it. They caught the trickle carefully in canteen cups, and served it with spoons. It worked out to four spoonfuls per man, with the single faucet running constantly. Its stream grew thinner and thinner.

Major Reginald H. "Bull" Ridgely, a Marine named for his thunderous voice, began with Beecher to try to take the roll from the referee's platform. It was a long and tedious task, with something particularly aggravating about it to the sunburned, hungry and thirsty men who sat in the court waiting for night to fall. A name would be called. No answer. "Well, anybody know what happened to him?" Half the men were not listening, trying in some makeshift way to better their position. "Well, doesn't anybody know what happened to him?"

A voice would say, "I think he passed out last night. I believe I saw him with the dead on the deck, way down under." As soon as there was a definite assertion, it would give birth to contradictory ones. "The hell you did! He was in the next bay to me. A bomb fragment got him." And from someone else, "How could a bomb have got him when I saw him swimming away from the ship?" At that moment the missing man might walk in from the latrine outside the court. Or the questioning might go for minutes longer, establishing something or establishing nothing.

"Take it easy," came the word from the referee's chair. "Conserve your strength. Don't move around."

As the sun went down the concrete suddenly lost its heat and grew cold. Men whom the sun had skinned red, men who had been putting their hands on their burning shoulders, now were shaken by chills and hugged themselves. Less than a third had shoes; many had only shorts or pants; a few were totally naked. Some of the Formosan sentries had been guards also at Cabanatuan and were known to the prisoners. These "Taiwanis" threw a couple of shirts over the fence, and pushed some casaba melons and a few cigarettes through the wire.

Some men were simply too weak to sit up in the rowers' formation devised to fill the court, and fell over. Some lines therefore devised a method of all 52 lying down together on the right side, intertwined, and then all 52, at the word "Turn over, boys," changing the position to the left. Cold, thirsty, hungry, and frequently brought to their feet by the prevailing disease of diarrhea, few slept.

The morning brought a few warming minutes that were neither chill night nor torrid day. Again there began the tedious calling of the roll, a rite always done centrally from the referee's chair, which took nearly two hours. About six more men had died during the night. A burial detail was named; the bodies were stripped of clothing; they were taken out the gate. Later the Japanese gave permission for them to be buried in an improvised cemetery down by the seawall.

The second day on the tennis court the prisoners received their first meal—two tablespoonfuls of rice, raw. Their standard measure had become the canteen cup for an entire line of 52 men, and the tablespoon for each man.

They asked Mr. Wada why they could not have more food and water. Nearby there was plenty of rice in the JNLP barracks, and water in several buildings. The hunchbacked interpreter would not give them permission to go for the water. As for the rice, he said that he could not get that for jurisdictional reasons. It seemed that while the prisoners were aboard the ship they were in the care of the Japanese Navy. But now that they were ashore again, they were under the Japanese Army. No matter if all 1,300 starved to death, the Navy could not be asked to provide food for Army prisoners.

This explanation seemed to please Mr. Wada; he and Lieutenant Toshino were comfortable and were eating well.

The naked men tried to adapt to the new situation of being fried on concrete by day, frozen by night. Chief Boatswain Jesse Lee, like many others, tore off the bottoms of his trousers to make caps for his friends, giving one leg to Gunner's Mate H. M. Farrell of Houston—who was still to lose an eye before he reached Japan—and the other to a machinist named Judy. They also got permission to move the worst wounded from the surface of the court to some shade trees outside. Lieutenant Commander John Littig, an intelligence officer who was known simply as coming from a socially prominent eastern family, died of wounds and weakness.

The days went by. On the fourth day since leaving Bilibid they got their first food ashore. On the fifth, as though to offbalance such generosity, there was no food morning or noon, and a light supper of two tablespoonsful of raw rice. Eventually some clothing came out from Manila. There was enough to tantalize, not enough to cover. A man without cap, shoes or socks got a pair of straw sandals; his head and legs remained uncovered. A man without shirt, cap or socks got the socks. A totally naked man got a pair of shorts.

The sixth day on the open tennis court, December 21st, a convoy of nineteen trucks arrived and about half the men were loaded aboard. The same convoy appeared the next day. Both convoys took the prisoners to San Fernando, Pampanga, stopping often under trees whenever airplanes were heard. The first convoy unloaded at the prison, which had been filled with Filipinos; the second unloaded at the theater.

The prisoners were in good spirits. They had lost strength but they had gained eight days' delay from the Japanese, and MacArthur was still on the way.

THE prison yard at Pampanga is about 70 feet by 60 feet, and a lemon tree grew in the center. The lemons lasted about fifteen seconds after the first prisoners entered; in five minutes most of the leaves were eaten as well. There were two cell blocks a single story high. The elderly officers and the sick were housed in them. The other prisoners lay down as they had on the tennis court, in the sun. There had once been toilets but they were long since broken. The open culvert six inches deep, which ran around the yard, became the latrine. "The flies," says one officer, "came from all over Luzon."

About 800 were jammed into the prison, and the other 500 into the dilapidated theater. The amputated Marine corporal Specht died almost on arrival in the theater. But still the prisoners' hearts were light. For the first time they had hot food. It was only rice and it was brought in on two big pieces of corrugated iron roofing, but it was hot and filling. And they had water, too, all they could drink. What if they had to fill their canteens at the toilet intakes? It was water, and it brought back life to their beady, shrunken stomachs.

An Army lieutenant colonel, Harry J. Harper, well known at Cabanatuan, died at Pampanga.

On the night of December 23rd four Red Cross boxes came down from Manila. For the needs of 1,300 men the drug quantities were minute, but they gave hope. On the same night several of the most ill were evacuated back to Bilibid.* The handful taken included, as well as survivors can remember, a lieutenant commander known as "Bull of the Woods" Harrington for his heavy voice, and a Marine lieutenant colonel who in Cabanatuan earned the nickname of "Caribou Sam" for his ability at rustling meat under the eyes of the Japanese field guards.

---

* In fact they were taken by a death squad led by Corporal Kazutane to a cemetery, where all were bayoneted and decapitated.

At three in the morning of the day before Christmas, the prisoners were routed out of the prison and theater and marched to the railroad station. An aged locomotive, whose multiple bullet holes testified to what the American planes were doing to Japanese rail traffic, awaited them with an inadequate string of 26-foot freight cars. The wounded were piled on top. The merely ill were packed in below. Curtis, the automobile agent, counted 107 men in and on his car alone. Mr. Wada soon explained why the wounded were placed on top. "If the American planes come," he said, "you must wave to them and show your bandages." The train, thus "protected" by its prisoners, was loaded with ammunition and supplies for two way stations along the line. "Wave white clothing," said Mr. Wada encouragingly, "so that your friends up there will recognize you."

The heat in the closed boxcars was so terrific that conditions soon equalled those aboard the *Oryoku Maru*. Perspiration plastered the rags of the prisoners to their bodies. But outside they could hear the indefatigable Filipino urchins yelling to the wounded on top, "Merry Christmas! Merry Chree-eestmas!"

The rumor spread through the train that they were going to be taken back to Bilibid to be clothed. But in mid-morning an air fight broke out overhead. They watched American planes dive bombing the Manila airfields. The train stopped amid wreckage that was still smoking. "We sweated out being raided again," says Major F. Langwith Berry, who was seated on the top of a boxcar with a fractured arm, "but fortunately the show was over." No man could get down even to relieve himself; the urinal was a canteen cup passed from hand to hand.

As night fell the train was still crawling northward. At three in the morning it reached the town of San Fernando del Union, on Lingayen Gulf. The freight doors grated open and the filthy, cramped men tumbled forth. They sprawled on the station platform, slumped in sleep. It was Christmas morning, 1944.

At daylight the Americans were marched to a single-story trade school on the outskirts of the town. A bush with green leaves and red flowers stood by the gate. They ate the leaves by handfuls. They lay there all day. The menu of their Christmas dinner was one-half cup of rice and one-third canteen cup of dirty surface water. They pulled up grass for beds and the soldiers gave them some disinfectant. At about 7 p.m. they were counted off by sections of 100 men, then marched three miles (nearly all were barefoot) over a coral shell road to a beach overlooking the Japanese anchorage.

Lingayen, being more than a hundred miles north of Manila, was freer from American fighter attacks. The docks were loaded with supplies recently arrived from Japan, and there were several ships winking their lights in the harbor.

The sand was bitter cold. The naked men shivered and pushed against each other for warmth. At least two died, one of them Lieutenant Colonel Edmundson of the Philippine Scouts, who had been suffering from acute diarrhea. A West Pointer, Captain Wilson Farrell of the 31st Infantry, who had organized a "swing shift" of cloth-wavers to get air into the suffocating boxcars, labored hard to encourage the downhearted and keep their heads up. But it was bitterly clear to all that they had been moved once again beyond hope of rescue by MacArthur. They were going to Japan.

The officers of the 200th Coast Artillery, almost all outdoorsmen from New Mexico, got together and began to lay plans for an escape. They would steal a rowboat and make their way up the coast. But Lieutenant Colonel John Luikart of Clovis, who was to die within a week, forbade the plan. He reminded them that on Bataan the Japanese had shot at one time several fellow officers—Major James Hazelwood, Captain Ray Gonzales, Captain Eddie Kemp, Captain Raymond Thwaits—along with Sergeant Barney Prosser and Charleston Miller, a Navajo Indian—simply for deviating from the line of the death march to O'Donnell in order to trade. "You cannot expose the lives of these other prisoners to reprisal," Luikart said.

Again the burning sun came up. Again the skins of the weakened men began to curl with sunburn. Commander Bridget begged and begged the Japanese to give water. A rice ball was issued for each man, but discipline was cracking again. Some got two; some got none. Bridget and Beecher then secured permission from the Japanese—Major John Pyzig of the Marines shared interpreting duties with Engelhart—for the men to enter the water and bathe their blisters.

They were allowed five minutes in the water, barely enough time to splash themselves. Many were so dehydrated that they scooped the salt water into their mouths. When they came out Bridget renewed his pleading for drinking water. An Army captain of engineers from Hope, Arkansas, lost his head, leaped up, and dashed into the water, drinking like mad. The Japanese raised their guns to fire, but he was pulled out in time. Finally the Japanese issued water: one canteen cup for twenty men. It worked out to four tablespoonsful for each thirsty mouth. But there was a rotation. After ninety minutes more in the sun you could have another four tablespoonsful.

Lieutenant Toshino and Mr. Wada had seen how the American planes spared the prisoners on the tennis court and atop the train. Here at Lingayen they put this immunity to use. "We want you to be warned," said Mr. Wada. "You are sitting on a gasoline dump. If we are bombed—well. . . ."

All that day they did not believe him. But toward nightfall a detachment of soldiers drove up, unlimbered shovels, and began to dig. Mr. Wada, for once, had been telling the truth. Drum after drum of gasoline was uncovered directly under them, loaded and driven away. "You see?" said Mr. Wada. "We lose our gas, then you lose something else—eh?"

Again they lay down on the cold sand, shivering, thinking of Christmas at home; too hungry, thirsty and cold to sleep. Somewhere between midnight and dawn Mr. Wada again stirred up the sentries, who ordered the Americans on their feet. They marched along the waterfront to a dock loaded with Japanese supplies. It was still dark and the guards could not watch all 1,300 men as they moved between high piles of boxes. Hungry, the prisoners plundered some of the boxes. They found some aerial film, pulled it out and exposed it. The New Mexican artillery officers found bran and a little dried fish, which they parceled out among those who had shirts to conceal it.

The Japanese were suddenly in fearful haste. Lieutenant Toshino would scold Mr. Wada in Japanese, and the hunchback would say, "Get in the barge, quickly, quickly! You must hurry, hurry!" Some prisoners were literally pushed off the dock and fell in the barge's bottom. "Speedo!" shouted the guards. "Speedo, speedo!" With rifle butts and the flats of their swords they pushed back the fallen in the barge. "Back, back! Speedo, speedo!"

The sun was just coming up as the prisoners climbed on sunburned feet the iron side-ladder of their new vessel, whose propellers were already impatiently turning over. All this haste was for a good reason. Ordinarily, in wars hitherto, ships have considered themselves in danger from air or submarine attack only by day. If armed, they have felt themselves fairly safe against submarines except at the weak visibility hours of sunrise and sunset, when the low profile of a submarine gives it an advantage.

The American submarines, however, became specialists in night attacks. Thus the Japanese shipping controls were always in a dilemma: whether to face the subs by night or the bombers by day. Where they were within range of both, as at Manila, there was simply no answer but to take advantage of any bad weather and hope for stormy cover, which makes either torpedo or bomb sighting difficult. At Lingayen, however, more than a hundred miles to the north, they were out of range of scourging air attacks by day—though a long-range raid was always possible. And if ships sailed by day and lay up by night, they had at least a fighting chance to beat the American submarines, whose deadliest strikes were made by darkness. . . . The Japanese wanted to get out at dawn and widen the aircraft range as much as possible the first day, thus halving their possible antagonists.

Two freighters were leaving, a big one of about 8,000 tons marked *No. 2* on its superstructure, and another of about 5,500 tons marked *No. 1* on its funnel.* The first bargefuls of men were crowded aboard the *No. 2* in the midships hold, which had two levels. But as the nervous captain watched the rapidly rising sun, he lost patience with the slow crawl of tired prisoners up his ladder. Once the thousand-man mark was reached, he lifted anchor and the last batch climbed up while the freighter moved down the harbor.

---

* *No. 1* was really the *Brazil Maru; No. 2* was the *Enoura Maru.*

The remainder, some 234 men and a few Japanese wounded and sick, were hustled aboard *No. 1.* On the morning of the 27th both vessels set forth along the coast of northern Luzon. That same evening a submarine fired two torpedoes at *No. 2.* Both missed, and exploded on the Luzon shore.

The last cargo which *No. 2* had carried was horses. "The hold where we were," says a prisoner, "was like a floating barn, full of horse manure and the biggest, hungriest horse flies I ever saw. They immediately set to work biting our backs and legs. Then more flies came and covered our mouths, ears and eyes. We smelled already, and our smell drew them."

It was the Japanese practice to save the horses' urine for some chemical use, bringing it back to Japan in the bilges of the ship. "An overpowering smell like ammonia came up from the bilges," one man recalled. There was a ventilating system installed to keep the horses alive, but with Americans in the hold the Japanese shut it off.

The prisoners placed their wounded on the upper of the two decks in the hold, where the odor was less. The two Army doctors, Lieutenant Colonels North and Schwartz, were in charge of this sick level. In delirium several men fell or rolled off into the lower level that night. Below, in the fetor of the hold, Commander Bridget, almost indistinguishably hoarse now, was in charge. Beecher handled negotiations with Lieutenant Toshino and Mr. Wada.

The pit on *No. 2* was about 60 feet square, with bays 10 feet deep on two sides and bays about 4 feet deep on the other two sides. The horses had left scattered feed in the crevices of these stalls. The prisoners scraped up the remnants and ate them, mixed with the bran stolen on the dock.

The Japanese crew of this vessel seemed willing to give the prisoners rice and water. But Mr. Wada and Lieutenant Toshino and the Formosan guards were afraid to let the prisoners on deck. Lieutenant Colonel Kenneth "Swede" Olson, a regular Army finance officer who had been camp commandant at Mindanao, climbed up boldly and faced the hunchback. "These men are hungry and thirsty, Mr. Wada," he said. "They are dying. Sick men won't be any good to you. Dead men won't help you. Give us a chance. We're not afraid to work for our lives. All we want is a chance."

Finally Toshino and Wada relented. They allowed the crew to send down food, and eventually allowed the prisoners to send six-man chow details on deck to the galley. The prisoners each had rice and a quarter canteen cupful of hot soup. But the Japanese would not allow them to keep the rice buckets long enough to pass around; they had to send them up again immediately. So they dumped out the rice on dirty raincoats and on the manure-scattered pit. "The lineup was something to see," says one prisoner. "We were barefooted, bearded, dirty and full of diarrhea. We ate from our hats, from pieces of cloth, from our hands. You would see an officer who once commanded a battalion with a handful of rice clutched against his sweaty, naked chest so the flies could not get it, eating it like an animal with his befouled hands."

Again death was moving quietly among them. Of dehydration or diarrhea, or old wounds, a man died almost every hour. From the Japanese galley they procured rice sacks for shrouds. When a man died his body was stripped of useable clothing, bundled in a sack, and hoisted out. Tying up the bodies was the job of boatswains like Jesse Lee and corpsmen like Patrick C. Hilton of Pratt, West Virginia: "The trouble was that the second day we ran out of sacks. I would tie a running bowline around the feet of the corpse and a half hitch around his hand, then say, 'All right, take him away'. He would rise up out of the hold, and his friends could see him for the last time against the sky, swinging back and forth against the side of the hatch as he went out of sight."

Most of the chaplains were by this time beyond doing any duties, but a Catholic Army lieutenant, Father William "Bill" Cummings of San Francisco and Ossining, New York, who in a sermon on Bataan had first uttered the phrase "There are no atheists in foxholes", often managed to say a few words of blessing as the body rose through the hatch. A Navy chief carpenter named O'Brien, for example, stricken on the beach with nutritional diarrhea which not even food could check, passed his final moments and was eased by

Cummings. An Air Force sergeant named Brown, however, who jumped overboard off northern Luzon at night, was followed only by the scattered shots of the Taiwani guards.

Captain John Presnell, a graduate of the University of Maine, tried to climb the iron ladder to the deck, and was shot dead by the guards.

As the ships drew away from the Luzon coast it began to grow cold. The men who had broiled now shivered both night and day. As their losses increased the Japanese made a rule that bodies could no longer be hoisted out of the hold immediately after death. They had to lie out on the bottom of the hold in full sight of Lieutenant Toshino or Mr. Wada when they glanced into the pit. Once there were six or eight bodies, Wada would give permission for a general hoisting of corpses. The horse troughs around the hold were now latrines. "You could watch a single fly go from the latrines to the bodies, and then from the bodies to your rice," says a prisoner. Captain Jack Clark, a Marine, kept the death roll for Beecher.

The 234 men on *No. 1* were in a way worse off than those on *No. 2* because they were committed into the hands of their frightened Formosan guards. For the first two days they got nothing at all, except that the guards diverted themselves by dropping cigarettes through the hatch to watch the Americans scramble. Lieutenant Colonel "Johnny" Johnson, one of the few hardworking officers who came through, took firm hold and saw that every scrap of food on hand was rationed. Their first food was the leavings from the guards, and a Japanese guard does not leave very much. It amounted to a teaspoon of rice per man.

Johnson took a teaspoonful to the commander of the guard. He said, "If we must go on like this, my men will all die." The commander replied, "We want you to die. Your submarines are sinking our ships. We want you to die."

The Japanese crewmen sold a cheap rock candy to the prisoners for rings and fountain pens.

All sense of disorder and fight was now gone from the men. Johnson had set them off in groups of twenty, by areas. Bearded, dirty, shoeless and sunburned, they lay in their areas, awaiting death in the throbbing hold.

No. 2, though the newer and larger ship, broke its steering gear two days from the Philippines and had to be towed most of the rest of the way. The convoy reached the harbor of Takau, in Formosa, on New Year's Day, 1945. In celebration of safe arrival the prisoners aboard *No. 1* received five pieces of hardtack each, their New Year's feast. About a dozen men had died on *No. 1* and somewhat more on *No. 2.* Older men like P. D. Rogers, once General Pershing's secretary and later Governor of Jolo, passed away of general weakness, while young men like Captain Alfonso Melandez and Captain James Sadler, both of Santa Fe, died of dysentery and exhaustion. Major Reginald Ridgely, Jr., Beecher's Marine mess officer, kept up a ceaseless chant of "Take it easy, boys, at ease, now" in his deep voice.

After three or four days in Takau harbor, the Japanese decided to put the two parties together again aboard *No. 2.* The smaller party spent a day and night, in between, aboard a still smaller freighter with a bad list, apparently from bombing. After twenty-four hours without food or water they were moved on January 4th to *No. 2* and jammed down into the midships hold already occupied by about 1,000 men. The next day the Japanese decided to open a forward hold, where about 450 men under Captain Arthur Wermuth of Chicago, the "one-man army", were transferred.

The prisoners knew that they were now within range of more bombers: the U.S. Air Force in China. Their alarm was increased when a light warship approached and tied itself to *No. 2,* making an inviting double target.

The *No. 2* had already taken aboard two hundred sacks of sugar, which were placed in the lower part of the crowded hold amidships. The prisoners sensed that the moment of departure for Japan was at hand. The 37 British prisoners, with them since Manila, were ordered ashore to join their compatriots in Formosa's camps.

About eight on the morning of January 6th there was a sudden crackle of anti-aircraft fire. Practice or real? Under the closed hatches the prisoners could not tell. Then bombs began to fall. The first hit the side close by the forward hold, and the ship rolled with the blow. The others—two or perhaps three—hit close inboard.

The first American bomb not only tore at the side of the ship; it ripped holes in the partition between the two holds. "We looked through the holes," says Theodore Lewin, a big broken-nosed soldier of fortune who had been a reporter in Los Angeles on the *Huntington Park Record* and proprietor of an offshore gambling ship. "We could see bodies in the forward hold, all stirred up and scrambled. Almost nobody was even moving. In our own hold the whole place was covered with bodies. Then from the forward hold Captain Wermuth yelled up, 'I'm taking charge here. Get us some stuff for the wounded, quick!' "

The wild cascade of hatch planks had felled Major Malevic of the Fourteenth Engineers, but he was still alive. Three Army lieutenant colonels were lying in a row, Peter Kemp, Jack Schwartz and Bill Manning. The outer two had been killed by head blows; Schwartz was untouched. The gallant Marine, Major Andrew Mathiesen, who had helped so many, was knocked from the upper level to the bottom by a hatch plank and later died of shock and internal injuries. Even after the mortal blow he pulled himself up, worked and gave orders normally, but finally collapsed.

"We're going to need the last clothing you have for bandages, boys," announced Lieutenant Colonel James McG. Sullivan, a medico. "Tear off your pant legs and shirts. If you're cold, get a sugar sack. We've got to save these men."

The appearance of the wounded in the middle hold was peculiarly unbearable. The fumes coming from the bilges had made a yellowish combination that the engineers said was ammonium picrate gas. In the pit, the men's hair had turned an unearthly yellow blond color.

"A Navy doctor only a foot away from me," says Lieutenant Russell Hutchison of Albuquerque, who had built a tiny radio in Davao to time MacArthur's coming, "lost his eye right out of his head. I was eating a mess kit of rice at the time. On my left a man had the back of his head blown clean off. There were dark flecks in my rice that had not been there before. I only hesitated a moment, then I ate the rice."

In this hold amidships, from which come the only coherent accounts of what happened, about 40 were killed and about 200 wounded. In the forward hold, which resembled a human butcher shop, over half the prisoners, more than 200, were dead, and many of the rest gravely wounded.

The Japanese were now in a civilized harbor, with doctors, hospitals, barges, and all other medical services at their disposal. Did they move to help? They did not. The first day nothing whatever was done. The unwounded in the middle hold, where some doctors were still alive, were not even allowed to go above and then descend into the chaos of the forward hold to help. So the first night passed, with the bodies stiffening where they lay.

The second day a small detachment of Japanese Red Cross corpsmen arrived at the ship. They did not even attempt to enter the forward hold. They handed out some medicines in the midships hold, and went away.

By now the living men in both holds were pleading with Lieutenant Toshino and Mr. Wada for permission to lift out their dead. The bodies were swollen and bloated; the stench was beyond breathing. But the Japanese would not allow them to move the bodies. Still another night they spent with their mangled dead and their unrelieved wounded. On the morning of the 8th, two full days later, Toshino and Wada for the first time agreed to have the bodies removed.

Purely as physical labor, it was a task almost beyond the strength of the survivors. To move 300 living men, heavy and helpless, would have been a full job for a large hospital corps with stretchers, slings, and aidemen husky and strong. These men had lost as much as forty pounds each; they had not had a true meal in many months; they were battle-shocked; they had no apparatus; and the dead bodies they had to move were those of their comrades of nearly three years' imprisonment.

And yet they had not wholly lost the American's last resource: his humor. As they stripped the bodies of clothing, as they tugged them and stacked them, they laughed at what had happened to a rice-and-latrine detail that was on deck when the bombs struck. Their guard, a Formosan named Ah Kong, hardly heard the whistle of bombs when he dropped his rifle and took to his heels. He ran into a passageway and huddled there. The Americans were scared of the bombs, but more scared that the other jittery guards, seeing them without Ah Kong, would shoot them down. So they picked up Ah Kong's rifle and poured pell-mell after him into the passageway, where they returned their panting sentry his weapon, pointing it back as usual at themselves.

"We'll never forget," said one member of this detail, "when Ah Kong allowed us to walk forward and peer down for a moment through the twisted hatchway of the forward hold. We could see Wermuth standing there, looking around trying to get his bearings. There seemed at least 300 dead around him and about 100 wounded. About 50 men who were whole were still walking around, dazed."

Beecher took charge in the hold amidships, Wermuth forward. Captain Jack Clark of the Marines, who had kept the list of the dead in the tennis court, was now dead himself, as was also Captain Lee Clark, another Marine. A sergeant of the Fourth Shanghai Marines named Staley had been killed between two petty officers of Ah Kong's trusties.

Even the Japanese saw that *No. 2* was so hopelessly perforated that she could never make Japan. Light peeked through all her bulkheads. The prison ships had left a long trail of American bodies committed to the sea, but a mass burial could not be carried out in Takau harbor. A barge appeared alongside. The dead were going ashore in Formosa.

Out of the middle hold the dead could be hauled individually, stripped and tied to ropes. For the forward hold it was necessary to rig a broad wire cargo net, on the end of a boom and tackle. Here Wermuth, with the help of corpsmen like Hilton, hauled the bodies like fagots and had them swung away through the hatch by the dozens, hugged within the wire net as if they were bunches of asparagus.

Before a load was lifted, if there was a body in it who had not yet been identified, the question would be asked: "Anybody alive from this man's bay?" (Silence.) "Anybody know which bay this man comes from?" (Silence.) Some men were unrecognizable even to those who had lived with them.

For the ugly job of loading the dead there was little rivalry. The survivors were weak and extremely thirsty. Though the horses in the same cargo hold had presumably drunk gallons of water, and though the boat was in harbor, the Japanese kept saying, "No water—we have no water." The wounds were kept from healing and further sapped by abnormal loss of water as well as blood. Then came the command: "We need thirty men to go ashore for burial duty with these bodies. Who volunteers?" Almost every man who could totter to his feet volunteered. His offer was not without self-interest. He hoped that for once, if he went ashore, he could fill up his body with water and renew his thinning blood.

"I wanted to go ashore and try for some water with all my heart," says one officer. "But I could not move. So I just lay on my back and watched that wire cargo net—it was about twenty feet square when laid out, I guess—going down into the hold empty, being loaded, and then ascending, shutting out the light with naked bodies before it swung away out of my sight."

At length the barge, overloaded, moved toward shore. Among the ten officers who went were Lieutenant H. B. Wright of the Air Corps, Lieutenant Keene of the Cavite 6th Marines—a South Carolinian—and Major John Fowler, 26th Cavalry. They reached a breakwater, tied up, but found that they were too weak to carry the bodies ashore one by one. They attached ropes to the naked feet, dragged them to the point where the breakwater met the sand, and laid them out in rows. It was a coal dumping yard, and there were black mountains of bituminous coal, thousand of tons, nearby. They left the bodies on the beach that first night, beside the coal.

The second day they again loaded the barge with bodies and brought them ashore, placing them beside their predecessors. Each night the burial party drew up and gave a military salute before returning to the ship. The third day they took all the bodies back to a Japanese crematorium near a shrine, and rendered them into ashes.

By now an evening prayer had become a part of their simple routine. Of the estimated sixteen chaplains in the party, both Protestant and Catholic, only three were to live to Japan. The strongest seemed to be the Army priest, Cummings. One Navy man says, "I shall never forget the prayer that Father asked the first night after the bombing, when the Japs would not let us move the bodies. He had often said prayers before that, at other times. But a lot of men paid no attention, then. They kept on babbling or arguing or cursing. This night, the minute he stood up there was absolute silence. I guess it was the first real and complete silence there had been since we left Bilibid. Even the deranged fellows were quiet. And I remember what his opening words were. He said, 'O God—O God, please grant that tomorrow we will be spared from being bombed.' There was just something about the way he said those words that brought the men around. Then he prayed. He somehow managed to say everything that was in our hearts—what we had left as hearts after squabbling with each other. The last thing he did was to lead us in the Lord's Prayer. I think every man there, even the unbalanced ones, managed to repeat at least some of the words after him."

The prisoners kept alive partly by trading with the Japanese and partly by stealing sugar from the bottom of the midships hold. The Japanese set every kind of guard, but the prisoners always managed to trick them. The sugar was a two-edged prize. "It saved a lot of men's lives as food, but it killed more than it saved." It was coarse and brown. If more than a tablespoonful a day was eaten, it caused severe diarrhea, and brought death. Few men had the self-control to hold down their consumption.

The sugar led to a double drama. Beecher had warned the men: "Don't eat sugar under the hatch where the guard can see you. Crawl into a corner." The practice was for two men to eat alternately, one standing guard for the other. In the same way, when the sugar was stolen from below, an officer stood at the hatch where he could signal down into the sugar hold. Marine Lieutenant Keene frequently acted as lookout.

Two of the ablest sugar thieves were a lieutenant in the geodetic survey of the Coast Guard who teamed up with a Catholic Navy chaplain, Lieutenant McManus. They stole many mess kits of sugar before they were caught at last. The Formosans brought them on deck; first they slapped them, then knocked them down with rifles, and finally kicked them systematically. The Coast Guard lieutenant, seeing the chaplain was going under fast, protested that he alone was responsible. The Japanese then released McManus and concentrated on the lieutenant. They said that they were going to shoot him. But after an hour's beating they pushed him back through the hatch.

However, the sugar thefts went on. Each morning when the Japanese sentries descended, another sack of sugar would be missing. But no Formosan sentry could be found who was willing to spend the night in the putrid hold under the prisoners. Finally Lieutenant Toshino and Mr. Wada came to the edge of the hatch and looked down into the pit. "Who has stolen the sugar?" demanded Mr. Wada. No answer. Mr. Wada had a consultation with the spectacled lieutenant, then made a stiff announcement. "Unless the thieves give themselves up immediately, we will cut off all rice and all water from both holds."

The silver-haired Beecher called a general meeting. He said, "This isn't a question of finding who has been taking the sugar. It's a matter of saving the lives of men who will die unless they have rice and at least a little water. We've got to have two men who are willing to go up and offer themselves as hostages for all the others. I don't have any idea what Toshino and Wada will order done to those two men. They may have them shot. I just don't know. The only thing I can promise them is this: if they survive whatever the Japs do to them, I will see to it that they are taken care of and don't go without food the rest of the trip."

There was an English sergeant aboard named Trapp, husky and of medium height, who had not gone ashore when the 37 Britons were taken over the side to the Formosan camp. Trapp had known several of the 4th Marines during his duty in China, and he had made new friends on the road from Bilibid. And there was a husky medical aideman, an Ohioan, Sergeant Arda M. "Max" Hanendrat of the 31st Infantry, who had qualified for honors on Bataan by carrying a wounded man on his back for thirteen miles. Trapp and Hanendrat volunteered.

Everyone waited, penned below, listening for such volleys as had already killed several prisoners. None came.

The Japanese psychology is peculiar. Whereas the caught thief may lightly be killed, the uncaught one who confesses his crime may in some cases escape with his life. When corpsman Patrick Hilton was allowed to go up the ladder to empty a *benjo,* he saw the two men, marked with blows and faint, kneeling between guards. Every time one reeled and fell over, the Japanese would slap him to consciousness again. But they still lived.

Eventually the two sergeants were pushed back into the hold. They lived to clamber aboard the boat that took them to Japan. But, great-hearted men that they were, in the end both died.

No. 2, it was clear, could not reach Japan in her present perforated condition, and the Japanese were stubbornly persistent that to Japan the prisoners must go. The morning of January 13th, two weeks after the arrival in Takau and a week after the American bombing that had cost approximately 350 American lives, Toshino ordered the remaining men to move to another ship that lay a few hundred yards off.

Between 800 and 900 men were now alive of the 1,600 plus who had marched out of Bilibid precisely a month before. Many of them, however, wounded and untended, were at the very gate of death. To move them was to doom them. But the Japanese wanted them moved, and not slowly, but as fast as possible. Once again the sentries' cry was "Speedo, speedo!" A barge was brought alongside, like the barge that had taken the 350 to the beach and the crematorium. "Speedo, speedo!"

There were intestinal hemorrhages, extreme shocks, amputations: how could such men be moved? Corpsmen like Hilton figured out a bosun's chair to get them out of the hold. He put a Spanish bowline around each leg and a square knot around the waist to steady the torso, and up went the groaning man, hauled by sixteen of the pairs of hands still able to tug. When it came to moving the men who could not be held upright, the corpsmen took a hatch plank, tied the wounded man to the plank, fixed a scaffold knot around each end, and slowly tugged him through the hatch.

"In a way this was the most terrible job of all," says one officer. "For the first time we had to cause pain to ourselves, and we could not avoid it. What I remember most clearly was the smile on Mr. Wada's face as he watched us." A Navy pharmacist named Hogan died the moment he touched *No. 2*'s own deck.

When the barge reached the new ship, another obstacle awaited the wounded. On the side where the accommodation ladder had been lowered there were already a couple of barges tied up, whose decks had to be circumnavigated with each wounded man before the ladder was reached.

The ups and downs of this slow trip brought many of the worst wounded into coma. "I'll never forget," says one officer, "seeing Captain Walter Donaldson, a 200th Coast Artillery officer from Deming, New Mexico. He could not walk, but he could crawl, and he crawled the whole way. He had two sprained wrists and two fractured ankles, but he could still creep on his elbows and knees. He crawled all the way around the barges, up the ladder and onto the deck."

Approximately fourteen men who reached the new ship never saw its hold. They passed away on its decks immediately. But they were not taken ashore to be cremated; they waited, like the others, to make at least a start on the journey toward Japan. Dead in port, they were to be buried at sea.

On the new ship, an undersized freighter, the shrinking party was again forced all into a single hold, the next to the last one aft. The bays here were divided stanchion by stanchion and about 15 feet long by about 10 feet deep. Each bay accommodated around twenty men, counted off by Lieutenant Colonel Johnson. Two positions were possible: to sit with legs extended, or to lie down with knees drawn up. Standing, or lying down at full length, was impossible. Rapidly though the party diminished, the Japanese always managed to see that the men's pits were too small for their numbers.

After sundown on January 13th, the ship weighed anchor and slipped out of Takau. But her course did not turn toward Japan, but to China.

By now it was apparent that only the strongest would endure and live. The little food was rationed carefully, but not equally. The medical corpsmen, who were doing most of the physical work, did more and got more, by common consent. And the details which carried the slop buckets on the decks had opportunities for trading not given to those lying below decks.

The death rate took a wild jump upward. George Curtis says: "I counted 47 dead in all on the first day out." By now the Japanese also were calling the roll, standing like little gods at the edge of the hatch against the skyline for as long as two hours at a time and monotonously droning forth the names of the Americans. When one did not answer, they did not ask any questions; Mr. Wada simply drew a line through his name. Less and less was seen of Lieutenant Toshino. He may have been slightly apprehensive that his superiors would not be fully happy over his stewardship. After all, though, over half the Americans were still alive.

It immediately grew colder. A few straw mats were in the hold, but only enough for about a third of the men. Friends tried to huddle together under a single dry mat, while the cold wind swept under them. From the first day a bitter draft began to suck through the hold. It came from the ventilator in the Japanese quarters just astern, sucked through the stern bays on the starboard side of the prisoners' pit, swept across the opening in the middle and up through the hatch. On this wind of death the lives of many Americans rode their way out.

More than once Beecher pleaded with the Japanese to allow the prisoners to stuff one of their straw mats in the ventilator. The Japanese always refused. And so the wind of death brought pneumonia, a new visitor.

The hatch in the center of the hold, covered with tarpaulin, led to the deck below and was never opened. It lay there, bare to the sky, with the cold draft sweeping and swirling over it. The rain and later the snow and hail fell through it, fell on the bodies of those who lay exposed on the hatch.

The hatch was the center of all their life, and since their life pointed always toward death, it was natural that the dead should be piled there. Things were reversed from the other ships, where to be under the hatch was a favored position. Here, if you moved to the hatch or were moved there by the corpsmen, it was the equivalent of euthanasia or mercy death. It meant that you were so far gone that the food of those who might still be able to live could no longer be spared for you. It placed you neighbor to the dead whom you would soon join.

The dying on the hatch were also looked on covetously by the shivering men in the bays who were already mentally dividing up their clothes. A medical committee for clothing—itself grotesquely naked, a kind of skinny parody of such social committees at home—was supposed to handle the equitable division of clothes. But men died at night, and the committee members could not always get to their feet, and there was connivance. The ladder guard—the man who had been placed to keep the demented from climbing the ladder and being shot by the sentries—might look away. When he looked back, a man not yet quite dead would have lost his shirt, and no questions asked.

A few life-preservers, the kapok-stuffed vest kind, torn and dirty, overlooked by the Japanese in their final search of the hold, lay in the far corners of the bays. Immediately the prisoners tore these open and pulled out the wadding. They parceled out the kapok. The few rolls of it were stuffed into the few pants that still had full legs and the few shirts that still had arms. "The luckiest ones walked around looking like fat teddy bears," says one survivor. "But they never stopped scratching. The kapok was a hive of lice, and the lice never gave them any peace to enjoy their warmth."

It was unmistakable from the beginning that the Japanese had not lost their intention of killing their prisoners by thirst. Here was a freighter fresh from the principal harbor of Formosa, whose water tanks should have been filled to the brim. Of rice the prisoners

received a one-half canteen cupful daily, but of water they received
less than they would have if cast away in an open lifeboat. The ration was 2 to 4 spoonfuls daily.

"If you forgave the Japanese everything else," says one survivor,
"I cannot see how you could forgive the way they denied us water all
the way from Manila to Japan. Some starved, some were suffocated,
some were shot by guards, some died of sunstroke, some died of cold;
all things that were deliberately caused and avoidable. But everybody was thirsty, and everybody was kept thirsty all the time."

They soon found that they were in a submarine zone. Three days
from Takau they picked up a crippled, torpedoed ship and towed it
for a day. Their steerage way was barely five knots. Then the prison
ship was ordered to turn back for another distressed ship. They
towed that one for two days. Then they began to approach the islands off the China coast. "We passed unholy looking little islands,
ugly and completely bare," recalled one man. "The water around
them was a nasty yellow. I supposed we were at the mouth of the
Yangtze or the Whangpoo. But if you'd been on deck and seen the
water, there was something you dreaded almost more than dying:
the idea of being slipped over the side and descending into that yellow Chinese sea-mud."

The Japanese had no water to give, but they had plenty to sell. At
the rear of the two passageways between the bays there were two
open gratings, through one of which swept the so-called "wind of
death". These gratings were the trading center. By now the Americans had little left to offer. The keepsakes a man parts with last
began to go.

The Japanese liked American wedding rings, the solid gold kind.
For a thick, heavy one a Japanese would bring you five canteens full
of water. Annapolis and West Point rings, the most valued possession of the professional officer, were always bad seconds to wedding
rings. They never brought more than four cigarettes, and an early
glut brought them down as low as two. For a pair of shoes you could
get two cans of tomatoes or salmon, or a handful of tangerines. For a
heavy Navajo turquoise ring, Lieutenant Russell Hutchison gained
two straw mats, enough to save his life and that of another officer.

A wristwatch—rare indeed—would get you an old rice sack. Captain William Miner saved his life and that of Major F. Langwith Berry by trading a fountain pen for a straw mat. "We considered that a tremendous bargain," says Berry.

The clothing issued on the Olongapo tennis court had been *skoshi*—insignificant in amount—but the cold Manchurian winds blowing out of the Yellow Sea did not induce the Japanese to issue any more. The prisoners lay huddled as far back in the bays as possible, staccato coughs coming from their parched throats. The icy wind seethed and sang through the cracked partitions and swept the bare passageways. Once Lieutenant Colonel Johnson said to a Japanese officer who knew a little English, "Listen, if our men don't have at least some more water, they will die—*die,* I tell you!" The Japanese looked him over calmly and said, "Everybody *potai* (dead)—okay, okay."

As the freighter wound her way through the desolate islands off the Chinese rivers, hiding by night against prowling submarines and proceeding by day, the prisoners began to die at the rate of twenty or more daily. A man whose husky constitution made him a body collector says, "Every morning was the same. The ladder guard would waken me and say that it was time to get busy. I would take a small handful of sugar and swallow it for breakfast before I touched the bodies. Then I would slowly make the circle of the bays. I didn't make any pretense of being dignified or tender. I would just stop at the bay and put my head in and say, 'Got any stiffs in there?' They might say, 'Yes, we've got a big one this morning.' 'Well,' I'd say, 'get him out to the edge here. I haven't got all day.' Sometimes they would help me, but sometimes they would just say, 'Come on in and get him yourself.' That would make me sore. I would dive right in there and knock them over until I got what I was after. I'd haul him out. Nine times out of ten he'd be stripped naked already and there'd be nothing for the clothing committee. It must sound callous to say so, but death meant nothing to us. If you made it, you made it; if not, you died. That was all there was to it."

The bodies were hauled up, feet first, with a rope around their ankles. Then every prisoner listened for the succession of scooting whishes as each comrade was slipped over the side. The Japanese kept the hatches closed, and shoved over the bodies themselves.

The fifth day out of Takau, Commander Maurice Joses—the regular Navy doctor in nominal command of the entire party but who had been failing ever since the Subic Bay bombing—called to his side Boatswain Clarence Taylor. Joses had been placed in an upper bay in the hospital zone and Taylor, who had worked with him at Bilibid, got in the next bay to be sort of nearby.

Joses was suffering from extreme diarrhea or dysentery. Even for its own commanding officer, the party could do nothing; the last of the hoarded handful of sulfaguanadine tablets from the Red Cross at San Fernando, Pampanga, had been finished days ago. "I'd like to talk to you a little, Ty," said Joses. "I don't think I'll be able to make it through the night." Taylor gave him the usual reassuring encouragement. But the doctor was right. When first light came through the hatch, their commander was gone.

Even in this filth, thirst and starvation, however, decency would send up occasional timid shoots. The Shirk brothers, Robert and Jack, had been mining engineers in Manila when the Army crooked its finger and gave them commissions. Jack fell sick first, grew worse, and finally the corpsmen saw that he would not live. They removed him from the sick bay and laid him out on the hatch, where he soon expired. Having stripped his body, they were about to tug it roughly from the dying to the dead side of the hatch, when a corpsman looked up and whispered: "Hey, handle this one with a little extra care. His brother is watching us from that upper bay." When they had laid Jack Shirk with the others, Bob Shirk climbed painfully out of his bay. He went and stood a little while looking at his brother, his matted head bowed. Perhaps he prayed. At length he shook his head slowly and went back to his own bay, where he too died.

Captain John G. Hudgins, an Army dental officer, had received at Takau four shrapnel wounds in the back and three in the legs, each the size of a silver dollar. His friend the corpsman Pat Hilton struck up an attachment with the Japanese cook, who occasionally gave him scraps of food. Hudgins' unattended wounds were weeping constantly, causing him to dehydrate rapidly. Hilton would bring him the food scraps which the dentist would trade for water. The pit's market rate was six tablespoons of water for one ration of rice. In this way Hudgins would build up as much as a quarter canteen cup of water in reserve. Then the corpsman would come around an hour later and find the canteen cup empty. "What became of your water, doc?" The dentist would look contrite. "Pat, I'm sorry, I simply had to drink it."

Hudgins had a second friend in another dentist, Major Arthur Irons; over and over he repeated to Irons and Hilton, "I firmly believe that when I leave this place I shall go to a better world." On Christmas afternoon on the Lingayen beach Hudgins and Hilton had agreed that their chances were getting thinner and each pledged to inform the other's family if one came through. A night came when the dentist passed away. Irons and Hilton stood over Hudgins—clad still in his Philippine army trousers and shirt, barefooted—and Irons said: "This man will be a bond between us."

When snow fell, the prisoners caught what they could in their unwashed mess kits, waving them back and forth like magic swords under the hatchway to entrap individual snowflakes. So as not to miss any flakes, they sometimes had to pull the dying out of the way. They licked cloth that had been wetted by rain or snow. The half-naked, barefooted men would pretend to have to go on deck to empty a toilet *benjo*. On the way back to the hatch they would furtively reach down and scoop a handful of snow from the deck and stuff it into their mouths. Of course, only one man in a hundred could get water this way, because more than six were rarely allowed on deck at a time.

What saved a few lives was a steam winch which stood on the deck near the hatch. The winch had a small petcock which dripped. For an adroit man, it was possible to pretend to be relieving himself over the side, and at the same time to catch three or four droplets, or even as much as a spoonful, in his extended hand. "One day," says Major Berry, "I got pretty near a canteenful out of that winch. I kept going up the ladder and approaching the sentry with my hands on my stomach, saying '*toxan bioki*', which means 'very sick'. When he allowed me to go to the side, I would maneuver so that the winch was between us, open my flask and hang it under the steam petcock. Then I would make sick noises until the guard began to act restless. I'd go down again and come back in a half-hour. I worked this ten or twelve times."

Men who had dysentery were placed on the hatch earlier than others. The weakened corpsmen grew weary of circulating to all the bays with the *benjo* buckets and were forced to centralize matters on the hatch, windy and exposed though it was. The corpsmen who worked all night were perhaps the most unqualifiedly admired of the hardworking medicos. "You not only had to hustle those buckets for the men on the hatch," says pharmacist Frank Maxwell of Birmingham, "but you also had to stop fights in the bays for the clothing of others who had gone." Deas Coburn of Charleston, John Istock of Pittsburgh, and Estel Myers of Louisville worked hard at saving lives, as did a husky New Mexican, Oscar Otero of Los Lunas. "The noise and nervous tension at night," says Myers, "were such that you could never lie down and rest. You tried to nap by day, when some patients could take care of themselves." The sergeant major, James J. Jordan, at fifty-three as tough as a bantam after thirty-three years in the rough world of the Marine Corps, says, "For the first time in my life, I was beyond knowing or caring what happened."

The hatch, lying barely eight feet below the wind-swept deck, became known as "the zero ward". When a man knew that his strength was ebbing, he would say quite openly, "Well, boys, I've had enough. I'm going out onto the zero ward tonight." Almost all who lay there ended in the sea, but Gene Ortega of Albuquerque slept there through all the voyage and is alive today.

Mr. Wada was fairly often seen, but Lieutenant Toshino came to the top of the hatch hardly at all. "I saw Toshino only twice in the whole voyage," says one prisoner. Once the Americans began calling for him, Mr. Wada came to the edge of the pit. "If you do that, I shall order the guards to shoot into the hold," he said. From the bays came a rumble: "To hell with him. We're going to die anyway, aren't we?"

Mr. Wada's rules were the most senseless tyranny. The pure sea was running past the bulkheads outside; it needed only a rope and a few bucketfuls of sea water to make the hold at least clean. But Mr. Wada would allow only one bucket a day to be used by the whole dead squad, to wash part of the grime of bodies from their hands. Mess kits and canteen cups were never cleaned.

Once Ted Lewin, the Los Angeles reporter and promoter, approached Joses' successor as commanding officer, the Marine Lieutenant Colonel Curtis Beecher, as he sat in his bay. "What are you thinking about, colonel?" Lewin asked. "I was remembering," said the gray-haired Beecher, "a fellow I heard talk at the Explorers' Club in Chicago after the last war. He described how the Armenians made their march of death with the Turks driving them along. I was just wondering whether it could have been any worse than this."

For a new infraction of his rules, the theft of sugar, Mr. Wada threatened to cut off all provender. "It doesn't matter," said Beecher wearily, "because if you don't give us some water and food, we're all going to pass out anyway." By this time Beecher looked, in the words of an aide, "gaunt, matted, gray and weak."

As the voyage drew into its second week the prisoners lost all discretion and robbed sugar from the hold at will. In the pit the price of sugar fell, to six spoonfuls for one spoonful of water. The Formosan rice they were not eating was rough and full of hulls; it aggravated bowel action and increased diarrhea, while brown sugar seemed to make the diarrhea chronic.

The violent rages, the bloodsuckings and murders of the Manila–Olongapo trip were no longer possible. The men were too weak. They were broken or at least submissive. For them it was no longer their affair; they belonged to God or fate.

Father Cummings still carried on his evening service. His Protestant colleagues—the redheaded Episcopalian Navy chaplain, Lieutenant Quinn, and the Army chaplain Lieutenant Tiffany—were both gone. Gone too was the spectacled Jesuit missionary, Captain Joseph G. Van der Heiden, whose suede jacket had fallen to someone else. Lieutenant Zerphas, a priest from the 26th Cavalry who had given many last blessings, was now able to help little, and Lieutenant John E. Duffy of Notre Dame was in a condition where he insisted on being brought ham and eggs.

Major F. Langwith Berry, an 86th Cavalry officer, remembers these services thus: "Often at evening the call 'at ease' would be given. The hubbub of talking would diminish but still continue. Then we would hear above the noise, 'It's the chaplain, boys, it's the chaplain.' The clear, penetrating voice of Father Cummings was unmistakable. Immediately complete silence would fall in the blackness of the hold. First he would give a few words of encouragement, and next he would say the Lord's Prayer. During those few seconds, we thought of home, of our mothers, of gardens, lakes and mountains in America. And then—'that's all, boys'—our vespers were over."

Once, when a man hurled a curse in the middle of the service, a Marine lieutenant felled him with a swipe of his sun helmet. The ex-missionary from San Francisco was, after all, the man who first said, "There are no atheists in foxholes." His service became an expected part of the day's routine. Then came an evening when Father Bill was unable to stand up. Forty-three years old, he was weakened by severe dysentery and thirst. He never spoke again, and eventually he lay on the hatch where he had blessed so many others, a body deserted by the spirit. His body was hoisted high, and the Japanese delivered him to the sea.

The only Negro aboard was Sergeant Robert W. Brownlee, a genial, cheerful and diligent soldier who had been much prized as the top mess sergeant of the 26th Cavalry. He had a family of five children awaiting his return to Manila. Having helped many others on the ship, he contracted both dysentery and cerebral malaria and died fourteen days out of Formosa.

An athlete sometimes called West Point's greatest football center, Lieutenant Colonel Maurice F. "Moe" Daley, wounded in the Takau bombing, passed away from acute dysentery.

A civilian engineer whose wife and children were in the Baguio camp had simple last words: "Take care of them."

One wounded soldier asked George Curtis, the New Bedford and Manila auto agent, whether he might rest his head in the elder man's lap. Another gave Curtis a card for his mother. A middle-aged civilian paced around the hatch whispering: "I just can't take it any more," then lay down forever. A young soldier was weeping and saying, "If I could only make my life worth four Nips before I go."

One man kept repeating, "I have such pain in my chest I can't stand it, I simply can't." A companion in the same bay would soothe him with, "Hold out just another two days." This dialogue went on until the wounded man managed to save a half-canteen of water. Making his complaint with a new note of determination, he held the canteen off at arm's length and, with all his summoned force, struck himself in the brow. He keeled over, and when his companion felt him the same night, he was already cold. "We could not believe there was any way that a man could commit suicide with a canteen," said one survivor, "but we saw it done."

Commander Bridget had been fading rapidly. He had an extreme case of diarrhea, so acute that he sometimes moved in a daze. The last tablets of sulfaguanadine had been given to him days before, but had not eased him. He even ate mouthfuls of straw in the hope of being cured. Once, wandering on the open deck, he must have clashed in the dark with a sentry. He was found at the bottom of one of the forward holds, beaten up but with his clothing still intact. When death came, like many of the prisoners, he probably did not even know that he was going.

Lieutenant Colonel George Hamilton inherited the gray gabardine riding breeches Bridget had worn, washed them up in seawater by especial permission of a guard and the aid of Boatswain Taylor, and drew them on with pride. These famous breeches made Hamilton the best-dressed prisoner after Major Robert V. Nelson, an Army dentist who possessed the warmest wardrobe in the pit. Yet when this prized clothing reached Japan, it was worn by other men, the secondary owners having gone to join the originals.

Frequently an officer would tap a recumbent, shivering man on the shoulder and murmur, "You'd better go over and say goodbye to your friend over there. He's pretty nearly gone." And the man's garments, like those of Christ, would often be parted among his companions before he entered his next world.

As the men scratched brown sugar from the hold, Lieutenant Murray Day, a field artillery officer from New England who had gone to Princeton, told them of his maple sugar business. "When we have a reunion of alumni after the war, we'll serve my maple sugar," he said. He never reached Japan.

An Air Corps warrant officer, William Keegan, had gone through bombings and thirst with unbowed head, and been strong enough to help bear the dead ashore at Takau. Suddenly he collapsed of malnutrition and thirst and immediately died.

Lieutenant Arthur Derby, a Harvard graduate from New York City and Virginia, had been suffering amoebic dysentery when he left Bilibid. Often he said, "I'd give $1,000 cash for just two sulfaguanadine pills." Though unwounded, he drooped away with malnutrition and finally faded out.

A field artillery officer, Lieutenant Dwayne Alder of Salt Lake City, who had become unbalanced after the Takau bombing, recovered his reason but passed away.

Lieutenant Colonel Louis Barnes of Massachusetts, of the Army medical corps, had been able to help his fellow physicians little. "A tough-spirited and charming old man," a younger officer called him. His 240 lbs. shrank and he died of exhaustion and exposure.

The Navy Senior Lieutenant Douglas, nephew of the famous tree ring historian of the University of Arizona, showed himself particularly unselfish, giving his strength to wash the befouled wounded and cheer them up. He'd say, "God is looking after us—we'll make Japan safely, I know." Some of his patients did, but not Douglas.

Cold and starvation erased the perpetual game grin of Lieutenant Commander Arthur Bryan.

It was not all heroism. Theft and quarreling never ceased. A whole bay full of interlocked men would dispute loudly over such a matter as when to turn over and rest on the other side. All had to turn or none; there was not room for differing postures. But some had worse wounds on their right side, some on the left.

Not only was clothing stolen from the dying, but water from the healthy and well. "There were fellows who taught themselves how to slip down beside you while you were asleep, open your canteen and without a sound of swallowing drink all your water. You would try hard to sleep with your fingers locked around the plug. But every morning someone would sit up in his bay and yell, 'Where's the dirty so-and-so who stole my water?' "

But there was also Lieutenant Colonel Charles "Polly" Humber, a football man at West Point, who shared his water with many others before diarrhea and thirst took him.

The search for water was as remorseless as if they were in the Sahara. "I remember a morning four days out of Japan when someone peeked over the ladder and saw there was sleet and snow remaining on the deck," says Chief Yeoman Theodore R. Brownell of Fort Smith, Arkansas. "I sneaked up the ladder, crept on deck and saw the most beautiful thing in the world—a long, thick icicle. But just as I reached for it the Jap sentry saw me. *'Kudai!'* (Look out!) he yelled, and came for me with his bayonet. I had scooped up a snowball to make sure I had something even if I missed out on the icicle. But in scrambling out of the way of his bayonet I lost even the snowball and fell back into the hold again, empty-handed and thirsty as ever."

The Navy chief, slender and medium-sized, had found a comrade in a long Army beanpole, Private William Earl Surber of Colorado Springs. "We lay together like a tablespoon and a teaspoon," says Brownell. "But I got the best of it. He was long enough to keep me warm, but I wasn't long enough to keep him warm at the ends." Surber, the more ill of the pair, had alternating periods of delirium and normalcy. In normalcy he talked about wanting two things: to eat one more dish of meatballs and spaghetti, and to have a regular baptism. The men talked often of the hereafter which they both expected to enter shortly, and repeatedly Surber said, "I'm worried. I want to get baptized." Brownell, a Catholic, thought it proper that Surber, a Protestant, should be baptized by a Protestant rite. By now the prison ship was in Japanese waters and not a single chaplain still alive was sane and strong enough to approach Surber. The chaplain Brownell counted on was Lieutenant Commander H. R. Trump, an Episcopalian who was lying a few bays off, unable to move. Since Surber could not be moved to Trump, Brownell was trying to build up the chaplain's strength enough to walk to the soldier's bay. The chaplain would accept food but no water from the

Navy chief, and he died on the 27th. "Ted, you've got to get me baptized," Surber kept saying. "I've got to be baptized somehow today. If there aren't any chaplains, can't you baptize me?"

Since any lay person can baptize another, Brownell could not refuse. But he had no water, not even a tablespoonful. "I didn't see any way out," says Brownell. "So I did something that I guess any clergyman would think pretty awful. I baptized Earl with my own saliva. I simply put my fingers in my mouth, got enough moisture on them so he could feel it, and I said, 'I baptize thee in the name of the Father, the Son and the Holy Ghost'."

Surber's expression became more peaceful. Before first light on the morning of January 28th, about 4 a.m., Brownell noticed that his friend's body had grown cold.

They saw and smelled Japan on the 30th. The bays by now had much more room. In Brownell's, for example, four out of nine had died; this proportion was about representative, though some bays were better, some worse. On the last night, off the entrance to Moji, there was a submarine attack, with American torpedoes blasting the night with flame as they struck the shore. But finally they were in the harbor of Moji in northern Kyshu, and the net closed behind them.

THE neat little Japanese officers came aboard and asked for the senior officer present. "They tried hard not to show it," says one officer, "but you could see that they could not help being shocked. When Lieutenant Colonel Beecher walked out, his shirt clotted with filth, a dirty towel wound around his brow, his beard and hair hanging down, and gave them a feeble sort of salute, then leaned back against the bulkhead as though just doing that had exhausted him, with slop buckets on one side of him and the morning's dead piled on the other, you could see that the Moji officials were taken aback."

It was mid-winter, the temperature just above freezing. The Japanese lined the prisoners up on the deck and ordered them to strip naked. They were then sprayed with disinfectant from blowguns—hair, face, beard and then the whole shivering body. Many prisoners were in pneumonia's first stages already. Meantime the

Japanese doctors were looking down into the pit, where some of the unmoveable wounded still lay. An overpowering odor of urine and excrement arose to their nostrils. "Dysentery!" said the doctors, and ordered a general examination.

In Japan, where things are never done the easy way if a painful one exists, the diseases of evacuation are not checked by the stool test in use everywhere else. The Japanese use a long glass rod, which they insert up the rectum. Laying down their atomizers, the Japanese interns went for the Americans with long glass rods. The prisoners below, whose infection was unmistakable, were spared. But for reasons fathomable only to the Japanese mind, the corpses lying on the deck, about fifteen in number, had to be tested too. Every dead man underwent the same ignominy as his living comrades. The Japanese officials were also very dissatisfied that there were several among this last batch of dead whom nobody living could identify.

A little clothing was distributed; some men got their first shirts, others their first shoes. An Army warrant officer, while changing back to his clothes after the "medical examination", collapsed and died on the deck under the eyes of the Japanese doctors.

The last muster aboard the ship was called. It showed 435 men still alive (a few survivors say 425). Many were sinking and beyond recall. But the last voyage by sea had ended with about one-half the men living who survived the Formosan bombing, or a little more than one-fourth of the 1,600 men who left Bilibid prison on December 13th.

The Japanese now ordered the prisoners ashore. They marched off the ship to the second floor of a pier, limped downstairs to the street, and then made a slow walk about two blocks to a factory auditorium in a large warehouse. "I took a fall making a six-inch curb," says one officer. "Most of the men walked with sunken heads, dragging their heels. I could not understand why, as soon as we reached them, people on the sidewalks would put handkerchiefs to their faces. Then I realized it was because we smelled so terrific."

The first arrivals in the auditorium, which was without seats, looked for water. "We found it, delicious and bitterly cold, in the inflow tank of a toilet. Before the Japanese could do anything, hundreds had lined up. They drove us back, but later they loosened up and allowed us to go in a few at a time."

The Japanese ordered them to take off their shoes. Few obeyed; they were beyond caring. The prisoners squatted on the concrete floor. Rice was brought in, hot and tempting. But the Japanese ordered it put aside until the roll call was made again, a matter of nearly an hour. Then there was an uplifting talk by a new interpreter. "In Japan," he said, "food is very valuable. You must not waste any food. If you waste food, you will be shot."

The prisoners listened apathetically. It would not have moved them if he had said they would be boiled in oil. What mattered was that the rice was clean and white and even had some gingered radish in it.

Volunteers were mustered to carry the extremely ill to the hospital. The party began to break up. One group of officers able to walk were taken by streetcar to a camp near Moji where a few American enlisted men were housed already. "Never did officers feel so grateful to enlisted men as we were to them," says one officer. "They had a little coffee, some powdered milk, and sugar hoarded from a Red Cross package. They prepared some for us. I cannot tell anyone how that tasted to us. I can only say that tears broke out of our eyes. We had come so far. We had suffered so much."

Of approximately 135 survivors, officers and men, who were carried to the Moji hospital, about 38 died in the first two days. In all, about 85 died there.

Of about 100—chiefly officers—who went to Camp #3 near Moji, about 31 died.

Of 97 prisoners, mostly enlisted men, taken by train to Camp #17 near Omuta, 15 died.

Of about 100 officers who went to Camp #1 near Fukuoka, about 30 died.

Thus, of the 435 who reached Japan, about 161 died subsequently. Only about 274 of the 1,600 who started from Bilibid Prison are believed to have survived the terrible ordeal. Some others died of other causes.

The hand of a long-dead comrade intervened to protect the lives of the weak but living. An Army warrant officer, Lacey O. Jenkins, had caught diphtheria in Takau. When the Americans had asked for serum to cure him, Lieutenant Toshino and Mr. Wada simply turned their backs. Jenkins, a man of 200 pounds, shrank rapidly and soon died. Now, in Moji, the case of Jenkins was resurrected. For the home authorities it reflected little foresight on Toshino and Wada. And for the prisoners diphtheria meant quarantine. Quarantine meant that they could not be sent down into the Mitsui coal mines to labor for a cent a day, not at least for several weeks. They did go down eventually, and one man of every six died there.

A Cavite naval officer, Edward Little, who was one of the original 'old 500' prisoners who had opened Camp #17, seeing the thin line of survivors from the death cruise march in, asked the camp physician, Captain Thomas Hewlett, how many had died.

"If you want to see dead men," replied Hewlett, "there they stand before you."

An officer who survived, telling his story to an American rescue party after Japan surrendered, listened in silence as his hearers said what they thought of the Japanese. When they had finished, he said, "Yes, the Japanese are as you say. But we, the three hundred or so living, we were the devils, too. If we had not been devils, we could not have survived. When you speak of the good and the heroic, don't talk about us. The generous men, the brave men, the unselfish men, are the men we left behind."

VII

The Weller Dispatches
by Anthony Weller
(2005)

I

Every great war correspondent has an important story that got away—that was banned by someone in authority, censored into silence, and never appeared. Too often, such reporters die beset by a sense that their duty to history, of which they are well aware, remains unfulfilled. With my father, it was linked to one of the cataclysmic events of the twentieth century. His odyssey on Kyushu, pulled together here for the first time, raises many questions not just about the atomic bomb and the prison camps, but about censorship in the United States and Japan and the larger responsibilities of a reporter. History is written by forgetfulness as well as memory; this essay will try to provide a backdrop for who he was, for what he saw, and for what he wrote.

George Anthony Weller (1907–2002) was among the most eminent American foreign correspondents of his era, recipient of a 1943 Pulitzer Prize and a 1954 George Polk Award. He first made his name as a courageous reporter during World War II, and was one of the few to cover every principal theater of war.

Having begun as a novelist during the Depression, Weller, with a more literary style than most foreign correspondents', spent much of his life overseas, and across six decades he reported from all the continents. During the 1930s he wrote on the Balkans for the *New York Times,* and joined the *Chicago Daily News* foreign staff in late 1940. Then syndicated in over sixty papers, the paper could boast such famed reporters as Leland Stowe, Paul Ghali, Richard Mowrer, Webb Miller, and Robert J. Casey. From the mid-1950s, Weller covered principally the Middle East, the Mediterranean, the Soviet Union, and Africa. In 1975 he retired from the newspaper but continued to write, and was awarded the Premio Internazionale di Giornalismo of Italy. He died at his home there in December 2002.

Inevitably, this book is as much about being a war correspondent in 1945 as it is about what one man saw. The ease of modern communications can make us overlook the fact that, until recently, a reporter's challenge lay in surmounting the problems not only of "getting in," but of swiftly being able to get a story out. There were no instantaneous satellite links, only cable offices within reach if one were lucky, where—along with normal, excruciating delays—the tendrils of military and government censorship could be too muscular to remove.

Their equivalent nowadays is still effective: to stop a story at its source by limiting access. If you can control what is witnessed, you can mold what is reported. Since news organizations are rarely anxious to announce their shortcomings, a credulous public remains, as usual, none the wiser.

II

In Japan and the United States alike, World War II chroniclers, historians of the atomic bomb, and scholars of press censorship have long known that these dispatches *had* existed once but, never having surfaced in the intervening sixty years, they were thought erased from the past. As did my father, who went to his grave deeply frustrated by their disappearance.

Their first importance lies in their visceral immediacy. We are so accustomed to reading about the atomic bomb and its consequences, wrapped in a half century of hindsight, that it comes as a shock to walk with George Weller among the still-smoldering ruins of Nagasaki, to pass through the city's broken wards and speak with Japanese doctors, or to hear the sagas of Allied prisoners whom he has just told the war is over. These dispatches represent a tireless attempt by one of the most battle-experienced reporters of his day, typing at speed under challenging conditions, to come to grips with scenes unlike anything he knew and to accurately, unsentimentally, convey them to the American people.

I also believe that the dispatches hold a particular relevance not just from their content, but from the official will to silence them back in 1945. In our era of the controlled, hygienic "embedding" of journalists in war zones, amid current disputes over a government's right to keep secrets, the Weller dispatches represent a kind of rogue reporting that many militaries may have snuffed out, but which is still essential to learning the truth.

It is always problematic to inhabit the past, to enter its differences; to re-create all its assumptions, all it took for granted—for we must first try to understand it fairly, on its own terms, before we judge it on ours. (The very names *Hiroshima* and *Nagasaki,* for example, carry a charged, self-sufficient meaning now that they did not then.) Reading this book, one is constantly reminded of all Weller did *not* know that we know today, and how much he was witnessing for the first time and trying to make sense of as he sat in that borrowed house in Nagasaki, writing deep into each night and sending his dispatches off each morning with the *kempeitai,* hoping that they were getting through the Tokyo censors, to be safely cabled to his editor in Chicago and, nationwide, onto tomorrow afternoon's front page.

They were not, of course. And I think that once the other journalists had come and gone and he realized he'd lost his best chance to leapfrog MacArthur's censors, his shift of attention from a bombed Nagasaki to the prison camps must have carried a dose of frustration, amid a hunger to wring everything he could from the opportunity. During three weeks on Kyushu, as the first Western correspondent into the atomic site as well as the camps, he wrote over fifty thousand words, in itself a two-hundred-page book.

Weller, like all the other reporters covering the surrender in Tokyo Bay on the battleship U.S.S. *Missouri,* September 2, 1945, at that moment had no hard information about what had gone on in Hiroshima and Nagasaki. He was unsure what awaited him if he proved successful at getting into either, since no outsider had been

in yet, not even from the U.S. military. He only knew he was forbidden to visit both places. But since Japan had signed the peace treaty
and was no longer in a state of war with the Allies, he felt he had
a right to go wherever he wanted. More important, the world had a
right to know what the nuclear sites looked like, to learn first hand
how the war had been concluded.

III

There were limited reports throughout Japan. Weller, reaching
Tokyo from China via the Philippines a couple of weeks after the
Japanese surrender (August 15), had filed this dispatch with his
newspaper on August 31, two days before the treaty signing:

> The atomic bomb holds first place over any other element as
> the cause of Japan's decision to surrender, according to Japa-
> nese civilians with whom I've talked. At first the authorities
> held down newspapers from announcing the bomb's effect on
> Hiroshima, but leakage began after four or five days. Now the
> newspaper *Asahi,* with two million circulation, is planning a
> book detailing the bomb's effects on Hiroshima and Nagasaki.
>
> Japanese censorship was doubly effective because internal
> circulation was almost halted, and therefore refugees from
> Hiroshima—and therefore the truth—could not reach Tokyo
> masses even by gossip.
>
> When authorities decided to inform people of what might be
> in store for them, [Japanese] Army members of the Censorship
> Board had cushioning stories released saying that people in
> white shirts with sleeves escaped burning, and also that those
> underground went unscathed. The last story was partly true
> since the only survivors came from dugouts.
>
> The government was compelled to release the truth by the
> fact that many who escaped—as they thought—the effect of
> the atomic bomb with light wounds went to live with relatives
> in other cities and died as much as a week after.

Sadao Maruyama and Keiko Sonoi, an eminent stage actor and movie stage actress, were living in Hiroshima. Both escaped. Maruyama came to Tokyo. After three or four days he began claiming that he felt excessive warmth in his stomach. After five days, the warmth had turned to burning. At the end of a week he suddenly cried to the friend with whom I talked, "I feel as though my insides were burning out." He rushed to the bathroom, guzzled water and stepped into a cold shower where he abruptly died. An autopsy showed his entrails eaten away.

Actress Sonoi, after Hiroshima, went to Kobe and telegraphed Tokyo, "I am happy to have been saved." She had only a small swelling of her wrist. But the swelling spread and soon covered her whole body. Her hair fell out. In approximately a week, she too died. These seemingly healthy persons who died many miles from Hiroshima many days afterward were the actual breakers of censorship, who compelled the military to allow the truth to be told about Hiroshima. Small wonder that some Japanese have been asking correspondents: "When will we get scientific equality?"—meaning the secret of the atomic bomb.

Army censors, not yet on high radiation alert, let that story through; the manuscript is stamped *Passed By Censors*. But the newspaper never ran it.

Sneaking into a nuclear site for an entire series of articles a week later, however, defying both a travel ban and a media blackout, was not going to get past those same censors. (It's unclear if MacArthur ever learned that Weller also impersonated an officer.) By some accounts, the general—trying to ensure his glory as Supreme Commander of the Allied Powers while hiding the bomb's lethal radiation and the fact that no medical aid, not even an observer, had been sent to the dying even weeks after the surrender—was absolutely livid at Weller's effrontery. And because the reporter was still under MacArthur's control in Occupied Japan, had he succeeded in getting the censored dispatches out, his newspaper could never have published them without losing its invaluable accreditation there, which was unthinkable.

Many months later, of course, their timeliness was ended; there was no more scoop; with victory, the gaze of the people had moved on.

That MacArthur successfully prevented their appearance always infuriated Weller; that the war was over only made it more outrageous. He saw it as part of a larger failing in MacArthur, and after the general's death in April 1964, wrote an evenhanded critique which didn't mention Nagasaki:

> MacArthur perceived that publicity was the lever of American power and he used it openly.
>
> MacArthur's censors, by suppressing almost everything political and meaningful from the Southwest Pacific, reduced the war to a series of banal hero stories costing the American people a generation of political education in Southeast Asia.
>
> To MacArthur ruthless censorship was a means not to deceive the Japanese enemy but to keep his material supplies increasing in an uncritical atmosphere. When I tried to cost-analyze the sending of 25 bombers to destroy a single Japanese Zero parked on a field, the story was instantly killed. To MacArthur this was the way to keep the public happy and tractable.

Like many correspondents, Weller thought the international political naiveté of Americans was almost total. In *Singapore Is Silent* (1943), written during the first year after the United States entered the war, he was blunt: "Asia is the kindergarten of American geopolitics, and the American people are the reluctant pupils who dislike the lessons they must learn, and have not yet understood that the old, simple life of play in the garden at home is gone forever." Later in the war, in *Bases Overseas* (1944) he wrote:

> The American people have been politically bewildered about their foreign policy for fifty years. In war they are alternately drugged with the promise of bloodless and easy victory, then whipped up with official warnings that peace will be expensive and is far off . . . Politically this new American is not only igno-

rant; he is indifferent. There is the United States, or Home. And there are all the other places . . .

The key to the political life of the American abroad is . . . he must be loved, or at least liked, or he withers. His foreign policy, therefore, represents an attempt to become popular by being benevolent, rather than to be respected by being responsible . . .

[U]nsupplied with statesmen capable of building him an enduring peace consonant with his own sacrifices, the American turns by *reductio ad absurdum* to an emotional apprehension of war. If you cannot think about the war, can you not at least feel about it? Besides the escapism away from the war there is in the United States a unique escapism into war, into atrocity stories, into magic-weapon stories, into hero stories, into sex-and-war stories, that defeats the political teacher . . .

Today the fighting man overseas is waiting for the statesman at home to do something. The statesman at home is waiting for the people to suggest for him to do something. The people are waiting for the press and radio to suggest what they should ask the statesman to do. The press and radio are waiting for their foreign correspondents and war reporters overseas to suggest to them what they should suggest to the public. And the reporters and correspondents are unable to analyze, much less suggest political action, because the fighting men (officers and censorship, that is) say that politics is the affair of the statesman back home.

IV

A big, gusty man with extraordinarily alive blue eyes and a powerful head suggesting steel-reinforced bone structure, Weller always seemed larger than a mere six feet. As someone who felt at home everywhere and went deep into what he called the secret history of each place, his reportorial gift was a mask of complete innocence that was misleading and trapped his subjects in unwitting revelations, followed by the question that went for their vitals.

He was most of all a man of the world, in an old-fashioned definition: a type of American gentleman who existed midcentury, at ease in all situations. He spoke five foreign languages fluently (albeit with a Boston accent) and was exceedingly literate, charming, and stubbornly confident about his place in the order of things. At the same time he never forgot having grown up poor—his Harvard tuition was generously paid by a man he had caddied for as a teenager—and he remained frugal all his life. A career under fire or trapped in difficult places, from the Hindu Kush to the wilds of New Guinea, stopped him from worrying about eating well or dressing stylishly.

His first job after Harvard was as an actor in Max Reinhardt's theater company in Vienna. Freelancing in Athens, Capri, and Dubrovnik, he wrote two novels (*Not to Eat, Not for Love* and *Clutch and Differential*) that were highly praised but made him little money. Throughout the 1930s he managed to publish both reportage and fiction regularly in *The New Yorker, Story,* the *Nation, Esquire,* and the *Atlantic* while getting a political education in the Balkans as a stringer for the *New York Times.*

Barely solvent, once he joined the *Chicago Daily News*—leaving behind a wife and an eight-year-old daughter in the States—he had a nonstop war. From Lisbon to Belgrade to Bucharest he stayed one step ahead of the German army. He wrote the first eyewitness accounts of the airborne invasion of Crete. As the last reporter out of a burning Salonika (he escaped on a Greek fishing boat), he was soon captured by the Nazis in Athens and taken to Vienna and Berlin. Traded for a German journalist held by the Allies, he made his way through Spain and Portugal via Léopoldville (Kinshasa) to Brazzaville, Central Africa. There he did a famous interview with General de Gaulle, who used it to make military overtures to the Americans. After Churchill reacted angrily, de Gaulle scolded Weller for revealing the offer, trying hard but unable to fully deny having made it. (An account may be found in A. J. Liebling's *The Road Back to Paris.*)

From there he followed the Belgian Congolese Army to the Sudan, where they attacked the Italians in the highlands of western Ethiopia. In Addis Ababa he interviewed Haile Selassie on his recovered throne, learned about the Japanese attack on Pearl Harbor, and was ordered by his editors to proceed east—via Cairo, Basra, Karachi, Calcutta, Rangoon—to Singapore.

For six weeks he covered the doomed British colony as the Malay Peninsula fell to the Japanese. He got on one of the final boats safely out of Singapore and spent the next weeks covering the collapse of Java, fleeing on the very last boat to escape under heavy strafing and bombardment in March, 1942. (*Time* referred to him as the "much machine-gunned George Weller.")

On reaching Australia he sent out the first account of the epic Battle of the Java Sea (a disaster for the Allies) and rapidly wrote a now-classic book of war reportage, *Singapore Is Silent.* For the next year and a half, amid bouts of malaria, he covered the struggle for the Pacific islands: the Solomons, New Guinea, Samoa, Tonga, Fiji, the Cooks, the Gilberts, the Society Islands, and Australia. He even trained as a paratrooper, the first correspondent to do so, in order to understand the type of warfare he was writing about. During this time he received a 1943 Pulitzer Prize in foreign reporting for the story of an emergency appendectomy performed by a pharmacist's mate while on a submarine in enemy waters.

En route back home in late 1943 for leave he wrote *Bases Overseas,* a controversial book proposing a global system of U.S. bases. ("The largest army, the largest navy, and the largest industrial plant in the world: such are the unthinking aims of strategically incurious minds . . . In a country dominated by this cult of production, the *where* of its conflicts are nothing.") In the States, his divorce took up an unexpected amount of time and he was not able to return to the war until autumn of 1944; he couldn't help feeling, professionally, that he'd missed the big story, the Allied invasion of Europe.

Hoping to get back to the Pacific and what he later called "the battles of the U.S. Navy versus MacArthur," he returned the long way round: via Italy, where he was much hampered by British censorship; to the siege of Athens; through Palestine, Cyprus, Lebanon,

Iraq, and Iran. In Burma Weller wrote his own analysis of Yalta, a story which MacArthur's censors blocked because he called it a U.S. defeat by Stalin.

Weller later ran into the same blockade over a story about Corregidor, a Gibraltar in the mouth of Manila Bay. Many American servicemen had been killed or captured bravely trying to defend this U.S. base for six months in 1942. When it was finally taken back by MacArthur's adroit paratroops in February 1945, thousands of enemy died in the tunnels atop the island. Weller, en route to Tokyo, visited Corregidor soon after Japan agreed to surrender, but ran afoul of a captain stiffly in charge of censorship.

Having seen and described Japanese skulls from Buna to Myitkyina, I saw no harm in mentioning that there was one skull still underfoot in the exploded tunnels of the Rock. "You can't mention that skull; it would allow the enemy to know we have not been able to bury their dead respectably," said this unusually deft player. "But there is no enemy," I said, a little wildly, perhaps. "Japan caved in early this month. Didn't the news come through channels yet?" The censor, without replying, took a nice easy stance and thudded my Japanese skull into the corner wastebasket.

When Weller outsmarted MacArthur's restrictions to reach Nagasaki, he had, at age thirty-eight, already witnessed a vast range of bloodshed and destruction. He was also fed up with battling press censorship. The fates of a number of colleagues—correspondents he'd known all over the world for a decade since he began this work—were particularly on his mind at war's end.

V

Though Weller did not know this at the time, another independent Western journalist beat him into an atomic site: a colleague from the Pacific war, the Australian reporter Wilfred Burchett (1911–1983).

Burchett made his way into Hiroshima on September 3. Without U.S. military interference or guidance, he saw what he had to see, and got out. Better, he got the story into London's *Daily Express*. He succeeded precisely where Weller failed.

And just as Weller would be obsessed for the rest of his life with the three weeks he spent around Nagasaki and the pile of dispatches he wrote but failed to lay before the eyes of the world, Burchett would remain obsessed with the day he spent in Hiroshima, the repercussions of all he saw, and the lone dispatch he did send. In a peculiar way these two reporters, who had earlier crossed paths in New Guinea (and, nearly four decades after the bomb, managed to finally compare notes), are linked to a third, the *New York Times* science reporter William L. Laurence (1888–1977)—whom, I feel it is safe to say, neither regarded as a colleague.

All three are part of a story that may never be fully known: how the U.S. government was determined that the actual nature of the atomic bomb and its radiation not be allowed to explode over the American psyche.

Burchett had covered the war in the Pacific, and written favorably about the B-29 incendiary raids on Japanese cities. Like many journalists, he reached Tokyo two days before the *Missouri* treaty signing. The movements of the Allied press were already meticulously controlled. Determined to get the Hiroshima scoop, Burchett planned a series of feints. A U.S. Navy public relations officer in whom he confided, with no love lost for MacArthur and "delighted at the prospect of a correspondent accredited to the Navy getting into Hiroshima ahead of anyone accredited to the Army," provided him with a month's food supply, including beef—impossible to come by. A contact at Japan's Domei news agency got him a ticket on the 6 a.m. train to Hiroshima, along with a note for their reporter, to accompany the food and plenty of cigarettes.

Very early the next morning, when a U.S. press officer came to wake up Burchett for the treaty signing, the Aussie was groaning on his bed with diarrhea, regrettably indisposed to join the hundreds of other correspondents.

After twenty hours jammed into a train with glowering,

demobilized—but eventually drunken and friendly—Japanese soldiers eager to share his cigarettes, Burchett managed to reach Hiroshima late the next night. Though the war was over, he was arrested by station guards. At dawn he showed them his letter of introduction and his portable typewriter, and eventually Bin Nakamura of Domei and a woman translator were brought round. Nakamura agreed to help Burchett, relieved to learn that his own dispatches (the first from the city, for Nakamura had survived the bomb) were getting through. For days he'd been transmitting by Morse code on an apparatus which could send but not receive. Hiroshima was still out of radio and newspaper contact.

Nakamura and the translator took Burchett to one of the few buildings standing, the Fukuoka department store, where the city's police had set up headquarters. The police debated shooting them all, but decided instead to provide a car and driver so that Burchett, whom they took for an American, could report on "what his people have done to us." He visited one of the few makeshift hospitals, then sat on a chunk of rubble and typed out the story which the *Daily Express* would headline on September 5 as "The Atomic Plague," with the subheading "I Write This As a Warning to the World."

Like Weller, he arrived four weeks to the day since the bomb. Not surprisingly, their descriptions of the doomed in hospital wards are similar. But the estimates Burchett received from the Hiroshima doctors are much higher than Weller's in Nagasaki: 53,000 dead, 30,000 others missing and presumed dead, with 100 more each day. "People are still dying, mysteriously and horribly—people who were uninjured in the cataclysm from an unknown something which I can only describe as the atomic plague. . . . Hiroshima does not look like a bombed city. It looks as if a monster steamroller has passed over it and squashed it out of existence."

Like Weller in Nagasaki, he pointed out that Hiroshima's air-raid warning system had failed (the "all clear" had sounded) and people were not in their shelters when the bomb detonated. Decades later he would describe the attitude he found in the streets as "almost total apathy . . . a state of trauma."

Nakamura that afternoon transmitted the dispatch to Tokyo,

tapping it out "letter by letter on a Morse hand-set." While Burchett was waiting in the rubble, who should arrive but the same junket of American pressmen, flown directly out of Washington and thus not answerable to MacArthur, who six days later (September 9) would surprise Weller in Nagasaki. Astonished to find an Aussie interloper—having been led all over the world for two months while promised the scoop of the century, learning they'd missed the actual bomb, and now expecting to be the very first reporters into Hiroshima—they were, as Burchett recalled, chagrined.

"'Who the hell are you?' asked one of the colonels, eyeing me with distaste bordering on hostility . . . 'How long have you been here?'" Burchett's request for a lift was refused, as was his plea that they at least get his article up to his colleague in Tokyo. (One correspondent, Homer Bigart, protested, to no avail.) Burchett does not specify if the colonel's refusal came after he suggested they go see radiation victims in the hospital.

This junket was more elaborate than Burchett and Weller surmised: a lumbering elephant of newspaper and radio correspondents accompanied by still and newsreel photographers, with an unexpressed purpose. It included reporters from the AP, the United Press, NBC, CBS, ABC, the *New York Times,* and the *New York Herald Tribune.* Summoned to the Pentagon back in July, they were delivered into the hands of a guiding press relations officer, Lieutenant Colonel John "Tex" McCrary of the U.S. Army Air Corps, who promised (as Clark Lee of the International News Service recalled) the chance "to witness and report an earth-shaking event which would change the course of history." (*What, another?* commented one wag.) Facilities included plush transport on two B-17 Flying Fortresses equipped with desks, lamps, long-range transmitters, and best of all, a CENSORED stamp that hung over McCrary's desk. "Help yourself, guys," he told them cheerfully. "You're the censors on this show."

The intention, naturally, was to make sure the bomb got portrayed as the U.S. government wished. From Washington they'd been flown to Florida, New York, and London; to Hamburg, Berlin, and Munich for fact-finding views of damaged cities; to Paris and

Rome for several days so that (according to Lee) Tex could snuggle his "beautiful and athletic" wife, Jinx Falkenberg, on tour with the USO. Presumably Tex was not privy to the exact date when the bomb would be dropped. From there it was more time-wasting in Cairo and Casablanca while the journalists wondered when they might start satisfying editors back home who were paying their salaries and getting little in return. In Calcutta they read in the papers about their "world-shaking assignment . . . They were to have seen this historic and terrifying explosion—if they had reached Guam on time. . . . [but] love proved stronger than the atom bomb."

Perhaps. Tex did get his charges into Hiroshima, which was part of the unstated goal of the mission: to report appropriately the bomb's ability to demolish a city with one strike. Whether or not the junket members realized, a corollary purpose was to make it evident there was no dangerous radiation involved. That might be arguably too much like the use of, say, poison gas.

The junket landed twelve miles away, and drove to Hiroshima in two borrowed cars and a truck. They toured the ruins, walked across tracts so barren it was impossible to locate where streets had run, and spoke to doctors. Yet as Burchett recalled, "To one old acquaintance from some of the island-hopping campaigns, who asked for my impressions, I replied, 'The real story is in the hospitals.' He shrugged . . . fog was closing in and they were anxious to get back to their plane and take off while there was still visibility." They ended up spending the night on the airfield.

A day earlier, in Tokyo, MacArthur had signed the peace treaty that was portrayed as "an unconditional surrender." It was not; despite Japan's wars on the Dutch East Indies, the Malay States, the Philippines, China, Korea, and the United States, Emperor Hirohito was allowed to remain in power. MacArthur immediately pronounced all southern Japan, including the atomic sites, off-limits to the press, as was firebombed Tokyo. Reporters would be sequestered in Yokohama, the nearby port. Besides (the brainwashing continued), the pre-atomic bombings had been so efficient that there was no reliable rail or road system southward. All principal bridges were supposedly out; no way to get anywhere. As one MacArthur spokesman flatly explained, "It is not military policy for correspondents to spearhead the occupation."

By the night of September 3, Burchett's colleague Henry Keys had been moved, along with the rest of the Allied press, to a drab Yokohama hotel. On two attempts to reach Tokyo he was hauled off the train by U.S. military police. Improvising, Keys hired (cigarettes and food, as usual) a local journalist to await the Morse transmission at the Domei offices.

By now Burchett had left Hiroshima and was on his way back by train.

Late that night the Japanese journalist banged on Keys's hotel-room door, Burchett's dispatch in hand. Keys rushed it over to the press center for transmission. The duty clerk assessed the dateline and insisted the story had to clear the censors. *Why,* Keys demanded, *since the war is over now?*—only to be told it was a special case, and could not be sent without approval.

Keys, another resourceful Aussie, snarled his way from officer to officer over the duty clerk's telephone, waking them up and climbing the ranks until finally someone "was glad to yield." It helped that the story was for a non-U.S. newspaper. Keys stood over the cable operator until the *Daily Express* acknowledged that every word had reached London.

Weller was now (the morning of September 4) airborne, en route in a DC-3 south to Kanoya with sizable troop transports. He would stay there all that day, file three long dispatches, then slip off in darkness.

On September 5 England's largest-circulation daily carried Burchett's story on the front page. His editor astutely offered free worldwide reprint rights. In the United States, no newspaper bothered with it.

Burchett took his time returning; near Kyoto, and on Honshu, he visited several prison camps. He reached the capital on the morning of September 7, not yet aware how very unpopular he had become. Tokyo, reduced in many parts to fire-ravaged debris, was now occupied by U.S. troops.

By this time Weller had spent a full day in Nagasaki, written his first dispatch late into the night, and sent it north by *kempeitai* to MacArthur's censors. His note at the bottom, requesting radio acknowledgment from two fellow *Chicago Daily News* men in Tokyo, implies that he felt someone might need to help slide or bully the dispatch through official channels, and that he presumed the press center's cable operator would contact them.

Burchett, unwashed, exhausted, ran into a colleague at the train station who urged him to come straight to the Imperial Hotel. A press conference had been called by the top brass to eviscerate his article about radiation sickness.

Burchett got to the formal rite in time to hear General Thomas Farrell, deputy chief of the Manhattan Project and its head man in the Pacific—who one month prior had overseen bomb preparations on the island of Tinian—explain how both atomic devices were "exploded at a specifically calculated altitude to exclude any possibility of residual radioactivity." Therefore, the symptoms Burchett described were either blast burns or sloppy reporting.

Burchett, feeling rather scruffy amid the uniforms and medals, asked tersely if Farrell had actually been to Hiroshima. Aha, he had not. After a scientist-versus-layman argument that ended with Burchett challenging the Army general on why, if all he claimed were true, fish died within seconds of entering a stretch of Hiroshima's river, the correspondent received the closing admonition of a press briefing enacted to disprove him: "I'm afraid you've fallen victim to Japanese propaganda."

Conspiratorial as it sounds, afterward Burchett was spirited away to a U.S. Army hospital for medical tests, which showed that his white corpuscle count was down—"a typical symptom of radiation sickness," he comments sourly in a memoir, though the doctors pretended otherwise. On his release he found that his camera containing a film shot in Hiroshima was gone from his belongings, as was the carbon of his story. As was his press accreditation: MacArthur ordered Burchett expelled from Japan for "having gone beyond the boundaries of military occupation." This proved futile once the objection was raised that he was still under the umbrella of Admiral Nimitz, based on Guam. The Navy, eager to seize an opportunity to simultaneously annoy both the Army and MacArthur, delightedly reaccredited him.

The point was not that nearly a hundred thousand Japanese might have died on a Monday morning from a sole bomb; more had died during a single night's incendiary raid over Tokyo in March (as Weller described in detail in an August 31 dispatch passed by censors, though never published by his newspaper). Indeed, napalm had been developed to aid those firebombings. Nor was the point that many of the atomic-burned would never recover. The priority for the military, the government, and the American people was to end the war as soon as possible against a merciless enemy who had, after all, started it. Few in the United States in 1945 had lost sight of the fact that the Pacific war was entirely Japan's doing; that their schoolmates and brothers had died of gunfire trying to capture some coral atoll in the Gilberts (as Weller phrased it once), rather than at Key West of old age.

No, the point to be carefully disproved and silenced was what Burchett called *the atomic plague* and Weller called *Disease X*. The city wasteland of Hiroshima that Burchett portrayed, far more devastated than what Weller saw in Nagasaki, was not what provoked a damage-control U.S. military press conference thirty-six hours after the article appeared, with editors round the world screaming through the cable wires for every reporter in Yokohama to get down to the nuclear sites and see for themselves. What provoked the official denials was Burchett's claim of a deadly radiation that confirmed the many Japanese rumors and reports—the invisible death that after a month had still not gone away. Suppose it lasted even longer? Suppose it hung around for the U.S. servicemen who were soon to occupy Hiroshima and Nagasaki? Suppose it drifted over the nearby POWs awaiting liberation? A lingering cloud of radioactivity floating in the wrong direction (like after the July 16, 1945, New Mexico test) was a lethal liability.

Weller's timing was perfect: his first dispatch from Nagasaki probably reached Tokyo on the heels of that press conference, either late the night of September 7 or the next morning. Worst of all, Weller—whose reputation was as every politician's nightmare, a bulldog who, once he got his nose in the doorway, was not backing down—was still in Nagasaki, unstoppably typing away. The U.S. military had an idea what he would find out if he stayed there. And he did: the next evening the Tokyo censors received four more stories from him, including descriptions of Allied POW camps that lay directly under the blast, with prisoners killed as a result. His dispatches, already enough to fill a week's front pages in Chicago and in sixty-plus syndicate newspapers for starters, never stood a chance.

(When U.S. forces finally entered Hiroshima and confirmed Japanese reports that several American POWs were killed by the bomb, the news was covered up. Families were informed only that their loved ones had died in Japan. The facts were not revealed until 1977, when War Department files from the occupation were declassified. Even then the Pentagon denied it.)

There had already been one important Hiroshima article to vindicate the U.S. government and subtly contradict Burchett. It appeared the same day, September 5, in the *New York Times*. This was by Bill Lawrence, who wrote as W. H. Lawrence (and not to be confused, as so many historians have done, with William L. Laurence, long-standing science writer for the *Times*, known to colleagues as "Atomic Bill").

Lawrence (1916–1972)—who inevitably was called "Non-Atomic Bill"—was a brash young reporter who would later be a buddy of Jack Kennedy and spend the last decade of his career with ABC News. He'd covered Moscow for two years and glimpsed the war in the Pacific before being invited along on this junket. Via Tex's airborne transmission equipment, he managed to speed his article home. Its thrust was to confirm U.S. strength. Lawrence called Hiroshima "the world's worst-damaged city . . . the final proof of what the mechanical and scientific genius of America has been able to accomplish in war." Without apparently entering a hospital, he referred—less markedly than Burchett—to "the other physical ailments of the bombs" and quoted Japanese doctors, who "told us that persons who had been only slightly injured on the day of the blast lost 86% of their white blood corpuscles, their hair began to drop out, they lost appetites, vomited blood and finally died." (Lawrence later claimed he *did* go to the hospitals; if so, this was not in the article as published.) But a week afterward, rather curiously—and despite encountering Weller in Nagasaki, who had interviewed Japanese doctors in depth about Disease X—Lawrence wrote: "I am convinced that, horrible as the bomb undoubtedly is, the Japanese are exaggerating its effects. . . ."

Among all the junketeers Homer Bigart of the *Herald Tribune,* a reporter's reporter, was probably the most trenchant. On the same day as the Burchett and Lawrence articles, he called the bomb "a weapon far more terrible and deadly than poison gas." He described the effects, related by Japanese doctors, of death by radiation, but without using the dreaded word.

As a result of the press junket, *Life* magazine would decide that while a few in Hiroshima had perished from exposure to radiation right when the bomb exploded, no Japanese "died from radioactivity afterward." *Time* was more skeptical, pointing out that "In a week when the first U.S. newsmen entered Hiroshima . . . and made plain the appalling devastation . . . the State Department issued a formal report on atrocities committed by the Japanese. The timing was not missed by many readers."

Up till now MacArthur had been largely kept out of the atomic loop, forbidden to make any statements questioning the necessity of the bomb. His plans involved a leisurely three-month timetable for occupying southern Japan. He was furious at this press caravan flown over from Washington and outside his control. He considered court-martialing all of the reporters and officers involved for traveling outside the occupation zone and risking an incident with the Japanese; instead he cut off gas supplies to any planes that might repeat the transgression. The junket was forced to drag a lieutenant general over from Guam to requisition fuel to keep their B-17s flying.

The press junket ran counter to MacArthur's interests to the degree that anyone who disobeyed him was profoundly annoying. Their reporting would inevitably enshrine the effectiveness of the atomic bomb at the expense of his own importance. Plus it got all the other journalists yelping about when they might see Hiroshima and Nagasaki for themselves, which only solidified his determination to keep a lid on the two cities and a firmer grip on Japanese censorship. The junket did, however, run parallel to his interests to the degree that it would create, in a home readership, a sensation of earned and absolute power in American hands over Japanese lives—of which MacArthur was now the supreme instrument.

Some historians, from the moral high ground of the present, have laid all sorts of collectively Byzantine accusations upon this U.S. military press junket. As Burchett puts it, the reporters had been selected "to participate in a great cover-up conspiracy, although some of them may not have realized this at the time." Weller saw them as hasty day-trippers, like "yacht passengers who have stopped to buy basketry on an island." They seem to have made no serious effort to investigate claims of deaths by radiation, and by the time they were whisked into Nagasaki they certainly had no excuse of ignorance. Although Burchett beat them into Hiroshima by only a few hours, his article has an utterly different flavor than theirs, partly because he was able to see the whole situation through Nakamura's experienced eyes, and partly because he was not there as a guest of the conquering government.

In any case, the U.S. Army went rapidly into a public relations spin cycle. They'd hoped to keep both nuclear sites virginal from the Allied press, but suddenly reporters, monitored or not, were thick on the ground in one of them. General Farrell, the day after his press conference excoriating Burchett, and hoping to counter alert Japanese diplomatic efforts abroad to present the bombs as a crime against humanity, took a research team of eleven scientists down to Hiroshima to see for himself (September 8). One member later stated he was openly told by Farrell that their mission was "to prove that there was no radioactivity from the bomb."

Meanwhile George Weller was still in Nagasaki, sending up dispatches to the censors' wastebaskets. On September 9, after having the story to himself for three days, he was upended by the junket's arrival—though his reception by McCrary & Co. was warmer than what they gave Burchett. Maybe this was because they expected him to be there; and once they let him know how furious MacArthur was at his relentless articles, Tex ("kindness itself," as Weller recalled) offered to send all his dispatches once airborne. Was this because Weller was American, not Australian? Or was it to control the stories? Yet Weller never discerned ulterior motives in Tex's offer. It seems more likely that the junket and its officers, having been denied fuel for their planes and even threatened with court-martial, were fed up with MacArthur's posturing, and saw Weller not as a competitor but as an ally. What did it matter, since they'd already published their Hiroshima stories? They could not guess at all he had seen that they had not, and he would speak of them only as cohorts who'd evaded MacArthur's blackout more adeptly than he.

Their encounter begs the question of whether Weller admitted to himself that MacArthur's reputed anger meant his stories were not getting through. If MacArthur's censorship had something of the personal vendetta about it, then Weller's refusal to seize the opportunity he was offered also carries a bit of the stubbornness of a feud. Clearly the press junket stopped him in his tracks; no dispatch by Weller written the evening of September 9 survives. The next day he temporarily gave up on Nagasaki. As he later wrote, "Then [i.e., once the junket left] I heard of an unopened prison camp at Omuta, full of human derelicts. I went there and found a strange group of awed prisoners who had seen two mushroom clouds on the horizon. . . ."

On September 12 Farrell held another briefing in Tokyo, to convey the results of his science expedition to Hiroshima. Bill Lawrence's coverage for the *New York Times* was headlined "No Radioactivity in Hiroshima Ruin." Farrell denied that the atomic bomb "produced a dangerous, lingering radioactivity." He also countered a frequent Japanese accusation, stating that "no poison gases were released" at the moment of explosion—which was literally true. Lawrence, from what he'd seen with his own eyes and even written a week earlier, would have known that the press conference was deliberately misleading, but there was no skepticism in his article. (As he bragged in a 1972 memoir, "even politicians know that I can keep a secret.")

Stateside, there was significant activity from the greatest atomic authority in the press. Whatever MacArthur's spokesman might have said when laying down the laws restricting correspondents' movements in Japan, it was now military policy for reporters to spearhead the *propaganda*—an equally significant occupation.

The lever of this propaganda was the science writer for the *New York Times,* William L. Laurence. Laurence had been born in Lithuania in 1888 of a highly religious Jewish family, some of whom were later killed by the Nazis. He made it to the United States as a poor young man, fought for his adopted country in World War I on the battlefields of France, and succeeded at the American dream. By age fifty-seven he had two Harvard degrees and a Pulitzer Prize, having been with the *Times* since 1930. But for four months he was paid dual salaries. On loan from his newspaperman role, without the knowledge of his colleagues he became the privileged witness, official chronicler, press-release author, reporter-at-large, and unnamed spokesman for the War Department, for the Manhattan Project (which developed the atomic bomb), and for President Truman. When the bomb went off over Nagasaki on August 9, Laurence was in one of the B-29s, having cradled the device in his tremulous hands scant hours before. It was, he wrote for the *New York Times* but on behalf of the government, "a living thing, a new species of being, born right before our incredulous eyes."

Historians have written much, especially recently, about this symbiotic relationship. What appears today a flagrant conflict of interest was little remarked on a couple of decades ago, and even praised by analysts of the press twenty years before that. Laurence had written about atomic energy since 1929 and, as the first and most eminent newspaper science reporter in the land, enjoyed an oracular status. General Leslie Groves, the head of the Manhattan Project, approached the newspaper's publisher and its senior editor on behalf of the War Department and arranged to borrow Laurence in April 1945 as special consultant for a top secret project. The implication was that when events exploded, the *New York Times* would have a monopoly.

What deepens the stain on all parties involved is how far it went. The *Times* abandoned any stance of impartiality or code of ethics; W. L. Laurence gave vent to his own sense of divine mission, and seems never to have felt his journalistic duties were compromised;

and the U.S. government proved a masterly puppeteer. As often with an embedded reporter, if the sense of privileged access is flattering enough, obedience will be total—the message will be delivered not only as instructed, but with an extra flourish.

Groves already had public relations people on the Manhattan Project, but a respected journalist was needed to supply an imprimatur and a gravitas. Laurence was proud of his new role, since he believed that atomic power would prove the greatest scientific achievement of the twentieth century, which he quotably dubbed "The Atomic Age." For 119 privileged days he flew all over the country to laboratories and test sites and plants, interviewed the Allies' top physicists, had his wastebasket contents burned daily, told his wife practically nothing, and turned out scads of press releases or official reports—which were stamped TOP SECRET and locked in a vault until needed.

From behind the Atomic Curtain, as he termed it, he witnessed the July 16 Trinity test in New Mexico, the very first, and thought it a "Genesis . . . as though one were present at the moment of creation when God said: 'Let there be light.' " Laurence even saw a gigantic Statue of Liberty take shape in the mountain of clouds. He drafted the War Department's worldwide press release that accompanied Truman's August 6 radio speech on Hiroshima, calling it "unique in the history of journalism . . . No greater honor could have come to any newspaperman, or anyone else for that matter." He'd written an early draft of the president's own statement, but it was rejected by the White House as "exaggerated, even phony." His role was proudly displayed by his newspaper on August 7, touting him as the voice behind "pounds of official reports and bales of War Department handouts designed to enlighten laymen on the working of the atomic bomb." It did not disclose his dual-salary status.

Laurence's role in the carom of the story was only beginning. In mid-August, rather than being allowed to visit Hiroshima and Nagasaki as was planned, he was yanked back from the Pacific to the United States. He was still on both payrolls. On September 9, the *New York Times* ran his exclusive eyewitness account of dropping Fat Man on Nagasaki ("a thing of beauty to behold"). This was a month after the bombing, the same day that three more of Weller's Nagasaki dispatches, including extensive interviews with Japanese doctors and visits to hospital wards jammed with the dying, were stopped by the censors.

All the other reporters had stayed in Hiroshima for a few hours, written one story, then moved on. Only Weller was turning out an entire series from a nuclear site, with each article pivoting on the last, enlarging it, deepening it, revising his earlier assumptions and impressions.

On September 12, the *Times* featured Laurence's front-page story from Ground Zero in New Mexico where, along with thirty fellow reporters and photographers, the job was to prove that at the very "cradle of a new era in civilization," two months after the Trinity test, there was no dangerous radioactivity. He quoted General Groves: "You could live there forever."

At this point all speculation becomes moot about any enthusiasm the *Chicago Daily News,* had they received Weller's dispatches, might've shown for challenging a competitor. On September 14 the War Department sent "in confidence" to all editors of newspaper, magazine, and broadcast media a note from President Truman asking that any information about the "operational use" of the atomic bomb be kept secret unless quite specifically approved by the War Department. The purpose was "the highest national security." In other words, no substantive coverage without approval. This was not, it was stressed, censorship. Of course it had the same effect.

By this time Weller was busy piling up dispatches among the prison camps of Kyushu—the eyewitness accounts of seeing both bombs explode.

On September 18 MacArthur enacted a new censorship regime for all media in Japan banning, among the code's ten clauses, "Anything . . . that would promote hatred or disbelief in the Allied forces." This meant the bomb. All newspaper or magazine articles and photographs had to be passed by a censorship board before publication. However, it was forbidden to mention that there was any censorship. These strictures were soon extended to books, radio broadcasts, movies, and mail. The censorship did not end in Japan until October 1949;* scientific papers were not liberated until 1951.

Truman's censorship in the States didn't apply to Laurence, though. Starting September 26—the day Weller gave up on Nagasaki and set off by ship for Guam—the *New York Times* ran a ten-part series that Laurence had prepared for the government, detailing the scientific history of the bomb, praising the past and future of atomic power, and all but omitting any mention of radiation. The articles were vetted by the War Department, but the biblical allegories, the references to pioneer America and other mythologies, were pure Laurence. The series was then offered by the government, via the *Times,* free to papers around the country for reprint, and made into a free pamphlet for distribution in schools and to the entire public.

And the reward? Laurence's *Times* salary was $150 a week. On loan to the U.S. government, he believed he would pocket a bit more by serving two masters. In 1977, the year he died, at age eighty-nine, he would claim he'd been diddled by both the War Department and the *New York Times* for his seventeen weeks of dual-salaried work. Expecting to more than double his income, he felt cheated out of just under $3,000 by the military and just over $2,000 by the newspaper. He wrote to the *Times* demanding the extra money; they refused. More than twenty years had passed, after all.

However, as a result of his work-for-hire stories on the atomic bomb, in 1946 Laurence did receive his second Pulitzer Prize and a commendation by the War Department. Those counted for something.

In *Shadows of Hiroshima* (1983), Burchett recalls a 1978 conversation:

> In getting my report through I was more fortunate than a colleague, George Weller of the *Chicago Daily News.* I learned of

---

* John Hersey's *Hiroshima,* published in the United States late in 1946, would not appear in Japan until more than two years had passed, and only after much protest from the Authors League of America.

what happened to his reports from Nagasaki only thirty-three years after the event. Passing through Paris where I was then based, he got my telephone number from a mutual friend and called to congratulate me . . . "But why now, after so many years?" I asked. "Because I've never had the chance of talking to you before," he replied. "I greatly admired your feat, the more so because you succeeded in doing in Hiroshima what I failed to do in Nagasaki . . . I wrote a series of articles, totalling 25,000 words. As a loyal, disciplined member of the press corps, I sent the material to MacArthur's press headquarters for clearance and transmission . . . Eventually I arrived in Guam with my leg in a plaster cast. I immediately looked for what I hoped would be congratulatory messages—or at least acknowledgment that my series had arrived. The paper had received nothing. MacArthur had 'killed' the lot. I had always been an enemy of MacArthur's censorship. Now I think he decided to punish me."

Weller, in a 1990 radio interview, praised Burchett for beating him in, and remembered the Aussie as "a very sharp and careful reporter whom I had known at the battle of Buna." In his view, Burchett succeeded by

not being troubled by the qualms I was of putting MacArthur on the spot. He saw the chink in the censorship—that the U.S. Navy had been involved for the entire war in a struggle for power with General MacArthur—sometimes cooperating, sometimes not cooperating. It was a bitter pill that MacArthur, who fought a relatively tame war, was getting chief command of the entire Pacific, and censoring whatever he wished to. Burchett figured this out and said: *I am sure, now that peace is here, that the Navy will allow me to see Hiroshima.* And the Navy did not prevent it. He went in, wrote the story of Hiroshima—more deaths, if you will, than Nagasaki—and got his story out. I instead sent mine straight to MacArthur to force the decision on him. His censors stopped them on the grounds I was there illegitimately. They didn't accept my idea that because peace had broken out, I had a right to report.

VI

"All censored information is fundamentally propaganda," Weller wrote in *Bases Overseas,* published a year before the war ended. He was speaking from deep experience, and with nuclear prescience. In a never-published 1947 satirical article called "How to Become a Censor" that he managed through gritted teeth (the taste is bitter: "If you don't get your chance *in* the next war, you may get it *after* the next war") he points out censorship's disastrous and overall effect on the public understanding of an event:

> The moment when it could have been understood politically is missed, suppressed. The possibility of comprehension will never return again . . . And the porcelain men of history will pose forever in these lying attitudes.
>
> The aim of well-timed censorship is to instill this simple idea: *it probably never happened.*

He adds that one of the most effective censors he knew spent the whole war perfecting a flawless sense of timing to be used only after Japan had surrendered. He was "trained in the MacArthur school of censorship":

> . . . a tall lean lieutenant-colonel, greyfaced and greyhaired, who smoothed out his swing on a whole series of stories of mine about Nagasaki. I went to the atomized port while the ruins were still smoking, when the only American alive—besides errant ex-prisoners—was a single survivor of a crashed B-29, who thought he was still on Saipan . . . I fed my stories by special messenger to the grey lieutenant-colonel in Tokyo. With one ashen shot after another he holed them into obscurity . . . The

war was over, but he . . . kept right on playing my Nagasakis
into the upper drawer of the "file and forget" until all were
wasted. That was timing.

Twenty thousand skulls pulverized in an hour beside Nagasaki's dour creek—who would believe them censorable
today?

All this suggests that Weller knew his nemesis on MacArthur's
staff. It seems plausible; he had turned out several Tokyo stories
prior to the treaty signing, and might've dealt with the man. Weller
had already encountered his double in the Philippines, en route to
Japan via Manila, then MacArthur's headquarters. There the following dispatch was blocked, as Weller's penciled scrawl indicates. It
provides a preview, only a week after Japan had caved in, of
MacArthur's muzzling of the press as a fundamental technique.

Manila, August 22, 1945—1830 hours

[Killed by censorship]

The iron curtain of censorship was clamped down today at
MacArthur's headquarters on all details regarding the coming
occupation of Japanese-held territory. In the meantime, Tokyo
Radio and the Domei news agency continued to pour forth a
flow of purported details of how, when, and where all Japanese-
held territory was destined to be occupied.

This curious situation of the vanquished announcing the details of a coming surrender which the victor grimly refuses either to confirm or to deny can be considered typical of the
Pacific situation today. Whereas in Germany, British, American
and Russian armies did their occupying first and their talking
afterward, Japan seems to be—at least in the eye of
MacArthur's headquarters—just as much a problem in logistics
and military secrecy after the "unconditional" surrender as
before.

In some senses, this attitude of supersecrecy is undoubtedly justified. Never conquered before in her history, Japan is still a land of the unpredictable. But the paradox has arisen that while MacArthur's planners have been forced to put most details of the forthcoming occupation in Japanese hands in order to insure their success, they cannot—for reasons which may well be good and sufficient—reveal them publicly.

Meantime, without hindrance or even rebuke, Japanese Radio continues broadcasting to the world that the first American party will land by plane at Atsuki Airdrome on the west side of Yokohama next Sunday, and that the main naval landing will occur on Tuesday at Yokosuka. Because—by reason of many imponderables—responsibility for security has shifted to the Japanese, the initiative for announcements is also theirs, causing some observers here to inquire: "Say, who's surrendering here, anyway?"

[*The rest of the dispatch is missing.*]

Defying a censorship, even through timing, could damage a reporter. In the 1966 memoir "First into Nagasaki," which opens this book, Weller writes: "At least I was not busted by my organization for bucking the system, like dour, funny Ed Kennedy, who was too early for Eisenhower with the signing of the armistice. Ed, who had covered the fall of Greece with me, had set up communications that were too good."

Kennedy, the Associated Press bureau chief in Paris, had—along with all the other reporters present at Germany's surrender to the United States on May 7—promised Eisenhower he would wait until the Germans also surrendered to the Russians before he broke the news. Once the peace was broadcast to the German people at large, however, Kennedy figured any agreements were off, and he went ahead and broke the story to America via the AP. Kennedy stirred up the ire of his colleagues, lost his credentials, was sent home in professional disgrace, and wasn't reaccredited by Eisenhower until 1947.

This wasn't Kennedy's first scrap; Weller had met up with him in 1941 in Egypt, "his Buster Keaton visage . . . concealing an expert newspaperman . . . Once, a year earlier, he had dressed himself up as an Arab and picketed a leading Cairo hotel, telling all questioners with sad nobility: 'I am picketing this hotel in protest against the British censorship.' "

Part of Weller's higher education had come in 1942 at Singapore, as one of the final correspondents to escape the island colony, which was being futilely portrayed by British information officers as impregnable long after Japanese characters were writ large, in blood, on the bomb-shattered walls. In *Singapore Is Silent* (1943) Weller devotes an entire chapter to censorship:

> Nearly every ship that left southward was bombed. The air was completely in Japanese hands. Yet the censors still blue-pencilled "siege." . . . After the causeway was blown, the troops having retreated across it, there was a conference in the press-room at the Cathay [an office building] which would have made Noah Webster smile. "Can we refer now to the 'siege of Singapore' as having begun?" the correspondents wanted to know. The army's strategist-lexicographer hesitated . . . it was a matter of hours, perhaps of minutes, before the very room in which the correspondents were sitting . . . would be under Japanese shellfire. But had Singapore's siege begun? The military censor did not like to think so.
>
> "I still don't like that word," he said. "I still don't think it's justified."
>
> There was a burst of expostulation.
>
> "But surely you can't deny that we are besieged," said someone.
>
> "Besieged, yes," said the military censor, "but I object to the noun 'siege.' "
>
> "We cannot say that 'the siege of Singapore has begun.' Can we say that 'Singapore is now besieged'?"
>
> The censor nodded. "Yes, I will pass 'besieged.' *But I still don't like the word 'siege.'* "

At least one newspaperman who missed the conference and still could not seem to get the hang of this rule even after his colleagues patiently explained it to him, led his dispatch off with "The siege of Singapore has begun." The next morning when the shells were dropping on the island, he received his censored carbon back, and it read "The besiegement of Singapore has begun." Naturally "besiegement" was changed in London and New York back to "siege," the cable editors reasonably considering that this was a time for plain language.

He goes on to describe several partial censorships. One is how news gets delayed until the official version catches up to reporters. ("It is difficult to mention the military, naval, and RAF censors temperately. They held the correspondents' noses fast to the grindstone of the communiqués, even when the communiqués were two to three days behind the facts.") He also points out how a rigid system ordains what a correspondent turns out, knowing that certain ideas are forbidden. ("The newspaperman's malady is to accept all the inhibitions of a bad censorship and to discourage himself by precensoring his own work.") Another constant danger is "the staff of robot censors," who can be ferocious, "cut an entire leading paragraph off a narrative and then send it 10,000 miles away to enter the newspaper office headless, its whole opening statement of topic, place, and circumstances amputated."

Though it may be difficult, in our era of instantaneous electronic transmission, to conceive of any blockage interrupting the channel of news from reporter to editor—save by a more cunning censorship on the part of a government—it is illuminating to remind ourselves that the correspondents' version of World War II was, in a sense, only what the censors failed to stop.

And there was always the threat of dire punishment: the withdrawal, in a war zone, of accreditation, without which a reporter could not function, leaving his news organization without a berth in an important dateline. Thus in Singapore, to control American press criticism, the British disaccredited E. R. Noderer of the *Chicago Tribune* and Cecil Brown of CBS, *Newsweek,* and *Life.* Both men were compelled to leave; it radically altered their careers. Regarding Brown, "a strong hint was dropped that he was being punished for matter which he submitted and which was censored, but whose very submission indicated that he was not disposed as he should have been."

Weller concludes:

> Military censorship always ends by being political . . . A censorship is supposed to keep political criticism under control. Is there any point at which a correspondent would be hauled before the authorities for being too optimistic . . . by filing a dispatch that outbuttered the most complacent greasers of public opinion[?] . . . Words, words, words. But these were words to remember. Those tiresome discussions in the Cathay involved the principles for which people were offering all they had, blood and sweat, tears and toil . . . In one way the American and British peoples were fighting to be informed. They did not want to be fooled. They wanted to hear the truth. They could take it.
>
> It is through knowing the truth that the people discover their hidden will.

Throughout the war, then, there was another war going on, all along, and it did not end with any treaty of surrender.

So why were virtually all of Weller's 1945 dispatches from Japan censored? Surely the prison camp stories would've played well back home, building the case against a brutal enemy—even if the Nagasaki reports each contained a dangerous radiation all their own, the unpredictable half-life of truth. Difficult as it may be to parse MacArthur's motivations, it's also hard to think of one good reason why the U.S. government might've wanted to encourage any correspondents outside their guidance to venture into the nuclear sites. After Burchett, Weller was unknowingly sending his dispatches into a hornets' nest in Tokyo, where he hadn't a prayer of success. And after Truman's confidential memorandum, one week into Weller's odyssey, anything that got through the censors would've still probably been silenced back home.

Weller always maintained that since MacArthur was determined to be known as the vanquisher of Japan (despite denials of presidential ambition), he did not want to promote the bombs' success at the cost of his own, having already been upstaged by a troupe of scientists in New Mexico.

Likewise, a candid report on the radiation suffering in the Nagasaki hospitals, contradicting U.S. government assurances, could only embarrass MacArthur before the American people, since even a month after the bomb he had failed, as supreme commander, to provide medical assistance to the devastated scene. Nor would there be any such aid in Nagasaki until six weeks had passed; and it would come via the Navy, not thanks to MacArthur. That, for Weller, remained the great shame of the whole event, and the largest humiliation of all buried in the killed dispatches.

Besides the public relations headache that there had been American and Allied POWs directly beneath the Nagasaki bomb, the fact that most of them avoided atomic incineration simply by ducking into a shallow trench was not a military secret anyone wanted exposed. The bomb was an all-powerful, divine weapon; W. L. Laurence had said so.

There was yet another reason. Weller had been MacArthur's nemesis ever since the correspondent escaped from Singapore and Java to Australia in early 1942, and came under the iron hand of censorship while reporting the struggle up the Pacific islands. The general would have taken Weller's entry into Nagasaki as a personal affront as much as a defiance of his authority.

Already, a year earlier, in *Bases Overseas,* Weller had written: "Political censorship under MacArthur's command was strict, the officially expressed view of his headquarters being that a war correspondent was not entitled to inform the American public of matters of controversial nature . . ."

He then quotes a letter received from one of MacArthur's censors:

We believe that a correspondent has a certain duty towards the Commander of the Forces whom he represents, and it is the Commander-in-Chief's desire that nothing of a political nature be released as coming from his staff of correspondents, and nothing that may be in any way criticizing the efforts of any Commander of any of the Allied nations.

"What the United States badly needs," Weller concludes, "is a long cold bath of reality."

Tantalizingly absent from the files is an exchange of cables which must have taken place between Weller and his *Chicago Daily News* editor over the strange silences between September 5—the date on his Kanoya dispatches—and when he reached Guam seven weeks later. Once he learned his worst fears had been realized, he would've had to describe the enormous scoops that got away, and explain the most damning censorship he had suffered in the entire war. It is not so surprising I found no trace of these cables, or the home-office replies, anywhere in the archive. They must have hurt deeply.

Just after MacArthur's death, Weller summed him up as

deliberately remote, intimate only with his peers at the top. Rarely casual, dedicated, nearly humorless . . . [with] the un-conscious assumption of effortless superiority that the British once bred into their elite. It drew to him very competent spe-cialists, who asked only to be firmly directed, and sycophants, especially newsmen who gave up the fight against his censor-ship. Every general wants more of everything than he has, but the difference between MacArthur and others was that he would break windows to get it.

Twenty years later, in 1984, at age seventy-seven, Weller wrote:

As sure as Judgement Day, his wrath fell upon me. I had al-ready tried to pass a dispatch saying that Yalta was an Ameri-can disgrace, but this was worse . . . Jealous of the fact that "his war" of four years had been won by two bombs prepared with-out his knowledge and dropped without his command, MacArthur determined to do his best to erase from history—or

at least blur as well as censorship could—the important human
lessons of radiation's effect on civil populations.

VII

Very little of this book has ever seen the light of day.

"First into Nagasaki" was written for and appeared, with significant editorial cutting, as "Back to Nagasaki" in a 1967 anthology of
reporters' memoirs entitled *How I Got That Story,* put together by
the Overseas Press Club of New York. (I have restored all the
deleted passages.) Weller had, in 1965, produced a short account for
his paper, the *Chicago Daily News,* on the twentieth anniversary of
the bomb. For the longer piece, written in Rome in July 1966, he
benefited from far more space, a sense of authorial independence,
and from Gilbert Harrison's army report, written right after their
shared journey and which Harrison—by then the editor of the *New
Republic*—kindly forwarded to him in Italy. Harrison's notes have
clarified questions I had about Weller's first few days in Nagasaki
and also suggest there may yet be some dispatches missing.

Weller appears not to have realized then that Burchett had beat
him to a nuclear site (his opening paragraph suggests as much), but
in later years he always spoke admiringly of the achievement.

One inaccuracy in his recollections concerned how much work he
produced in three weeks on Kyushu; over the years he called it anything from ten thousand to twenty-five thousand words. This probably comes from conflating the Nagasaki stories with the POW
stories, but it is still way off the mark, since the true figure is nearly
fifty-five thousand words. "The Death Cruise," researched on
Kyushu but largely written after he left Nagasaki by ship for Guam,
runs at over twenty-five thousand words. Thus, apart from the 1966
memoir and my present essay, this entire book was written between
September 6 and October 21, 1945, totaling about eighty thousand
words of material in unedited form.

All Weller's dispatches have been "expanded" from a ready-for-
telegram language which reporters of the day were accustomed to

writing in directly. Due to the costs of sending stories from around the world back home—rates were calculated by the word—this compressed "cablese" removed all obvious words. Numbers, acronyms, and punctuations were spelled out.

I have worked from my father's blue-ink carbon copies, typed on one side of each long, double-spaced page—smudged and often highly mildewed or even crumbling. The originals went to the Tokyo censors and disappeared.

Fortunately each dispatch was dated by the correspondent. Since it was obvious at the receiving end what year and month the article was written in, the more telling detail (especially in war) was at what hour a reporter actually was typing—meaning how up-to-date his information was, since a dispatch might sit in a cable office for days awaiting transmission. For example, in 1942 the entire (Allied) South Pacific only had two working cable routes, and one was the slow way around Africa; reporters nominally based in Australia while covering the war on New Guinea might queue up behind a logjam of four hundred coded government messages.

At the top of each dispatch Weller provided a number—say, 62300—which indicates (if one knows the month already) the sixth of September, at 2300 hours. Similarly, 100200 means the tenth of the month, at 2 a.m. In this way I have been able to order the stories accurately and reconstruct Weller's movements around Kyushu.

To illustrate, here is the beginning of the eighth dispatch as typed in its original version, written at 1 a.m. on the morning of September 9:

> press collect via rca
> chicagonews newyork
> nagasaki 90100 article to follow nagasakis hospitals stop atomic bombs peculiar quote disease unquote comma uncured because untreated and untreated because undiagnosed comma is still snatching away lives here stop men women children with no outward marks injury are dying daily in hospitals some after having walked around three or four weeks minimum thinking theyve escaped stop doctors here have every modern medica-

ment but candidly confessed in talking to writer dash first allied
observer reach nagasaki since surrender undash that answer to
malady is beyond them stop their patients though skins whole
are simply passing away under their eyes paragraph

This becomes:

> The atomic bomb's peculiar "disease," uncured because it is un-
> treated and untreated because it is undiagnosed, is still snatch-
> ing away lives here. Men, women and children with no outward
> marks of injury are dying daily in hospitals, some after having
> walked around for three or four weeks thinking they have es-
> caped. The doctors here have every modern medicament, but
> candidly confessed in talking to the writer—the first Allied
> observer to reach Nagasaki since the surrender—that the an-
> swer to the malady is beyond them. Their patients, though
> their skins are whole, are simply passing away under their eyes.

The Nagasaki dispatches, dated September 6–9, and the later
ones dated September 20–25, are entirely intact and have not been
trimmed in any way. I'm convinced Weller attempted to send other
articles during those first few days; in "First into Nagasaki" he mentions (as does Harrison in his notes) examining a hillside outside the
city where the most expensive Mitsubishi machinery was hidden,
yet curiously there is no resulting dispatch.

From Harrison's notes, written on September 8 as an official report, I've been able to answer several lingering questions about the
entire journey. (The notes judiciously do not mention Weller's im-
personation of a colonel.) Harrison is more forthcoming about the
general's hospitality than Weller: "We were given a large beautiful
home overlooking the bay where we had the entire house at our disposal plus servants who prepared our food, baths and sleeping ac-
commodations. We bathed with buckets of hot and cold water. For
supper we were served hot *sake* wine, lobster, soy beans and seaweed, whale meat, beef, rice and biscuits. We were hungry."

On that second day (September 7) they made an extensive tour by car of the area damaged by the bomb—the ruined Mitsubishi factories that had produced steel fittings, ship parts, and electrical engines. At the one building not knocked down, the concrete Mitsubishi headquarters, they found former employees sitting around and, in one room, a line of boxes, each five inches square, containing the ashes of unknown dead. The employees encouraged Weller to photograph this altar. After visiting two POW camps as described in the dispatches, they found an American radio operator (mentioned above) whose B-29, carrying POW supplies, had crashed a few days earlier. He was the sole survivor, but could remember nothing and believed he was still on Saipan. He had not yet been told that his crewmates were dead.

The morning of September 8 they were found by the two American doctors who had come down from Camp #3—survivors of the Bataan death march of 1942 to Camp O'Donnell, in the Philippines. These doctors confirmed that no one, neither prisoners nor Japanese camp officials, knew for certain where all the Allied POW camps were on Kyushu, or how many men were in them. Harrison suggests that Weller's intention from the very start was to visit these unopened POW camps to the north after he saw Nagasaki. Though in his 1966 essay he was dismissive of all the unpolitical, look-Mom-I'm-free stories, he seems to have been aware that these prisoners would have seen both atomic bombs go off, and have dramatic sagas of their own.

For the entire afternoon until early evening they visited the civilian hospital, accompanied by the Dutch doctor who'd been a POW. "We visited two hospitals, interviewed a battery of civilian and military doctors and a professor at the local medical college." That evening Harrison was asked by a Japanese his own impressions of the hospitals. "It had been hard to see," he recounts, "but neither Weller nor I nor the Dutchman who went with us to the hospitals could feel remorse."

The suggestion is that Harrison left Nagasaki on September 9 by train to somewhere where he could get a lift to Tokyo by military plane. Weller stuck around, ran into the press junket, and proceeded north to the prison camps at Omuta on September 10. My guess is that he got one of the general's men to drive him up there and await his first dispatches, to carry onward to Tokyo. I also suspect that Weller wrote at length, in a now-lost dispatch, about the U.S. prisoners who survived in proximity to the blast, since he referred to this paradox so repeatedly for the next half century. From Chungking, China, perhaps late in 1945 or early in 1946, he wrote an article entitled "Bringing to Earth the Atomic Bomb," published in October 1946 as "Atom-Bomb Myth Exploded" in a small magazine called *Progress Guide*—a would-be *Reader's Digest,* apparently. (This implies that better markets turned the piece down.) It appears to echo material from that early dispatch which must have gone astray, concerning a prison camp right in Nagasaki:

At the end of a long line of iron girders of the several Mitsubishi factories in Nagasaki, pushed over at an angle as though with a great foot, there are the remains of an Allied prison camp. A prison camp under the bomb? Yes. And you see the severed water pipes—among the big copper vats of the food kitchen— still giving out pathetic upward streams from the earth, like clams on an alarmed sand flat.

The Allied prisoners were not in their shelters. But were they all killed? They were not. Of about 200, only *four* were killed outright and four died later. Only about 40 were wounded, and all recovered with little more than simple first aid.

The camp was ruined. Yet some men were out in the open, even, and were not killed. Some wore white garments. The light color threw off the gamma rays that killed so many people, and they were unharmed.

Look at the signposts by the camp. One across the street that bore thin white letters on a thick blue background was burned till it looks like a piece of bacon. Another over here, black letters on a white background, has no mark that it was ever touched by the blast.

Discount many of the deaths by the fact that the people were outdoors, open and vulnerable. Discount some more by the fact that many died of thermal burns, plain heat burns, not due to the heat of the bomb but to being caught in the odd fires afterward. The heat of the bomb, of course, killed many.

I obtained the first anatomical reports of the effects of the gamma ray from two shivering doctors in the municipal hospital, with its floors covered with despairing family circles of the unmutilated but doomed. The gamma ray, one of the X-ray family, kills in three ways, all horrible.

It reduces the red corpuscles. It reduces the white corpuscles. And last and most serious, it reduces the platelets: the precious small elements that give the blood its power of clotting.

Reducing the reds means anemia. Reducing the whites means taking away the capacity to fight disease, for these are the disease-hunters. But reducing the platelets means that you die from a slight constriction of the throat, with just a few pimples on your legs. You die and they cut you open and your intestine is thick-choked with blood.

All this is very terrible, especially because the long, bony hand can reach out many days after the explosion and summon you by the shoulder. You can walk around perfectly normally for a month, and then you get the touch that means you have been tapped for death.

How could you have avoided this? Very simply. At a great enough distance, two miles or so, white clothing will beat back the gamma. Stand beside a wall; have any masonry between you and the bomb; and you are as safe as underground.

In the *shadow* of the gamma there is safety, not death.

Nagasaki is, of course, the neglected bomb, the one less written about; the name itself is not so charged as *Hiroshima*. Yet in several ways it is the more controversial bombing, and some historians who do not question the necessity of bombing the first question bombing the second. At the same time it seems far more fitting as a primary target, since the city was devoted to weapons manufacture; a great deal of Japan's armaments were made here. The original plan had been for a gap between the bombs of five days, not three—the second was to have been dropped on August 11—but a forecast of bad weather for the week to come pushed the schedule forward, not back.

Meanwhile there were conflicting reports in the Japanese hierarchy. A prominent physicist who reached Hiroshima on August 8, having failed to fly down a day earlier, reported back that evening to the prime minister in Tokyo that it had been, indeed, an atomic bomb, with a force of twenty thousand tons of TNT. He overestimated; it was probably about three-quarters that. He was awestruck and horrified, but he was also contradicted by a patriotic field marshal who had survived the bomb in his nearby headquarters and let his superiors know that it was "not that powerful a weapon."

During the day of August 8 the Soviet Union declared war against Japan, and during the night hurled a million and a half troops into Manchuria (now northeast China) against Japanese occupying forces, the Kwantung Army, which numbered close to 2 million. This tremendously powerful blitzkrieg meant Japan's loss of a region rich in much-needed raw materials as well as their grip on every crucial city. It was underreported at the time, because of Hiroshima.

At around 11 a.m. on August 9, Nagasaki received its bomb, armed with man-made plutonium 239 and known as "Fat Man" to the B-29 crew.

It is problematic to calculate deaths in either nuclear site precisely, especially those from radiation over the decades. The immediate death toll in Nagasaki was perhaps around forty thousand, the total possibly about seventy thousand. (Different figures in both directions are available, depending on one's source.) Nagasaki was not harmed as extensively as Hiroshima, largely due to topography. The death toll was lower by between a third and a half; parts of the city survived relatively intact.

Weller described it years later as "scorched and subdued but far from dead . . . there was a feeling of emptiness: streets empty of cars, sky empty of airplanes, a harbor empty of boats except one beached, slowly-burning junk that sent a mourning veil of black over the blackened docks and flattened warehouses. There were a few bicycles but generally it was a city of slow pedestrians, stunned and thoughtful . . . I climbed the hill, passing the unharmed homes of the well-to-do. As the panorama unfolded I could see the long black skeleton of the Mitsubishi aircraft and shipbuilding plant and the fields of ashes near it." This is a long way from Burchett's description of Hiroshima as a wasteland completely pulverized into dust and rubble.

Bureaucratically, once Truman ordered the first attack, the second was also put in motion. Kokura, with an army base—"a smaller city of greater military importance" according to Weller—was the preferred target on the morning of August 9, but it was covered with clouds. Thus Nagasaki experienced the plutonium bomb, developed at a specific extra cost of about $400 million.

No brief essay is the proper place to go into the peculiar psychology behind the manufacture and first use of an experimental weapon, which acquires increasing gravitational torque with time, especially during a costly war that has gone on for years and after a peace has already been made with one of two enemies (thereby inviting scrutiny from freshly budget-minded politicians). Whether one argues that it was right or wrong to drop the atomic bomb once, or twice, or at all, it is impossible on reading the history of the Manhattan Project not to conclude that short of an unexpected surrender from Japan, it was inevitable that it would be dropped.

Some have seen the Nagasaki bomb, politically, as the actual end of World War II; others as the commencement of an America-led Pax Atomica; still others (noting the timing with the USSR's entry into the war with Japan) as the start of the Cold War. Although Truman's secret news blackout may have done little specifically to sway any long-term discussion about the bomb, it had its desired effect. After Bill Lawrence, for example, no *New York Times* reporter visited Hiroshima for another five months.

On the afternoon of August 9, hearing the news that Nagasaki had been bombed, Emperor Hirohito called an imperial conference at which his ministers debated the wisdom of surrender. After hours of talk, at 2 a.m. Hirohito stated that he felt Japan should accept the terms of the Potsdam Declaration, terms of surrender proposed in late July by Truman (who had only become president on Roosevelt's death in April). But Potsdam called for the emperor to step down; and his ministers insisted that their acceptance depended on Hirohito being allowed to remain as sovereign—an astute demand that would ensure a sense of national exoneration. James F. Byrnes, the U.S. secretary of state, did not deal directly with this, and on August 14 Japan surrendered at Hirohito's command. The next day, the entire country heard with astonishment the first radio broadcast from a supreme ruler, now telling them squeakily, in the antiquated argot of the imperial court, that he was surrendering to save all mankind "from total extinction."

Until then, Japan's goal had been full, all-out war, as a country wholly committed; any Japanese famously preferred to die for the emperor rather than to surrender. (*One hundred million die together!* was the slogan.) Today the goal was surrender: all-out peace. It was the emperor's new will. Later that day a member of his cabinet, over the radio, formally denounced the United States for ignoring international law by dropping the atomic bombs.

In 1988, on the forty-seventh anniversary of the Japanese attack on Pearl Harbor, when the mayor of Nagasaki accused Hirohito of responsibility for the war and its numerous atrocities, he inadvertently stirred up petitions for his own impeachment, and nationwide protests and riots calling for his assassination.

A month afterward, in January 1989, Hirohito died at age eighty-seven, still emperor of Japan. Eleven days later the mayor, whom the Nagasaki police were no longer protecting, was shot in the back. He barely survived.

VIII

It is hardly surprising that a prisoner of war about to die from sustained torture on Kyushu in August 1945 and (for example) a political scientist sixty years later may hold a different attitude toward the dropping of the atomic bomb. The Japanese POW camps are one of the great omissions, one of the convenient erasures, of World War II memory. Not in the memories of those lucky enough to survive, but in the collective memory of those who read about the war from an armchair, or learn it in a classroom, or watch its mythologizing in a movie. If the only way to grasp the war's conclusion is to face, in Weller's phrase, "the anatomy of radiated man," likewise it is impossible to understand war with the Japanese without considering their POW camps. They are a chapter of the conflict that is largely ignored, at least in the United States, and especially so relative to the Nazi prisoner of war camps (Gavan Daws' is one of the few panoramic histories of great depth). As the decades pass, there is less and less motivation in any of the cultures involved to explore what occurred.

Weller's dispatches remind us of the individuals to whom all this happened. These voices rescued from the past each have their say, and if some seem repetitive that is part of the point. Like the Nagasaki dispatches, the prison camp stories exist as cablese that needed to be fleshed out into proper prose. I have trimmed judiciously, by about eight thousand words—around 20 percent. This was done to avoid highly redundant material, and also to remove the addresses of POWs which Weller included for a readership back home who, in any case, never got to see them. Such details were meant to let them know their loved ones were still alive.

When Weller left Nagasaki and shifted his attention to the camps, he knew they would soon be emptied and the former prisoners, his sources, scattered within days. He found men as eager to tell their sagas as he was to write them down. Weller was also aware there might soon be an internal pressure within the survivors to try to forget what they'd undergone, and their stories' flush of immediacy would soon be lost.

All the POW camp dispatches appear in shortened form. There are also two articles which Weller wrote just after arriving from Nagasaki in Guam. These exist as finished typescripts, and concern the "theater" put on to fool visiting Red Cross inspectors, and the aberrant Japanese prison camp commanders. Both were mailed not to Weller's newspaper but to his New York literary agent, Harold Ober, to be sold as magazine features. As best I can determine neither ever appeared. I have placed them among other Omuta stories about Camp #17.

Beyond the deprivations, degradations, and tortures these prisoners endured, each man often recounts how he got to the camps Weller visited. These conflicts, and all they implied, would have been instantly recognizable to the 1945 public. Many of the Dutch and the British, the Australians and Canadians, were taken in the defeats of Singapore (130,000), Java (32,000), and Hong Kong (14,000). Many of the Americans got captured on Guam or Wake; or in the Philippines (75,000), to then endure the Bataan death march, on which one in four died. Some built the Siam-Burma railroad, which claimed yet another 15,000 lives, same ratio. Nearly everywhere, in a hurry, the Japanese won and the Allies lost. The United States saw its navy smashed at Pearl Harbor and its Pacific air forces wiped out in Manila, just before MacArthur got himself safely out to Australia.

This litany of early military disasters added up to astonishing numbers. In a mere six months the Japanese, at a cost of only 15,000 of their own men (deaths and casualties), took 320,000 Allied soldiers out of the war, either as deaths, casualties, or prisoners; over half these were Asiatic. White prisoners, about 140,000 total over the course of the conflict, became slave labor across the growing Japanese empire. (Asiatic prisoners were often turned loose, as good propaganda among the subjugated peoples.) Japan had not signed the 1929 Geneva Conventions regarding treatment of prisoners of war, and a Japanese soldier would sooner be killed than captured: thus every enemy soldier who surrendered was a coward, a cur, a thing. Any notion of "inhumane treatment" toward a surrendered Chinese, much less a white man, was incomprehensible. White men were the foe, so their role was to work, then die. Whether their deaths proved painful did not matter to the Japanese.

Unlike the Nazi POW camps, there were few escape attempts, for it was obvious to any Allied POW in Asia that a white face was an immediate giveaway even had he succeeded, and the Japanese made it clear that they would execute ten men for every man who escaped. Statistically it was seven times healthier to be a POW under the Nazis than under the Japanese. By war's end, one out of every three white prisoners had died as their captives— "starved to death, worked to death, beaten to death, dead of loathsome epidemic diseases that the Japanese would not treat," as Daws puts it. Another year of war and there would have been no POWs still alive. (A Japan War Ministry directive of August 1944 iterated that "the aim is to annihilate them all, and not to leave any traces.")

Long-term survival amid such conditions, in what prisoners called "the University of the Far East," differed by nationality, and camps were largely segregated by country. The Dutch, as the only people with generations of experience at staying alive amid Asian diseases, proved most adept as POWs, with a death rate under 20 percent. (This disparity also reflects the fact that relatively few died in hellships.) The British died at around 32 percent, the Australians at 33 percent, the Americans at 34 percent. Some sources put all these figures higher.

Under the Nazis, who rather paradoxically subscribed to the Geneva Conventions, the Allied POW death rate was only 4 percent.

What the men only partially convey in Weller's camp dispatches were the conditions under which they somehow survived: few if any medical supplies—like anesthetic—or basic tools, even for amputations, because the Japanese refused to share the contents of regularly delivered Red Cross supply boxes; often no regular baths, and no reliable drinking water; little toothpaste or soap, so no chance to stave off the lower-torso diseases that accompany filthy latrines and flies, with dysentery and malaria the worst killers at up to 95 percent infected in some camp populations, plus crotch rot and all manner of vitamin deficiency diseases like scurvy, protein edema, and beriberi in which the body swelled up from giant bags of fluids that choked the lungs; ulcers that ate away the flesh so painfully that men peed in the holes in their own legs or poured in gasoline if they could get it; cholera and dengue fever; or all the inevitable diseases that came with multitudes of rats, fleas, maggots, and lice. For those who worked in the coal mines, standing for hours in water, pneumonia and tuberculosis were constant perils.

They starved, too, as the dispatches attest, on only five hundred to six hundred calories a day—a fifth of what a working man needs. A sad specialty, if it can be called that, of the American POW camps was trading in food futures. A man might trade two dinners against a single extra breakfast, to feel his stomach almost full for once. With everyone malnourished, it was possible to trade yourself into starvation this way. Such a practice horrified the British and Dutch and Australians, but it went on in all the U.S. camps, even when outlawed by the commanding officers. For men with serious nicotine fixations—in World War II three out of four servicemen smoked—trading meals for cigarettes was another way to starve themselves. The practice of self-mutilation, so detailed in Weller's dispatches, was another particularly American skill, though it often meant the difference between life and death if it bought someone a reprieve from the coal mines. The trick, if you were right-handed, was to be sure the expert broke your left arm, and did it cleanly.

Omuta, a small city and the site of several camps, was about thirty-five miles northeast and across the bay from Nagasaki. It was in the Fukuoka military district, about forty miles due south of that city. Weller possibly stayed in Omuta rather than in Camp #17 or #25, but knowing him it seems more likely he would've stayed at each camp, especially considering how much he researched and wrote in a few days.

Camp #7, which Weller identifies as at Izuka (now spelled Iizuka), is today referred to as Futase #7. The much smaller Camp #23, also placed by him at Izuka, is a few miles due south, and usually called Keisen #23. I suspect that Weller visited the Izuka camps with a prisoner recovery team which took him along after emptying the Omuta camps. A week later he accompanied a recovery team out of Nagasaki to visit Sasebo Camp #18, about fifty miles to the northwest.

Omuta Camp #17, which the bulk of Weller's dispatches describe, was the largest POW camp in Japan, and one of the harshest. Its facilities were somewhat better than others'; there was bathing water at least several months a year. Its thirty-three buildings, originally laborers' quarters built by the Mitsui Coal Mining Company, had some ventilation—a liability during winter. The coal mines were about a mile walk from camp. Theoretically men were given a day off every ten days, though sometimes they worked for four weeks straight.

The owner of the coal mines, Baron Takaharu Mitsui (1900–1983), a graduate of Dartmouth College in New Hampshire and world famous as a philatelist, was head of one of the two most powerful industrial families in Japan (along with Mitsubishi), and among the wealthiest men in the country. His mines produced half of its coal, though those at Omuta had been closed down in the 1920s as unsafe. He was well aware of the work and living conditions of the POWs, having visited the camp several times in his open touring car. Like other companies that used Allied prisoners as slave labor—Mitsubishi, Nippon Steel, Kawasaki—Mitsui paid the Japanese army a leasing fee per prisoner of two yen per day (above the average Japanese daily income), and the army kept the money. Though the prisoners were supposedly being paid a wage that was a minuscule fraction of this, very few ever received anything.

Because of this prisoner slave labor, such vast companies maintained full production throughout the war. Because of the delay between surrender and the occupation, they were able (unlike equivalent German companies) to obliterate a damning paper trail before the Americans arrived. They managed to persuade MacArthur's representatives that it was in no one's interests to slow down Japan's recovery by holding millionaire industrialists legally and financially responsible for what they had done in wartime—say, to extract the sort of POW reparations that the Dutch managed to. Indeed, many returning U.S. POWs were ordered by intelligence officers never to speak of their experiences at the hands of the Japanese unless they were given military clearance to do so; some were even compelled to sign documents to this end.

I have been unable to clear up the details on censorship of the POW dispatches. Weller arrived at Omuta Camp #17 on Monday, September 10. The fact that late the following night he typed up an emergency dispatch to Tokyo regarding B-29 supply drops to the camp suggests he had some way (perhaps still a *kempeitai* borrowed from the general) of getting messages up to the capital. Or perhaps there was domestic cable service from Omuta itself? Supporting either explanation, the *Chicago Daily News* ran an extremely brief piece on local-son Arthur Wermuth, "the one-man army," on September 12 (which I incorporated into the later one for this book). No other POW stories appeared around then, so they must have been censored in Tokyo. Had they reached Chicago, lengthy as they are, the paper could easily have edited out the bomb impressions, as per Truman's secret memorandum, and published just the accounts of imprisonment from each dispatch.

When Weller returned to Nagasaki on September 20 he seems to have made another concerted effort to send off stories or fragments, and succeeded in a minor way via the just-arrived Navy. On September 25 the *Chicago Daily News* published his first POWs dispatch, written two weeks earlier, entirely the remembrances by Chicago servicemen of their captivity plus a few bomb impressions; maybe this was let through as a "hometowner" story. On September 26 the newspaper ran a tiny portion of his long article from Izuka Camp #7, written nine days earlier—the few paragraphs about Chicago-area servicemen. On September 27 they ran his short piece about released POWs going home to the United States psychologically healthy (a preview of the military's coming lack of responsibility toward these men) and the editors cut Weller's cynical closing phrase questioning the official wrap-up. On October 1 they ran his short dispatch about the Dutchman on Java in 1942, tortured to madness, and on October 17–18 an abbreviated version of the Wake Island saga. It seems likely that the Navy was willing to send stories that had taken place nearly four years earlier outside Japan, or a smidgin of local-boy news for a Chicago readership, but otherwise little more.

Once Weller left Nagasaki by ship for Guam via Okinawa, Saipan, and Iwo Jima, he immediately wrote a short story on board which takes place in a camp evidently modeled on Omuta #17. "Departure, with Sword and Ashes" was sent to his agent Ober from Guam. It was published by the *Saturday Evening Post* in the issue of March 23, 1946. This popular weekly magazine, a top-paying market, frequently carried Weller's fiction and journalism, yet the delay suggests that editors thought it better to wait before running such material. The five-thousand-word story includes details of the camps after the recovery teams arrived that did not make it into any of the dispatches, written now not with a reporter's but with a novelist's eye.

For example, it describes the Baron Mitsui figure (here called Baron Satsumai) asking the prisoner recovery team over for tea; Major Toth, the senior officer among the prisoners, naturally refuses to go, and the head of the recovery team cannot understand why. These teams, to Toth, seem to have arrived from another planet— their hair "thick with an almost artificial brushiness . . . a hint of unexpended violence in their purposeful walk." An ex-prisoner named Mendoza has lost four fingers working in the coal mine: "Among the ulcers on his legs Toth recognized the old one which Lieutenant Bernstein, the medical officer, had nourished and kept alive with cap-lantern acid, so that Mendoza, after his amputation, would not have to go down the shaft again. It was the most famous of Camp 34's many acid-fed ulcers; it had flourished nineteen weeks, and even in its present fossilized or emeritus condition it still had an eye like a devilfish."

There is also, notably, a discussion of the food-trading among U.S. prisoners which so shocked other nationalities of prisoner and which Weller only mentions, I believe, once in his newspaper dispatches (" 'Halborn owed me four rice rations and two cigarettes . . . it's a legal debt' "). Toth reflects: "By sale, theft and compromise, Japan had crept in and occupied the fortress of each man's body. The Christmas before last, when he had had diarrhea, Borum had sold his own knife and fork for three rations of rice for him . . . Often he caught himself thinking whole sentences in Japanese."

But his greatest scorn is for the baron, trying to ingratiate himself with the POW officers ever since the news of Japan's surrender: "Disgust turned in Toth's stomach. 'Two weeks' admiration, after two years' starvation,' he said with unashamed bitterness. 'You know what we call that around #34? We call it atomic love.' "

He is aware that soon all this will disappear, will not be retained by either the Americans or the Japanese, eager for their own reasons to forget: "What the hell, who could come from outside and see the baroness pouring tea . . . and even the *kempeitai* ducking their little shaven heads, and believe it ever happened? All the most feared guards had disappeared—Fishface, the Growler, Donald Duck and the Fresno Kid—with their *kabokos* and their whips of motor belting and their challenges of '*Sabis?*' ('You want a gift?') followed by a bone-breaking blow. Gone, all gone."

The airdrops mentioned in Weller's dispatches were on a massive scale, parachuted from B-29s flying out of the Marianas. The drops began over the Japanese prison camps soon after the surrender on August 15, and they were a skill unto themselves. Location was everything. Thousands of pounds of canned food in crates on wooden pallets, or fifty-five-gallon drums, could easily kill if they crashed through the roof of a prisoner barracks or slammed into a farmer in a rice paddy. One camp was torched by a crate of matches that self-ignited on arrival. Many loads blew up on impact or even on the way down, and in fact more POWs were killed by unfortunate airdrops than by the atomic bombs. At Camp #17 one man was killed by a supply of fruit salad. The last Marine survivor of the heroic battle for Wake Island to die in the war was felled by a load of SPAM.

While this book was in preparation I received letters from former POWs at Camp #17 who, six decades on, recalled my father's arrival. Charles Balaza, who survived Corregidor, Camp Cabanatuan, Nichols Field, a hellship, and two years in the mines at Omuta, wrote, "I remember him as an angel that God sent, telling us that the war was over." Another, the late Billy Ayers, often joked with his nephew that "while he was saved by the bomb, he was rescued by a reporter." When Weller arrived, it was now eight days since the treaty and twenty-five days since Japan's capitulation. But the POWs did not know this. Balaza explains in his memoir why the men didn't leave the camp: "I got up one morning and discovered that the gates of our prison were wide open . . . A strange feeling came over me . . . Could it be some kind of trap? No one made a move for the gates, fearing the Japs may have machine guns lined up ready to fire . . . Trying to escape would have given them a very good excuse to kill us."

James Bashleben—quoted in Weller's first POW dispatch—wrote me the following account, sixty years and six weeks later.

I was a POW in Camp 17 and recall the day your father entered the camp—it was after the war ended. We were not aware of this, even though we were no longer working in the coal mine. Also, Red Cross boxes had been distributed, and we had been given new clothing. We suspected something was happening.

Another POW and I were near the front gate to the camp when a person in light khakis entered unescorted and went directly into the camp commander's office. We were stunned! The person was George Weller.

Shortly afterward we were told to assemble in an open area within the camp. There a large platform had been erected. [Four or five feet above the ground, remembers Major John Perkowski; it was around noon.] We lined up on one side facing the platform and the Japanese guards lined up on the other side. We noticed at once that they carried no rifles.

The camp commander [Isao Fukuhara], an interpreter and George Weller took the stand, and the commander began his speech. The only sentence I can recall is when he said, "Japan has laid down its arms in favor of a great nation." I do not remember any great emotional display at that moment. After years of our determination to beat the hell out of these guys, we just stood there speechless.

It was then that George Weller took over, and spoke to us. Sixty years is a long time ago, but as near as I can recall he told us about the A-bombs at Hiroshima and Nagasaki. Also, that the war was over and troops were already occupying Kyushu.

"The 21st Cavalry is already flying in troops and supplies from Okinawa," he said. "I have no authority to tell you what to do, but why should those planes go back empty?" Immediately, a couple of POWs took off for Kanoya field.

The following day a small plane flew over the camp and dropped a message it was OK to come down. I, along with a couple other POWs, tossed some Red Cross food in our shirts and took off. We reached the 21st Cavalry, boarded an "empty plane" and flew to Okinawa. Thanks to a subtle hint from George Weller we were on our way home!

Another POW, Wesley C. Browning Jr.—one of the original "old 500" prisoners at the camp—wrote me:

I remember very well one of the things that your father told us. It was: "I am a civilian and cannot tell you what to do, but if I were you, this is what I would do. About a hundred or so miles south of here is Atsuga Air Field, where our planes are coming in around the clock with men and supplies and are leaving empty. If you were there they would be glad to take you south to Manila."

After your father finished his talk Lieutenant Little, a Naval officer, proceeded to tell us, "If any of you leave this camp without my permission I will court-martial you."

As it turned out, Little was the one that was court-martialed. The next day three friends and I departed Camp #17, walked to the train station and found our way to Atsuga Air Field and were flown to Manila after a stopover at Formosa.

This incident is referred to in Weller's twelfth POW dispatch.

Among his Nagasaki papers I found a large sheet of lined paper handwritten in pencil, as if by a schoolchild, in English, and signed *The Camp Commander at Fukuoka,* which was Omuta's military district. It is impossible to say if this is the translated statement by the commandant of Camp #17, the much-feared Fukuhara, as scrawled out by the interpreter and read aloud just before Weller spoke. But its tone is probably not unique:

I am pleased to inform you that we received military orders for stoppage of welfare [!] on Aug. 18th.

Since you were interned in this camp you have doubtless had to go through much trouble and agony due to the extension of your stay here as prisoners of war. But you have overcome them and the news that the day for which you longed day and night, the day on which you could return to your dear homeland where your beloved wifes [sic] and children, parents, brothers, and sisters, are eagerly awaiting you, has become a fact is probably your supreme joy.

I would like to extend to you my most sincere congraulations [sic] but at the same time I sympathize most deeply with those who have been inable [sic] due to illness or some other unfortunate reason, to greet this joyous day.

By order, we the camp staff, have done all in our power towards your management and protection, but conditions here, we regret that we were unable to do half of what we wanted to do for you. But I trust in your great understanding on this point.

Several days ago at one camp the prisoners presented the camp staff and factory foremen with part of their valuable relief food stuff and personal belongings. This I know is an expression of your understandings open hearted gentlemenliness [sic] and we the camp staff are all deeply moved.

Until you are transferred over to Allied hands at a port to be designated later you will have to wait at this camp. Therefore I sincerely wish that you will wait quietly for the day when you can return to your homeland, behaving according to camp regulations, holding fast your pride and honour as people of a great nation and taking care of your health.

The Camp Commander
at Fukuoka

One of Weller's photographs shows the judgment of Fukuhara's earliest POWs, the original "old 500" in Camp #17. On a wall has been written, in careful, large capital letters: "THIS WAS THE H.Q. OF FUKAHARA, [sic] ONE OF THE MOST VICIOUS AND INHUMANE PRISON COMMANDERS." Fukuhara was found guilty of war crimes and hanged in early 1946.

Others, also guilty, even more vicious and inhumane, were luckier. Like the masterminds of Unit 731 of the Japanese army, near a Mitsubishi factory in Manchuria, who spent years performing imaginative experiments on white and Asian POWs, to learn how much suffering humans of all varieties could take before they died—atrocities to rival or surpass anything the Nazis thought up. MacArthur felt the U.S. military had use for such invaluable research in the coming fields of biological and chemical warfare, not to mention torture, and he provided dozens in Unit 731 with immunity in return for information. Many went on to become successful politicians and scientists, even millionaires, in Japan and in the United States.

IX

"The Death Cruise" would not exist had Weller never interviewed scores of prisoners. At some point early in those weeks he realized he had stumbled on another significant piece of history that was unwritten. Despite its descriptions of murder, cannibalism, and POW deaths by friendly fire, the story got through. This may be because the text was not delivered in cablese to a censor's office in Tokyo, but was sent from Guam, where Weller got accredited to Admiral Nimitz and the Navy. He finished the typescript on board the ship that carried him, encased in plaster, away from Nagasaki, and mailed it back to the *Chicago Daily News.* Neither his original nor his carbon bear a *Passed By Censors* stamp, nor is there any mention of censors in the correspondence. Yet alone of the 1945 material in this book (except for a few of the POW dispatches), it actually got published—albeit incomplete, with many of the more repellent passages omitted. It is also virtually the only wartime material here that exists as finished prose rather than as compressed cablese. "The Death Cruise" has never appeared complete, with all its hardships unsanitized, until now.

It is not so surprising that the two-hundred-plus Japanese hellship voyages have entered neither the general cultural memory, nor the cinema mythology, of World War II. They were unwaveringly horrific, and the deeper one goes into the details of each, the worse it all becomes. Though there have been books on the subject over the decades, those survivors still living quite reasonably feel their suffering has been neglected by the public and even by historians. The 102-volume official Japanese military records of World War II, for example, do not mention the ships at all. Nor do the U.S. records treat them as a separate area of study, deserving their own archival harbor. Yet more than a third of all Allied combatants taken prisoner rode at least one hellship.

Besides the documented voyages there were dozens of other hellships, for the most part undocumented, that are rarely mentioned because so little is factually known about them—like the ones that carried the 139,000 "comfort women," sexual slaves, all over the Japanese empire, or those that slogged Asiatic male prisoners as movable, expendable slave labor. These people suffered and died in their own hellships, too; no one speaks for them.

The ships were mostly merchant vessels (Mitsubishi owned and ran at least seventeen) used to transport Allied POWs from Malaya, Burma, the Netherlands East Indies, Borneo, the Philippines, and so on, either to elsewhere in the Japanese Greater East Asia Co-Prosperity Sphere or to Japan, to be crammed in prison camps and put to work. A single journey often involved several ships. As James Erickson points out, "Some of the *Oryoku Maru* survivors had been on six hellships; one to Davao, two back to Manila, and then the three to Japan." At war's end the Japanese were careful to eradicate a great deal of relevant documents.

As a result, statistics about the hellships are notoriously unreliable, and no two sources agree. It seems likely that between January 1942 and July 1945 over fifty thousand prisoners traveled by at least one hellship. About twenty-one thousand died, a rate of over 40 percent. The Death Cruise was among the most brutal in terms of suffering, and among the deadliest, both proportionally and in total losses. Only one man in six survived.

The hellships were, by themselves, the most deadly aspect of the war in the Pacific. A mathematical argument can be made that it was even more dangerous to be a passenger with the Japanese than to be in combat against them. Yet this is somewhat misleading, for as horrific as the hellships were—and there is no scarcity of quotes from men who experienced all the nightmares the war had to offer and still pronounced their weeks in a hellship's hold as the worst—the majority of deaths on board were a result of so-called friendly fire. Over 90 percent of Allied prisoner deaths at sea were the result of attacks on hellships by their own (usually American) planes and submarines, as with the *Oryoku Maru*. Death by friendly fire is one of the knottiest tragedies of war; once a conflict is over, it is discussed as vaguely and infrequently as possible. The sad fact is that fully one out of every three of *all* the Allied POWs killed in the entire war with the Japanese were killed by friendly fire at sea.

In terms of the *Oryoku Maru*, by autumn 1944 the movements of POWs out of the Philippines were accurately known to MacArthur's broad intelligence network. And yet American forces continued to sink Japanese transport ships that were carrying POWs. Of course, they were also carrying Japanese troops and military supplies, civilian passengers, and cargo. Weller does not provide a final tally, but out of the roughly 1,300 men who died as a result of the Death Cruise, at least five hundred died through U.S. attacks.

Weller's was the earliest serious extensive reportage on any hellship, and also the first to reach the American public. (There'd been earlier minimal reports in the United States on the *Shinyo Maru* and *Arisan Maru*, and about rescues of POWs in the water from a couple of other torpedoed vessels.) It remains the most in-depth contemporaneous eyewitness coverage of a hellship. Every other narrative of the Death Cruise has drawn substantially from it, almost invariably without giving credit.

Nearly all the men on board were Americans, and, unusually, two-thirds were officers. Though British, Australian, and Dutch prisoners suffered equivalent hells on their own hellships many times, it would appear that only American prisoners at sea ever committed acts of murder, vampirism, and even cannibalism to survive. Why, stretched to such extremes, did Americans behave differently?

It has been argued that each nationality was protected by its character against such a breakdown; that the Australians were better at mucking in together, or that the rigid class system enabled British officers to keep order and resist an every-man-for-himself mentality that American prisoners, for whatever reason, were unable to fend off. Cited along with these theories is the fact that in the POW camps only Americans seemed to re-create a harsh capitalistic system that resulted in food trading. Another possible answer is that the claim may not be accurate—that, instead, only Americans have had the self-possession to own up to such behavior.

The careful reader will have noticed that certain names recur a few times in these pages. Some men within the space of eight months survived the Death Cruise, the harsh conditions in the mines and the camps, and then watched both atomic bombs explode.

Throughout the war Weller often wrote longer articles that ran as series in the *Chicago Daily News* and its syndicate newspapers. "The Death Cruise" was the longest. Although most of Weller's research was done in the prison camps, it was supplemented with interviews en route from Nagasaki to Guam via Okinawa and Saipan. Evidently he wrote most of the twenty-five-thousand-word piece aboard ship, and mailed it to the *Chicago Daily News* on October 20. A letter from Guam on November 1 to his editor, Hal O'Flaherty— who had recently taken over from Carroll Binder—states:

> Ten days ago I sent you a set of rough drawings to go with this death cruise story, asking for an acknowledgment when you received them. No cable has come yet, but I am hoping you will have had them by the time this manuscript arrives. . . .
>
> I have felt enough faith in the subject to have worked on it every moment I could since I first heard of it at Omuta on September 10th. None of the survivors kept notes—they were not allowed to—and the army was way behind me on this topic at the time. So I have made over 70 pages of notes alone, plus many lists and cross-lists of names.
>
> I realize that it is confronting you with a new struggle for space to give you this just before Christmas. But I should have felt remiss in the correspondent's duty toward history if I failed

to record this before liberation had sicklied over the sharp memories these prisoners possessed. . . .

The orthopods are going to tell me this weekend whether they will let me go to China. Will you please acknowledge this MS and the October 20th sketches as they come in? A cable would relieve my mind very much.

As it turned out, the *Chicago Daily News* moved with speed once the story arrived. It ran in eleven parts, starting November 9. The *St. Louis Post-Dispatch* ran it in fifteen parts beginning on November 11, and the *San Francisco Chronicle* ran it in nineteen parts beginning on November 18. In all cases the story was cut, often very heavily, and differently from city to city. Perhaps editors felt that, after the war, the time for detailing such gruesome suffering had passed; references to murder among the POWs, much less to blood drinking, were minimized or eliminated.

The typescript also contains several partial lists of the dead at different stages of the journey. Weller included them with misgivings, aware that their numerous inaccuracies would not be resolved for months. Though the lists appear in some newspaper serializations, it seemed irresponsible to repeat them here. (I have corrected a few spelling errors in names in the text itself.)

Two years later, in 1947, following trials brought as a result of their conduct on the Death Cruise, Shusuke Wada received a sentence of life imprisonment and Lieutenant Junsabura Toshino the death sentence. Toshino was hanged; but Wada, who many of the men thought even more deserving of a noose, was let out of prison after serving only eight years.

X

From Guam Weller proceeded to Shanghai, then Chungking, China's wartime capital, and spent part of the winter in Beijing. He covered the hasty Soviet withdrawal from Changchun that deftly handed Manchuria over to the Communist Chinese, who imprisoned him for three weeks. Throughout those months Weller wouldn't let Nagasaki go, determined to pull some substance out of an experience still fresh in his memory. From Tsingtao, China, on May 19, 1946, no doubt as a result of a chance encounter, he filed this story.

> Some Japanese died at Nagasaki long after the blast from "atomic skin," the co-builder of Nagasaki's new "atomic airstrip" said today.
>
> Lieutenant Commander Paul O'Donnell of Peekskill, New York, said Navy doctors have concluded that small particles of radium-impregnated dust entered below the surface of bodies of some Japanese who died weeks later. The bomb's terrific blast lodged deadly particles under their skin, Navy doctors now believe, reversing the theory held earlier that irradiation entered directly in the form of the ray and had a permanent effect.
>
> All doctors are agreed that the bomb's main effect is killing platelets in the bloodstream: small elements which give the blood its capacity to clot.

From Chungking there was also that magazine article published in October 1946 as "Atom-Bomb Myth Exploded," and quoted from earlier:

> The atomic bomb which laid waste Nagasaki never struck that city. An atomic bomb does not strike its target; it murders the earth, but it bursts in the air far above it . . . The great rainbow shimmering cloud of gases builds into a tall, ghost-like figure of a genii, with the ghastly head of a foetus. It seems to throw man in its shadow. . . .
>
> What the small, drab people of Nagasaki saw around them a half hour after the cloud built its mighty, spectre-like column in their midst, was this: a great, flattened area of industrial slum. It was a sea of rubble, timbers at all angles, cries coming out

from under them. The heavy or concrete buildings still stood, though an air-push of death had moved through their windows.

Then smoke began to arise over the tossed sea of smashed buildings. The city had not caught fire immediately; it was crushed first . . . But these smokes multiplied. Some began to turn red, then yellow. Smokes began to appear in other places.

The little fire engines ran here and there, unrolling hoses. But there were too many fires. They broke out all around the firemen, who were cut off. Soon Nagasaki, which at first had been merely smashed, then smoking, was burning. Slowly the eczema of fire turned into a great inflammation. There was a joining of the great scattered group of blobs of fire. And finally it was all one fire . . . Hence the revolting cost in lives.

He goes on to point out the bomb's military limitations.

It is not greater than its means of delivery, and is wholly dependent on it . . . Moreover, the atomic bomb does not penetrate. Look at the air views of Hiroshima and Nagasaki, and you will see waste, but it is flat waste. It is desolation without craters. What this little desert says to man is simple: *Get underground, worm, if you want to live* . . . The earth is the protecting mother still. Get under her blanket and you are safe. . . .

The mystic atmosphere of the bomb is more than anything else due to the fact that the bomb did conclude the war. But it did not *win* the war. Japan was dead when the bomb "landed" on Hiroshima, dead, but she wouldn't lie down. The bomb poked her . . . and over she went.

In another article written at about the same time (I think) and never published (I think), entitled "Seapower and the Shattered Atom," he writes:

By being at the edge of the sea, Hiroshima and Nagasaki nearly became the objects of a quite different kind of attack . . . Under consideration was an underwater explosion, a deathly pillar of water projecting itself upward gigantically . . . a tidal wave greater than any nature has made. The bomb would be laid and detonated by a submarine which would take the place of the twin bombers which appeared over each Japanese city. A great roll of water, perhaps a hundred feet high, would sweep over the city and simply drown it . . . The effect of an atomic bomb detonated underwater might conceivably be much greater on a coastal metropolis than a bomb dropped from overhead. There is no defense against the all-pervasiveness, the merciless seeking quality of water. A tidal wave searches out all.

And he cannot help remembering:

I walked along the waterfront of Nagasaki, not long ago, looking at the upended ferryboat driven by the blast into the shallows . . . I turned down the far side of the great, bottle-shaped inlet, and crossed over to the other side, opposite the city. Here I was nearly two miles from where the bomb burst over the main serpentine of Mitsubishi plants. Here were the Mitsubishi shipyards, with scores of rusted baby submarines that would never touch water. Over them the blue sky showed through the lattice of steel where the roof had been ripped off.

I stood here, just inside the neck of the inlet, and imagined the atomic bomb burst underwater by an American submarine just outside the entrance to Nagasaki. Through the neck of the bottle I could see a scattering of islands. There was the answer. Unless the submarine could actually get inside the harbor— unlikely—the islands would break up and subdue the incoming mesa of water.

But he also cannot help imagining:

The same would be true, in my own country, of Boston Harbor, which is full of miscellaneous islands. But it would not be true of Chicago, were a bomb detonated underwater a short way offshore in Lake Michigan. And in San Francisco an atomic wave created just outside the Golden Gate would sweep through the narrows with concentrated, funnel-strengthened power, with nothing but Alcatraz Island in the center of the harbor to interfere with its fury. Los Angeles or San Diego, of course, would be pushovers, as would be Miami or New Orleans . . .

It is important always to keep in mind the limitations of the atomic bomb, as so few writers on the subject do today.

XI

To increase the frustration of the Nagasaki censorship, as the decades crept on, was the tragedy of Weller's carbons vanishing, by then the only copies extant. To him it was as if posterity—which has its own hunger—were determined to complete MacArthur's crime. For the rest of my father's long life he felt immensely troubled that he had betrayed a commitment to see that the truth got out, and that the American people deserved no less. Somehow his invaluable dispatches from September 1945 had gotten permanently lost in the aftermath of war, the tumult of a globe-girdling life. All he'd uniquely seen, as he wrote it at the time, would never see the light of history. He died at ninety-five, haunted by the certainty that they were gone forever.

I have now determined that they eventually made their way to Kyrenia, on Cyprus (where he was based on and off in the 1950s), to several houses he rented. They ended up stored for over a decade, along with many other World War II papers, in the crumbling stone garden shed of a house he'd bought. After a civil war they got moved inside to a cupboard beneath a staircase. At age seventy (1977) he went back and happened on them under the Kyrenia stairs, shipped them rather trustingly across the Mediterranean and home to Italy—then promptly lost them again. He also eventually forgot he'd ever located them, since whenever the subject came up they were described as having gone astray "soon after the war." This story will not seem incredible to anyone who is friends with a foreign correspondent.

Six months after he died, in his whitewashed Italian villa gazing out on a sun-blasted sea, I discovered them in a vast room of paper confusion—a tumultuous archive of half a century's eyewitnessed gore. In a mildewed wooden crate, apparently unopened since being shipped over from Cyprus and perhaps only opened once since 1945, among sheaf after thick sheaf of miraculously preserved typescripts from the final months of the Pacific war, I at last found the missing carbons: crumbling, moldy, brown with age, but still afire with all they had to say. For the last decades of his life they had been waiting twenty feet from where he sat, ever more faintly remembering.

XII

Sixty years may not seem very long, yet the pulling-together of this book, and my attempts to contact anyone living who saw my father on Kyushu, have reminded me of how quickly a generation of young men vanishes. The human need to remember and examine the past is not nearly so strong as the present's determination to erase all of it. Had my father died knowing most of these dispatches had survived, he would have surely understood that, ultimately, they would appear.

Are they all here? I have no way to be certain. Perhaps the word counts he always asserted were accurate; perhaps the atomic bomb dispatches I found are only a third or half of what he wrote. And it's possible that the entire censored archive still exists in the bowels of some U.S. government vault. A few years ago an American scholar cordially let me know he'd spent a week trying to track them down in Washington. A Japanese TV producer from Nagasaki who made an award-winning documentary in 2003 on the censored dispatches—and who interviewed me a month before I found them— also did his best to locate the originals, yet came up empty-handed.

It may be that they were misfiled in government archives over the years. Or, as my father believed, it could be that all were immediately torn up by U.S. censors in Tokyo. Why preserve what you have no wish to reveal?

Perhaps this book will flush them from hiding.

XIII

As a subject, the atomic bomb searches out a writer's weaknesses and has no mercy. My father's attitude to what he experienced in Nagasaki was complicated, and did not grow less so over the years— *I lost my war in Nagasaki,* he used to say. It is necessary to keep in mind exactly when Weller was writing—what year, what month—to assess whether he was recording faithfully, with a critical eye, what he saw. It is no use reading a reporter's words from the past and try- ing to frog-march them into the present. The goal, while remember- ing what you know that he did not, is also to ask yourself if he knew anything that you do not.

Weller was careful not to let himself be trapped in polemics on whether the atomic bomb was "wrong." To say that he hoped it would never be used again is an understatement; by 1945 he had seen enough death for one lifetime, and he still had many wars left to run. When I was a boy he always refused to tell me about Na- gasaki apart from the adventure of making his way in. Later, he de- scribed it as the most horrible human destruction he'd ever witnessed—but he was careful to point out that it had to be eval- uated alongside, for example, the firebombings of Tokyo and Dres- den. And each belonged within its much larger military and political context.

He was frustrated, as we have seen, that the issue of radiation was so deliberately silenced at the time. But he also felt strongly that because the atomic bomb was so dramatic, it was not clear- mindedly assessed as a military weapon compared to others, and that its newness inevitably led to a tendency in the public to misre- member or ignore the destruction of which our other weapons were capable.

Not only were there no straightforward answers, there were no non-complex questions. In interviews, or casual conversation, he could wind along these paths for hours and you would never be sure where he stood. You would only realize how few of the problem's dimensions you had considered.

When pointing out that Nagasaki should be spoken of in the same terms as those two famously firebombed cities, he was not diminishing the nuclear deaths so much as trying to put them in perspective. He usually reminded an interviewer that one single night of the Tokyo incendiary-bomb air raids was more costly than Nagasaki in human lives as well as buildings destroyed. His point was not that people should not critically analyze Nagasaki, but that they had failed to analyze Tokyo. (The effectiveness of those raids—the colossal number of dead Japanese—was poorly understood in the United States at the time of the atomic bombs.)

He was careful, in public and in private, not to take a position on the decision to drop the atomic bomb—to the degree that I'm not sure he ever made up his mind. He felt the reporter's task was not to follow the blind trails of *what-might-have-happened* (referred to by him as "condition contrary to fact") but to unearth the hidden, important truths of what actually *did* happen. The American instinct to simplify all politics, to look for an unpolitical, emotional right or wrong no matter what, stymied him. He believed profoundly that it was the reporter's duty not to simplify.

He was dismissive of Japanese propaganda putting the atomic bomb in its own separate shrine, turning an apparent plea for world peace and nuclear disarmament into a moral condemnation for the United States using the bomb in the first place. He felt there were, to be sure, arguments to be made against either bomb—but most did not suffice. If the victims of Nagasaki were civilians, who had placed the arms factories in its heart? Were the majority of dead American servicemen not likewise civilians yanked out of civilian lives to defend themselves in a war not of their own making? Was the United States uniquely reprehensible for using a weapon that Japan would have been morally quite content to use first, had they invented it first?

Because he was so critical of Japanese conduct both during the war and afterward, it has been easy to conclude that he "endorsed the bomb." But to criticize the Japanese for being eager propagandists with a bad case of amnesia is not an endorsement of the bomb, only a characterization of how they managed to curve the discussion.

He was not looking for a national apology; but he was looking for signs of self-understanding from the Japanese, an acknowledgment of their militaristic role across Asia and in waging war against a long-time ally. He was perpetually annoyed (though never surprised) at the pressure he would get, whenever Japanese journalists came to interview him, to apologize on behalf of the United States for having won the war, said apology to be delivered in the guise of guilt for having used such a terrible weapon, or in the guise of vows never to loose such a barbaric evil on the world again. He spoke with admiration of how astute the Japanese were as propagandists, and with dismay at how ready Americans were to feel sorry, even guilty, for not losing.

That said, he was never reluctant to connect his censorship to the fact that Americans—who as a people were generous both by conviction, and whenever they could think of nothing else to be—would not have forgiven either MacArthur or the U.S. government had they known we were doing nothing to offer people in Nagasaki all medical assistance. The weeks dragged on, and people perished, he felt, who might not have had to.

A key phrase in his thinking crops up in "First into Nagasaki," when he states, having seen those dying of radiation in the hospital: "I felt pity, but no remorse. The Japanese military had cured me of that." Another came up in a 1990 radio interview conducted by the Swedish journalist Bertil Wedin—"the worst crime of any war is to begin it."

Weller:

MacArthur didn't want anybody to go there because this would lead to a lot of compassionate stories about what had happened to the people. I wanted to get these stories. Most of the deaths had already occurred.

Even though MacArthur tried to stop the story by not having anyone see Nagasaki, I wanted to be completely straightforward toward him once I got there. The war was over for a month; he had no military right at all to stop the story, in my judgment. But I was going to treat him as a gentleman, and have him see the dispatches first. If he were an intelligent officer, now in a peacemaking situation, he would allow them to pass, because they were extremely valuable.

Why were they valuable? The excellent Japanese doctors had examined the cadavers, and found out fascinating things about the effect of the ray on all the organs of the body. That was the scientific preciousness, in my mind, of my whole mission. Everybody in the outside world thought that all the people were fried to death immediately by the bomb, cooked like a piece of meat. That wasn't the case at all. For some it was a slow death.

One of the first places I went was to the hospitals . . . I made the point of being not a conquering visitor but an inquiring visitor. People were still dying. They were sitting in pathetic circles, with families trying to comfort them in their last hours.

I had a strong sense that everything written about this bomb had been wrong. These people were dying with an intact machine of life, and the first thing to do to fight the effects of the bomb was to find a way to pump platelets into them. I didn't know whether one could, and the Japanese doctors didn't know yet whether they could. It was like a leak in a boat, there was no way to stop it.

Wedin:

Was it difficult not to become too emotionally involved?

Weller:

I became involved in every way. I reached instantly the level of compassion that still obtains throughout the world. But I also had a checking machine working on me, so that I could have a different story than simply a compassionate story—so I could analyze the atomic bomb as a new weapon of war that would be used throughout the world unless it was outlawed.

People thought it was a super-bomb, that more people had died than ever before at any one time. In fact this was not true. More people had died earlier in the heavy incendiary bombardment of Tokyo itself. Here, as a result of the bomb, Nagasaki's wooden houses caught fire from each other; streets were blocked; people were trapped in their homes. There was a medical story in these exotic platelets, but most of the dead had burned. It was a Dresden.

Wedin:

It sounds as if you do not feel the atomic bombs were justifiable.

Weller:

This is an immense problem, in which the victims have their right to be heard and the West has to decide what its position is. The Japanese—a very alert people politically, and quick to exploit a moral position—did not hesitate to remind me of this instantly.

The worst crime of any war is to begin it, to start the conflict. That is the problem here. The Japanese, after years of friendship with the USA, sent with great adroitness under the leadership of Admiral Yamamoto a force that completely and successfully deceived us and on a Sunday morning struck at Pearl Harbor. A very successful military operation. But was it successful morally, to strike them on their holy day of worship? America had taken the steps to make an advantageous peace in the Russo-Japanese War; they were the referees, and helped Japan to win that war. Was this, then, an ethical act? It destroyed a friendship that had gone on for many years.

And what to make of all that George Weller saw and heard and wrote down? Beyond any human impulse to take sides, beyond an overwhelming sense of regret, lies—I hope—a healthy outrage that in a free society it can still take sixty years for some of the missing pieces to come together. At least this book adds another sliver to the mosaic of what happened, what was witnessed. For me it is a small triumph that these words, the deaths and lives that were written about, and the deep determination behind them to get at the truth, were not lost forever.

In 1984, for *GEO* magazine, I asked several foreign correspondents to each recount their most important story that was silenced. My father wrote about Nagasaki, and called the piece, which never appeared, "Confessions of a Temporary Colonel." His final sentences, for me, hold great poignance.

I was once an illicit colonel, assuming that rank when I was actually only a rather troublesome war correspondent. A month after the bombs fell on Hiroshima and Nagasaki, both south Japanese cities were still off limits. But their hospitals were full of civilians dying under the inner glow of radiation. What was happening to them? There was a story waiting to be told, and I was determined to get it.

I expected that MacArthur would by now have let doctors and nurses reach Nagasaki. Or were they being detained for one super publicity shot of the general bringing mercy in victory? Yet the Japanese doctors who crowded to shake my hand, and show me their reports, were not resentful. MacArthur was only doing what one of their generals would have done: *punish.*

In the hospitals I met a strange sight. The patients, all doomed, had left their beds and were sitting on their haunches in the matless halls, surrounded by their kneeling relatives. They were pale, tearless, formal, withdrawn, dignified. Death was a matter of days.

These people squatting before me had run around, salvaging, unworried, believing they were safe because they were unburned. Then, carelessly, they scratched a finger on broken glass, or bit off a hangnail. And they bled. And bled.

I thought that perhaps there was still some way that MacArthur could save some of these lives, if he was told what was going on. So, instead of smuggling out my news myself, I began writing the story of the anatomy of radiated man. I wrote it all—besides the sight of blistered Nagasaki—with no false compassion, but with full details of every organ: heart, kidneys, stomach, pancreas, lung, genitals, everything. I mixed it with single stories, the lives of people who now lived in urns.

There was something else MacArthur didn't want known: right in the heart of Nagasaki, where a last black hulk still smoldered in the harbor, a hundred skinny American prisoners, now free, had actually been under the terrible light in the sky. When the bomb-bearing B-29 came over, they leaped in the slit trench surrounding the plant where they worked, and cowered flat. "Deep enough to put us in shadow," they said. "That's all you need." Four failed to lie flat enough, and died. For MacArthur they had a message: "Tell Uncle Doug food drops aren't enough."

In four days I sent 25,000 words by the hands of the obliging *kempeitai,* the secret police, directly to MacArthur. I figured that, since his officer had not followed the *kempeitai* back and arrested me, he would be interested enough—I had won a Pulitzer Prize, the first in his command—to let them pass.

I was wrong. MacArthur could not halt history or science, but he did his best to take the bloom off death by atomic radiation. All my dispatches were suppressed. Every one of my 25,000 words was killed by MacArthur's censorship, which went on afterward, month after month.

I relinquished my colonelcy, and began another enlistment in a war that is still unfinished.

Selected Reading

Due to the vast scope of the subject matter, what follows are merely a few suggestions for further reading which I found especially informative or helpful in the course of researching my father's saga. (Many books are, alas, out of print.) There is, of course, no substitute for contemporary newspapers and magazines in acquiring the flavor of an era.

For a general background to the bomb, along with histories of World War II or the Manhattan Project, try *Before the Fallout: From Marie Curie to Hiroshima* by Diana Preston (New York, 2005). Also *Hiroshima and Nagasaki: The Physical, Medical, and Social Effects of the Atomic Bombings* (Japanese Committee report, New York, 1981). Ian Buruma's *The Wages of Guilt* (New York, 1994) raises many other questions, fifty years on.

On the complex issue of how the bombs were dealt with by the press, the military, the U.S. and the Japanese governments, one starting point is the monumental *Hiroshima in America* by Robert Jay Lifton and Greg Mitchell (New York, 1995), a work with countless tributaries. Another is *Living with the Bomb: American and Japanese Cultural Conflicts in the Nuclear Age,* ed. by Laura Hein and Mark Selden (New York, 1997).

Monica Braw's *The Atomic Bomb Suppressed: American Censorship in Occupied Japan* (New York, 1991) covers authoritatively the pawn-takes-pawn strategies which followed the surrender.

An account of Tex McCrary's press junket may be found in *Off the Record,* ed. by Dickson Hartwell and Andrew A. Rooney (New York, 1953). One member, Bill Lawrence ("non-Atomic Bill") published a memoir, *Six Presidents, Too Many Wars* (New York, 1972). The most penetrating junket dispatch sent from Hiroshima appears in *Forward Positions: The War Correspondence of Homer Bigart* (Arkansas, 1992).

Wilfred Burchett detailed his Hiroshima saga in at least three books: *Democracy with a Tommygun* (Melbourne, 1946), *Passport* (Melbourne & Sydney, 1969), and the posthumous *Shadows of Hiroshima* (London, 1983) as well as many articles and interviews over the years. Though occasionally contradictory in small details, each has its own revelations.

The skirmishes of censorship crop up in war correspondents' memoirs like unscythable weeds. Cecil Brown's *Suez to Singapore* (New York, 1942) is especially vivid. Hugh Baillie's *High Tension* (New York, 1959) contains an eloquent portrait of MacArthur. Edward W. Beattie Jr.'s *"Freely to Pass"* (New York, 1942) contains a brief but eloquent portrait of Nagasaki from 1937.

The epic work on the POWs is Gavan Daws' *Prisoners of the Japanese* (New York, 1994), one of the greatest histories ever written about World War II; many other books are alive within it. I also recommend tracking down the personal memoirs, often self-published, of prisoners, among them notably *The Remorseless Road* by James McEwan (U.K., 1997), Charles Balaza's *Life as an American Prisoner of War of the Japanese* (New Jersey, 2002), and *No Uncle Sam: The Forgotten of Bataan* by Tony Bilek (Kent State, 2003).

Gregory F. Michno's *Death on the Hellships* (Annapolis, 2001) is the finest single work on the subject which I have found. Also in that category is *Unjust Enrichment: How Japan's Companies Built Postwar Fortunes Using American POWs* by Linda Goetz Holmes (Pennsylvania, 2001). And, from W. L. "Atomic Bill" Laurence to the present, Beverly Ann Deepe Keever's insightful *News Zero: The New York Times and the Bomb* (Maine, 2004).

There are several books on the defense of Wake; none seem to mention the Robinson Crusoes. I particularly liked *Wake Island: The Heroic Gallant Fight* by Duane Schultz (New York, 1978).

—*Anthony Weller*

Acknowledgments

Quite a few people took part in rescuing this book.

If anyone deserves the most gratitude, it is probably Barbara Somers, who meticulously retyped the text of the original "cablese" dispatches into a "computerese" I could deal with. She was, I suspect, the first person to read some pages in sixty years—and though the material was often repellent or difficult to decipher on those smudged carbons, her undaunted labor made this book possible.

Photographer Kirk Williamson, a friend for decades with much experience at dealing with historical photographs, faced the problem of the hundred pictures my father took, which survive only on contact strips or as tiny prints. He not only saved them all from oblivion, he guided me through the process of putting them in their original, meaningful order. He also found a way to capture the reality of the paper archive itself, in all its decrepit glory.

Many thanks are due to Jeffrey Donovan, Tim Crawford, and David Deans, who each looked after my father in Italy throughout his declining years, which they made not only coherent for him and gratifying, but even comfortable; their loving companionship was an immeasurable gift. A handshake, too, for Jean-Pierre Darnis, who spent a couple of dusty days helping me search fruitlessly through steamer trunks containing moldy typescripts from all over the world.

It was James Crabtree who, in the mid-1970s, salvaged the crate of Japanese dispatches from a tumbledown stone shed in our garden at Kyrenia, in the Turkish Republic of Northern Cyprus, brought them safely out of the rain, and stashed them under the stairs in Hope Cottage. There my father rediscovered them in 1977 then shipped them home to Italy, to be lost again amid the residue of innumerable wars.

Thanks also to my friend Patrick Thoze, who demonstrated how my father's worn and shiny Leica, on which I'd given up hope, was still ready to work just as faithfully as it had at Nagasaki, half a century earlier.

Photographer Macduff Everton put me in touch with Peter Howe, who in turn kindly sent me to agent J. P. Pappis and his superb Polaris Images, who now handle worldwide rights on my father's photos. Everyone at Polaris (especially the unflappable Meg Handler) has been tireless.

The following either answered difficult questions or steered me in the right direction: Simon Bourgin, Barbara Bruns, Dr. Janet Doran, Hans Herklots, Willis and Lee Hulings, Alen MacWeeney, Calvin Mitchell, Metin Münir, Emmett Thomas, Alan Weisman, and Michael Weller.

Sumire Kunieda of *Mainichi* (*Tokyo*) broke the story of the dispatches' existence in a series of June 2005 articles, having seen them mentioned in a profile of me—connected with a recent novel—written for the *Boston Globe* by David Mehegan.

On Turkish Cyprus, Halil Baştuğ, Allan Cavinder, Valérie Moniez, Richard Oldroyd, and Arman Ratip at different times helped extract parts of the story from my father; much gratitude in particular to journalist Bertil Wedin, whose long interview with him for Radio Bayrak on "Magazine North" in 1990 has been essential to me.

Bob Herguth Jr. and Monifa Thomas of the *Chicago Sun-Times* helped me to ascertain what little of my father's reporting actually filtered through from Kyushu in 1945 to the now long-defunct *Chicago Daily News*. At the New York Public Library, researcher nonpareil David Smith attacked the same mystery from another direction.

Special thanks are due another old friend, Kevin Buckley. As editor of *GEO* and a war correspondent himself, he commissioned my father to write, late in life, an account of Nagasaki which (owing to the magazine's untimely demise) never appeared. Beyond this, it was Kevin who first sent me out on writing assignments to the Middle East and Asia, and got me exploring that larger world. I owe him a lot.

Along with Kevin, the following comrades-in-arms helped with my essay: Geo Beach, Dan Connell, Barnaby Conrad III, Reuel Gerecht, Greg Gibson, and Eddie Lazarus. As always, I am indebted to them for perseverance, unending good humor, and much wisdom.

For me, one of the great rewards of the book has been the opportunity to make contact with the far-flung, close-knit world of former prisoners of war who still survive. This was in large part thanks to the omniscient Linda Dahl, who answered many of my questions and knew exactly to whom I should write. The following brave men were generous with their time and memories, no matter how painful those were: Karel Aster, Charlie Balaza, Jim Bashleben, Wesley C. Browning, Wayne Carringer, Bertram Freedman, Evans Garcia, Lou Goldbrum, Wes Injerd, Harold Kurvers, Joe Johnson, John Perkowski, Sol Schwartz, Leland Sims, Frank Stecklein, Donald Tapscott, Lester Tenney, and Joseph Vater.

In some cases, pertinent recollections found me from across several generations, thanks to descendants for whom the stories remain powerful: Alan Boyd, Jim Burnett, Scott Dood, Margaret Garcia, John Jensen, Kathryn Jones-Lucas, Tony Martinez, Michael Murray, Frank A. Nederhand, and R. Bruce Smith.

Jim Erickson very helpfully shared his knowledge of the hellships.

At Crown, I am grateful for the support of my editor, Luke Dempsey, his assistant, Lindsey Moore, my publicist, Jay Sones, and my publisher, Steve Ross: their enthusiasm for this project has never wavered. I also wish to thank Walter Cronkite—among many other distinctions, one of our last surviving correspondents from World War II—who was kind enough to offer his strong and timely foreword.

I have been fortunate to have Henry Dunow as my literary agent and close friend since 1989; the crucial balance between those roles, thanks to him, has been central to a bond I value enormously. (At his New York headquarters, Rolph Blythe unknotted a myriad of problems.) My literary agents in London and Tokyo—Daniela Petracco, Sarah Nundy, Andrew Nurnberg, and Asako Kawachi—provided helpful suggestions as well as representation, and read many versions of the material without complaint.

If I have inadvertently misspelled anyone's name in deciphering the original dispatches, I would very much like to correct it for subsequent editions.

My father would, I know, wish me to thank the community of San Felice Circeo for many kindnesses during his final decades.

Lastly, it is my wife, Kylée Smith, who saw me through the short but intense odyssey of this book. She was much loved by my father and much moved by how, as the years went on, the past seemed more and more to slip from his grasp. Six months after his death, she ran up his stairs in Italy to share my wonderment at seeing these dispatches spread out on the floor when I found them. Her constant support and counsel are incalculable.